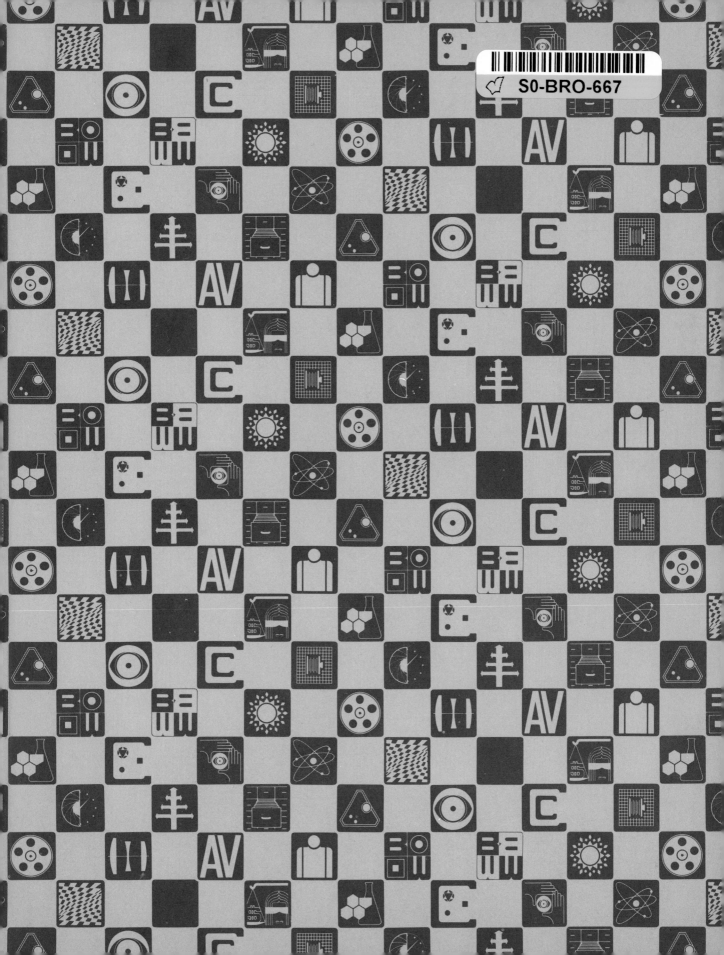

S0-BRO-667

Encyclopedia
of Practical
Photography

Volume 14

Trav-Z

Index

Edited by and published for
EASTMAN KODAK COMPANY

AMPHOTO
American Photographic Book Publishing Company
Garden City, New York

Copyright © 1979 by Eastman Kodak Company and American Photographic Book Publishing Company, Inc.

Library of Congress Cataloging in Publication Data

Amphoto, New York.
  Encyclopedia of practical photography.

  Includes bibliographical references and index.
  1. Photography—Dictionaries. I. Eastman Kodak Company. II. Title.
TR9.T34   770′.3   77–22562

ISBN 0–8174–3050–4 Trade Edition—Whole Set
ISBN 0–8174–3200–0 Library Edition—Whole Set
ISBN 0–8174–3064–4 Trade Edition—Volume 14
ISBN 0–8174–3214–0 Library Edition—Volume 14

Manufactured in the United States of America

Typesetting: Com Com (Haddon Craftsmen Inc.)
Printing and Binding: W. A. Krueger Company
Separations: Spectra Graphics Inc.
Index: Richardson Associates
Paper: Westvaco

Editorial Board

The *Encyclopedia of Practical Photography* was compiled and edited jointly by Eastman Kodak Company and American Photographic Book Publishing Co., Inc. (Amphoto). The comprehensive archives, vast resources, and technical staffs of both companies, as well as the published works of Kodak, were used as the basis for most of the information contained in this encyclopedia.

Symbol Identification

 Audiovisual

 Color Processing and Printing

 Picture-Making Techniques

 Biography

 Equipment and Facilities

 Scientific Photography

 Black-and-White Materials

 Exposure

 Special Effects and Techniques

 Black-and-White Processing and Printing

 History

 Special Interests

 Business and Legal Aspects

 Lighting

 Storage and Care

 Chemicals

 Motion Picture

 Theory of Photography

 Color Materials

 Optics

 Vision

Guide for the Reader

Use this encyclopedia as you would any good encyclopedia or dictionary. Look for the subject desired as it first occurs to you—most often you will locate it immediately. The shorter articles begin with a dictionary-style definition, and the longer articles begin with a short paragraph that summarizes the article that follows. Either of these should tell you if the information you need is in the article. The longer articles are then broken down by series of headings and sub-headings to aid further in locating specific information.

Cross References

If you do not find the specific information you are seeking in the article first consulted, use the cross references (within the article and at the end of it) to lead you to more information. The cross references can lead you from a general article to the more detailed articles into which the subject is divided. Cross references are printed in capital letters so that you can easily recognize them.
Example: *See also:* ZONE SYSTEM.

Index

If the initial article you turn to does not supply you with the information you seek, and the cross references do not lead you to it, use the index in the last volume. The index contains thousands of entries to help you identify and locate any subject you seek.

Symbols

To further aid you in locating information, the articles throughout have been organized into major photographic categories. Each category is represented by a symbol displayed on the opposite page. By using only the symbols, you can scan each volume and locate all the information under any of the general categories. Thus, if you wish to read all about lighting, simply locate the lighting symbols and read the articles under them.

Reading Lists

Most of the longer articles are followed by reading lists citing useful sources for further information. Should you require additional sources, check the cross-referenced articles for additional reading lists.

Metric Measurement

Both the U.S. Customary System of measurement and the International System (SI) are used throughout this encyclopedia. In most cases, the metric measurement is given first with the U.S. customary equivalent following in parenthesis. When equivalent measurements are given, they will be rounded off to the nearest whole unit or a tenth of a unit, unless precise measurement is important. When a measurement is considered a "standard," equivalents will not be given. For example: 35 mm film, 200 mm lens, 4″ × 5″ negative, and 8″ × 10″ prints will not be given with their customary or metric equivalents.

How Articles are Alphabetized

Article titles are alphabetized by letter sequence, with word breaks and hyphens not considered. Example:

> Archer, Frederick Scott
> Architectural Photography
> Archival Processing
> Arc Lamps

Abbreviations are alphabetized according to the letters of the abbreviations, not by the words the letters stand for. Example:

> Artificial Light
> ASA Speed

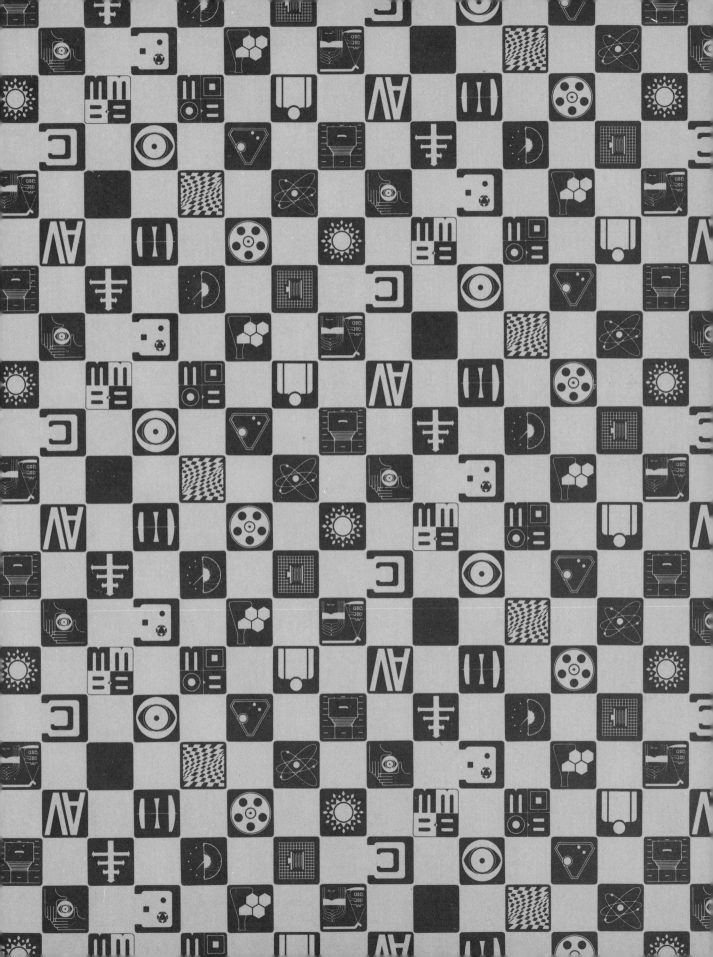

Contents
Volume 14

Travel Photography

Whether for a beginner or a professional, travel photography consists of getting ready, getting there, and getting the pictures. A good part of getting ready is knowing one's limitations and capabilities, and staying within them when planning travel and selecting equipment to take. Transportation problems may limit the kind and amount of equipment that can be taken, but this may be an advantage, since the tendency is to include too much. If you own only one camera and one lens, equipment selection is not a problem, but film, accessories, and the kind of pictures to try for will still have to be decided upon.

Experienced travel photographers frequently make up checklists of equipment for different kinds of photographic travels and for trips that involve overseas air travel. The lists are different and change with the seasons and various destinations. Leaving California in the heat of midsummer can make one forget that it is winter in New Zealand. Winter subjects require slow films for snow scenes, but close-up lenses for flower pictures will not be needed at that time of year. If it is going to be really cold, a selenium-cell light meter may be needed because battery-operated CdS meters do not work well in sub-zero weather. Some automatic camera shutters may not work at very low temperatures, and this should be checked out before leaving the summer of the Northern Hemisphere for a skiing vacation in South America in July or August.

Weather and season, together with expected subject matter, should determine the preliminary selection of film and equipment. Good travel guidebooks contain weather strips showing the average high and low temperatures and the average number of days of rain for each month of the year, and it is advisable to check these.

Practicing with Your Equipment

Being familiar with equipment is more than just knowing how to work the various features of the camera. You should be able to change lenses in a crowded moving vehicle, change film on a street corner, and keep up with the tour group while carrying your own gear. Get on a local bus and take pictures of interesting objects or scenes that you pass. Try photographing from the open window of an automobile while someone else drives. Until you can confidently adjust exposure for changing lighting conditions, rapidly focus the camera, or zoom the lens, you should practice beforehand.

Equipment should be organized in such a way that nothing gets lost or delays you, and your home is the best place to try out packing arrangements. First, however, consider the serious business of selecting the equipment that you plan to take on the trip.

Selecting Equipment

On aircraft, all cameras, lenses, and film must be carried as hand luggage for reasons of security. The maximum size for hand luggage on planes is 20 × 35 × 53 cm (8″× 14″× 2″) so that it can stowed under the seat. Most airlines allow two such pieces of luggage to be carried aboard, but if both are full size, there may be a problem finding space for them. Make sure the photo gear all goes into one unit, while personal items occupy a smaller bag. Incidentally, fitted cases are great space-wasters because the padding takes up a lot of room.

Cameras and Lenses. On every trip you will need to take one camera with a "normal" lens. The standard 50 or 55 mm lens is fine for 35 mm cameras with interchangeable lenses, but if you prefer a 28 mm or an 85 mm lens, that is what you should take. Indoors—and often outdoors—you will need all the speed you can get. However, if your favorite lens is not an $f/2$ lens or faster, it may be better to take the 50 mm $f/1.7$ or $f/1.4$ lens that came with the camera.

If you own them already, a medium wide-angle and a medium telephoto lens will complete the kit. Alternatively, a 35 to 105 mm zoom lens can be substituted for these two lenses with a slight saving of space. If you own a second camera of the same make, and the lenses are interchangeable with those of the first, consider taking it along and keeping it loaded with a second kind of film. One camera can be loaded with color and another with black-and-white film, or the second camera can be loaded with high-speed color film. Film choices will be discussed later in this article.

Unless you are going on a nature photography tour, stay away from the very long telephoto lenses, and the same goes for fisheye and other specialty

Even a much-photographed scene such as Mont St.-Michel can be given a new look by putting the structure in the context of the countryside around it. Photo by Neil Montanus.

lenses. If you do not have a specific picture in mind for one of these lenses, you will only waste space carrying them. Instead of carrying macro lenses or extension tubes, save space by carrying a set of +1, +2, and +3 supplementary lenses, which can be screwed together to give up to +6. These will allow as close a distance to the subject as the heavier equipment will, and they do not require any special calculations when flash is used.

Flash. It is advisable to have a small flash unit with you, and this should operate from standard pen-light cells, because a charger for rechargeable batteries not only takes up space but it also may not work on the odd voltages and frequencies found in some countries. Fast film and a fast lens will let you take pictures in many places that do not allow tripods or flash to be used. Besides, a good, solid tripod is difficult to carry on trips.

Batteries. Do not count on being able to get common items in foreign countries or even in smaller communities in the United States. Always put a fresh battery in your camera before leaving on a trip, and pack a spare camera battery for each camera in your gadget bag. If you have two cameras of the same kind, you should carry two spare batter-

ies. Seal spare mercury batteries in small polyethylene envelopes to protect them from humidity.

Film. A photographer should be reasonably selective about subjects to be photographed, but he or she should not be placed in a situation where there is fear of running out of film. A good rule is to carry a minimum of one 36-exposure roll of color film for every day you expect to be away from home. Since many days are consumed in travel from point to point, carrying film for days when you will not be photographing tends to balance things out. Some photographers carry about half as much black-and-white film as color material.

For travel, an ASA 64 color transparency film is the best choice because it allows you to cope with a much wider variety of lighting conditions than does a slower film. In addition, carrying a few rolls of fast transparency film is a wise procedure.

If you are going to do a lot of photographing in low light, substitute fast color film for part of your one-roll-a-day quota of ASA 64 film. You can carry Kodacolor 400 film and have either slides or prints made up from the resulting negatives. It is even possible to make black-and-white prints from color negatives; internegatives can also be made.

Travel Photography

About X-Rays

Repeated exposure to x-rays at airport security checking areas may fog film. The result can be anything from overexposed washed-out slides to strange light spots in shadow areas and streaks of many kinds on prints and slides.

The following procedure should minimize problems. Pack your gadget bag with spare lenses on the bottom and put cameras and film on top. Film should be removed from boxes, and if it is 35 mm, the plastic film containers should be marked with masking tape showing the type of film. The containers go into Sigma film shields that can be purchased at any large camera store.

The idea is not to rely entirely on film shields to protect film from radiation, but to take additional steps to avoid x-ray hazards, if possible. Before approaching the security checking station, remove the film and the cameras from the gadget bag. As you walk up to the counter, place the gadget bag and any other hand luggage you may have on the conveyor belt that passes through the x-ray machine. Somehow this simple step goes a long way toward putting the security people at ease, because they realize you are making an effort to speed up the process of hand-checking the items you do not want x-rayed. Remove the clip from the film shield and hold the sack open so the guard can see that it really contains film. If the guard suggests that you run the "protected film" through on the conveyor, tell him the shield may have been damaged and is no longer x-ray proof. In many areas you will also be asked to open up the leather cases on the cameras so that the guard can see that they too are real. Most of the time you will have no trouble getting your cameras and film hand-inspected without delay, but make it a practice to get to the airport well ahead of the departure time so that you can avoid the last-minute rush when security people are apt to be hurried. By being early and making the job easy, you can avoid having your film and cameras x-rayed at most airports around the world.

These additional precautions may not seem to be needed if film shields are used, but it is necessary to protect your film both from defective equipment that emits stray radiation and from equipment that is being improperly operated. Consider, for example, the fact that if an x-ray unit is turned up high enough to detect a gun in a film shield, the film would be subjected to an excessive amount of radiation regardless of whether it is in a shield or not. For x-ray inspection to be effective, the shadows on the fluoroscope screen must outline the shape of the objects in any package, and the outline of a partly filled lead shield might—if not penetrated—be no different from that of an explosive device. Worse yet, the shield could be used to hide weapons from the x-rays. All in all, it is advisable to rely on the shields only for protection against stray emissions from defective inspection equipment until better methods of inspection are adopted throughout the world.

Never pack film in luggage that is to be checked through and carried in the cargo hold of the plane. Much of this is routinely x-rayed by far more powerful units than are used at security counters.

To conserve space, film can be taken from its original box. The plastic containers should be marked as to contents. As each roll is exposed, it should be taped across the top and identified as to subject and assigned a roll number. Photo by Parry C. Yob.

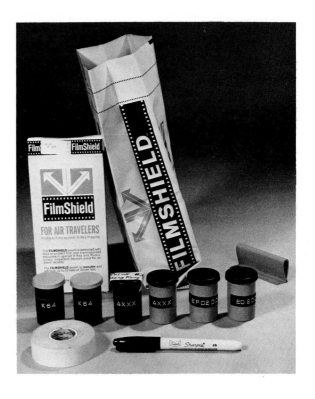

Checking Your Camera

While it may seem logical to have your camera cleaned, oiled, and adjusted just before leaving on a trip, this often turns out to be a mistake. If the camera has been giving good results for the last few months at home, a tune-up can lead to disaster. The camera repair person will adjust the shutter and meter either to factory specifications or to what the test equipment indicates are factory specifications, and this can make big changes in your results. If you have been using a higher or lower setting on the ASA scale of your camera's meter and getting good results, an adjustment of either meter or shutter could leave you guessing.

Do not buy a new camera and start off on a trip. Not only will you be unfamiliar with the camera's controls, but you will have no background data about the tolerances of the meter and shutter. Modern cameras are marvels of accuracy, but if you need a new camera, buy it a few weeks in advance and check out everything at home.

Some Tests. Do not trust that everything is continuing to work well whether the camera is new or old. Every time you change film, point the open camera toward some source of light, cock the camera, and push the shutter release. If the camera has a focal-plane shutter, watch the areas of the shutter as you cock the camera. If you see a slit of light as the camera is cocked, the mirror is not coming down

properly and at the same time there is a shutter problem. If you do not see a flash of light when you release the shutter, either the mirror is not coming up properly or the shutter curtains are not opening properly. If the camera has a blade shutter, check to see that it opens and closes properly when the release is pushed. These checks will not tell you anything about shutter speeds, but they will prevent major malfunctions from causing you to waste roll after roll of film.

Finally, always check to see that the handle on the take-up spool knob rotates each time you cock the camera. Be sure to do this on the first frame, and periodically throughout the roll. Sprocket holes sometimes strip out when a cassette jams, particularly in cold weather, and when this happens the same frame is exposed over and over.

If you expect to be using electronic flash, plug it into the camera's X-sync socket, and adjust the shutter to 1/60. Then place the light as far in front of the lens as possible, and with the aperture set at $f/11$, cock and fire the camera while looking through the open back. You will see a bright, almost blinding point of light if everything is working properly.

Exposure. One thing that travelers often do not know, or have simply forgotten, is the *reasonable exposure rule*. Most professionals keep a close check on their exposures by asking themselves if the expo-

(Left) While the photographer will certainly want to photograph well-known attractions, he or she should look for special views, such as this scene from the gardens of Versailles.
(Right) Quiet, sunlit streets such as this are also part of the traveler's vision, and should not be overlooked merely because they are obscure. Photos by Michael Fairchild.

sure they are using is reasonable. A reasonable exposure for a sunny day under normal conditions is 1/ASA at *f*/16. If the ASA is 64, the exposure would be 1/64 sec. at *f*/16. For an ASA of 400, the exposure would be 1/400 sec. at *f*/16. If the camera seems to be straying far from this reasonable exposure, stop and check. First check to see that you have not accidentally changed the ASA setting on the meter; then check to see that the battery is all right by using the manufacturer's battery checking procedure. If you cannot remember the instructions, it is a good idea to take along a photocopy of the battery checking page from the instruction manual. Finally, be sure that you have not pushed the meter beyond its capabilities. Many through-the-lens metering systems will not make readings at 1/1000 sec. when the ASA of the film is only 25. Nor will they read properly at very slow speeds such as 1/2 or 1 full second when the ASA rating is 400 or greater. You may forget this in the excitement of the trip, so if the meter is giving a false reading, adjust the shutter speed to some other setting and check to see if you get a reasonable reading.

Customs

Most foreign countries are not usually overly strict with tourists about cameras or film, although many have laws regulating the amount of film and the number of cameras a tourist may bring in. But in most cases, this is not a problem.

A little preplanning can avoid delays and problems that might occur when you get back to the United States. Before leaving the U.S., you should

Real people and real places are better photographic subjects than staged events seen only by tourists. Pictures such as this street scene (above) and the weathered face of a farm woman will help the traveler understand a country and its people better than photos of churches and monuments of a past era.

While photographs such as this bullfight scene are among the most common available, there is a certain satisfaction for the photographer in having a record of an event that he or she has personally attended. Additionally, for the photographer who is interested in selling his or her work, pictures like this are always in demand.

register your cameras and lenses with the U.S. Customs Department. This is done on Customs Form 4457, Certificate of Registration for Personal Effects Taken Abroad. You will have to present the actual equipment to the customs officer when you register it, but you will not be asked to produce sales slips or other proofs of ownership. You will be asked to fill out the form with serial numbers and descriptions and to sign it, after which the customs officer will mark the number of items and then stamp and sign the form.

Carry the original form in your wallet and a photocopy in your gadget bag. The photocopy has no official standing, but it could help if you lose the original. Most seaports and all international airports have customs offices that can clear the equipment for you, but if you plan to take care of registration at your port of departure, make sure that the customs office will be open and arrange to get there two or three hours earlier than you would normally arrive for other departure formalities. The form will allow you to bring your cameras back into the United States, and very often you will not be asked for it.

There are also questions about buying cameras overseas to save money. Unless you are visiting a country where U.S. currency enjoys a very favorable exchange rate, and which has long been noted for lower prices, like Hong Kong, your chances of saving money are not as great as you may think. If you are determined to hunt for bargains, you should write down the best price you can get from your local camera store before you leave. Do not trust your memory on prices. Next, be sure you know and have handled the latest model and are aware of its full retail price as well as the best "advertised price." The same goes for lenses and accessories. If you do find a real bargain, be sure to get a sales slip that shows not only the serial number but also the price in both local currency and in U.S. dollars. The duty you pay is determined by the price you paid abroad, not by the U.S. retail price. The actual duty ranges from 7.5 percent on cameras to about 15 percent on certain accessories, and it is subject to change. Make an honest declaration on every item you buy, and present the declaration to the customs officer when you re-enter the U.S. Most customs people are pleasant to deal with, but if your declarations are not valid, you can have your possessions confiscated and be fined in addition. If you paid $300 for a camera in Hong Kong, your personal $100 exemption would lower the duty price to $200, so there is no point in making an incorrect declaration to save $15 in duty.

Protecting Equipment from Theft

Valuable cameras and accessories are prime targets for thieves wherever you travel. They can be stolen at any time in any place, both at home and abroad. Generally there are more thieves in big cities than elsewhere, and the most probable places from which the goods can be stolen are hotel rooms and automobiles, locked or otherwise. If the thieves know the equipment is in the car, the locks will not prevent the theft.

Most hotels are glad to protect your property by locking it away in a safe. Thefts are as bad for the hotel as for the guests. If a safe is not available, keep the equipment with you at all times. However, do not display it unnecessarily. A large array of professional photographic equipment is particularly attractive to thieves.

Just as a lady's handbag can be snatched, so can a camera. Watch out for this in crowded places, particularly when you are carrying several other packages or pieces of luggage.

Aside from the possibility of theft, many cameras are lost by being left behind in restaurants, buses, airplanes, or elsewhere.

(Left) These Egyptian fishing boats offer a rather different view of a country generally pictured in terms of sand and pyramids.

(Right) People at work are an integral part of any environment, especially when they are engaged in such near-legendary crafts as are these Iranian rug-makers. While the subject's permission should always be asked before he or she is photographed, most people are proud of their skills and seldom mind the intrustion.

Travel Photography

Hints for Better Pictures

The best pictures are often the result of adopting the simplest philosophy for travel photography. Far too many photographic opportunities are missed by ignoring the interesting things along a route because people are convinced that there are better pictures awaiting them in Tokyo or Honolulu or San Francisco. This means passing up good photos because they represent things you sometimes see at home. Remember that exotic costumes or native boats are not required to make a good travel picture. The folks back home will be as interested in seeing the modern skyscrapers of Hong Kong as the colorful boats at Aberdeen.

Far too many travelers bring back roll after roll of pictures of staged events visited only by tourists. You would not tell a foreign visitor that the daily costume gunfights in Old Sacramento or Old Tucson represent America today, or that everybody in Hawaii wears grass skirts; so, when traveling, you should not ignore opportunities to photograph real people and the real places you are passing through.

Everywhere in the world, workers, merchants, street people, traffic, and machines make interesting subjects. Never overlook an opportunity to photograph a colorful fruit stand whether it is in Boston or Bangkok. Workers seldom object to being photographed. In fact they are usually pleased that you are interested in them and their work, and they do not expect tips as do the natives who frequent tour routes.

Use available light, reserving flash for times when it is absolutely necessary. In this way, you will get better pictures and you will not distract your subject. Use some discretion and observe common courtesy. Just because a funeral is being held in a foreign country does not make it a tourist's holiday. The Indians of the American Southwest have closed many photographic treasure areas to visitors because picture-taking tourists insensitively assumed every tribal rite or custom was something staged for their entertainment. Never enter any home anywhere unless the occupant has invited you to do so. If a local resident or official of any country objects to photography, put your camera away and move on to another place. Remember, you are there to take pictures, not to offend people.

• *See also:* COLOR PRINTING FROM TRANSPARENCIES; INTERNEGATIVES, COLOR.

Tripods

A tripod is a widely used, three-legged camera support. It provides a sturdy, yet relatively portable and compact means of holding the camera steady during exposure. A tripod is primarily used for steadying the camera when exposures are longer than 1/30 sec.—especially when telephoto lenses are used, and the natural vibration of the photographer's body would cause motion blur. With large motion-picture or view cameras, the tripod is essential, since such cameras are difficult, if not impossible, to hand-hold. Inasmuch as the view camera uses a ground glass for finding, it must remain fixed on the subject for the whole sequence of finding and picture-taking; it therefore requires a tripod. In making a panoramic sequence, a tripod with a calibrated pan head makes it possible to shoot a series of frames without overlap or missed sections.

Construction

Virtually all of today's tripods are made of lightweight metal, such as Duralumin, which is sturdy yet light. The heavier models—usually used in studios—are made of steel, brass, or wood and do not fold as compactly as the aluminum ones. Often these heavy models are transported via truck or a strong assistant, so lightness is not necessary. Such tripods can hold very large cameras (8″ × 10″ view, for example).

When buying a tripod, it is always best to select one that can support more weight than it is intended to hold. When working in a high wind, an extra-sturdy tripod will lessen the chance of blurred shots. By paying a little extra for a stronger piece of equipment at the start, it will not be necessary to buy a second tripod later. How well a tripod will perform and how long one will last is dependent on how well the unit is constructed. When choosing a tripod, carefully consider all the elements of construction.

The Legs. The legs make up 90 percent of the tripod. Two very good types of tripod legs are tubular ones made of extruded metal, and those of the U-channel design. Extruded legs are made from a single piece of metal drawn into shape without seams. Being round, they resist denting and bending. U-channel legs use less metal and are therefore

A typical tripod of the portable type. The head tilts, pans, and has a sturdy locking device. A crank allows the center post to be elevated some distance without adjusting the legs. The two-section legs have knurled locking rings to provide a sure grip.

adjustments. If a leg is being adjusted, or if a lock is flipped open by accident, the tripod can fall over. Legs with twist-lock collars can be adjusted while remaining locked tightly enough to keep from tipping under the camera's weight.

Feet. To prevent slippage, the feet of tripod legs usually have rubber caps to grip a smooth floor, and/or spikes for use outdoors. Some tripods have caps that can be raised above the spikes. On loose ground, such as sand, this design can be useful in keeping the legs from sinking into the soil. Care of the tripod should include keeping the caps free from dirt and moisture.

Braces. The tripod's legs have some arrangement to keep them from inadvertently opening too far. Some tripods have a simple stop where the legs meet at the top. A tripod designed for lightweight cameras does not need much more than this type of stop, but with heavier equipment there may be enough stress to break the stop or damage the area around it. For this reason the heavier tripods usually have center-braced legs. A light bracing bar extends from the center column to each leg, completing a sturdy triangle, and taking a great deal of stress off the portion of the leg above the brace.

On some tripods the center braces can be moved up the legs, permitting them to be opened wider than normal. This design is useful when the camera needs to be placed lower than the shortest height of the tripod's normal settings, or when a wider base is required.

Center Post. Many tripods have center posts that permit the camera to be raised without readjusting the tripod's legs. Inexpensive tripod models have center posts that slide up and down and are held in place with a locking screw. Better ones have crank-operated elevating mechanisms with locking devices to prevent the post from slipping under the camera's weight. Often the bottom of the post is threaded to accept the tripod head upside down for low-level photography. The center post should never be raised to its full height, as this makes the camera more susceptible to wobble. The center post should be used for "fine-tuning" rather than as a quick means of raising the camera.

The Head. The head of the tripod is usually made so that the camera can be turned and tilted in almost any direction. The most common type of head for lightweight tripods is the ball joint. A single

lighter. Being open on one side, they are easy to clean and lubricate, but are somewhat more susceptible to denting and bending. They are also likely to flex more than tubular legs.

The legs of most tripods are made in sections that telescope into each other. Two-section legs are normal for studio tripods, while three- or four-section legs are common on the lighter portable models. Tripods with more sections are generally weaker—each moving part is a potential weak spot—but they fold up to a shorter length for easier carrying. The telescoping legs make the tripod compact, portable, and easy to adjust.

Locks. Each section must lock securely at any point along its length. Twist-lock collars are usually employed on tubular legs. U-channel legs normally have flip-type locks that are released by flipping a lever. Flip-type locks and others of similar operation are either fully locked or fully released; most have no provision for controlled slippage to make fine

Tripods

screw unlocks the ball joint to permit turns and tilts in any combination. More sophisticated heads have separate controls for panning and tilting. Tripod heads made for heavy cameras tilt by means of a geared mechanism. This provides a great deal of control with virtually no slippage. Some heads have double tilt controls: one to tilt the camera right and left, and the other for forward and back tilting.

As is the case with all other parts, the tilting and panning controls must lock securely. All screws and moving parts should be made of steel or brass, and must be kept clean and free of corrosion. With very few exceptions, tripods are sold with heads that are made proportionate to the tripod's capacity. A different head can be attached for a particular shooting situation. Remember that the head adds weight, and a head that is too heavy for a lightweight tripod not only adds stress but also creates a problem of balance by raising the tripod's center of gravity.

Special Tripod Heads. A few camera manufacturers produce special pan heads for making panoramic sequences. Typically, such a head allows the camera to be turned after an exposure, stopping exactly where the next frame should line up with its predecessor. An ordinary head with calibrated panning controls will do just as well.

To calibrate a pan head for panoramic sequences the following will be necessary:

A spirit level
A piece of ground glass (to fit
   the camera back)
A marker
Some heavy tape
An empty camera

Set up the tripod in an area where there are many vertical lines on the screen—a city street for example. Adjust the tripod until it is perfectly level. Set all tilt controls to zero. Attach the camera to the tripod, open the back, open the shutter ("T" setting or "B" setting with locking release), and tape the ground glass—ground face down—to the camera, making sure that the ground face is exactly in the film plane. Focus the camera; the scene will appear on the ground glass. Make a mark on the top of the tripod and one on the pan head directly opposite it. This is the mark for the first frame. Note a point exactly on the left edge of the image. Turn the pan head until the point disappears beyond the right edge. Lock the pan head and make a second mark on it opposite the stationary mark. This is the second frame mark. Continue until you have panned a complete circle. (*See:* PANORAMIC PHOTOGRAPHY.)

In making motion pictures from a moving vehicle, it is necessary to keep the camera fixed on the subject. For this purpose there is a special tripod with a head that "floats" in liquid and is kept fixed by means of a gyroscope.

Quick Release. Since the attachment and removal of cameras can be a slow process, some tripod heads are made with a quick-release feature. This is, in effect, a two-part camera platform. One part is attached to the camera, and is locked in turn to the tripod head. It is most useful when more than one camera is employed in rapid succession, such as for taking the same picture on different films. There are also accessory platforms that can hold two cameras.

The Finish. A shiny chrome tripod can reflect unwanted light on the subject while a tripod with dull or gray finish will not. The best finish is dull black, but if you plan to work in the desert sun, black equipment should be avoided. It absorbs heat, and expansion can cause the parts to bind. In this case a shiny tripod is better, but a black cloth should be draped over the front to avoid unwanted reflections on the subjects when shooting close up. If secondhand equipment is being purchased, check the finish for dents and deep scratches. There may be other damage underneath.

Testing

Any tripod can be tested before buying by taking the following steps:

1. Extend the legs to maximum height, raise the center post to full elevation, lock all locks, and tighten all controls on the pan head.
2. Press your hand on top of the camera platform with about twice the weight of the camera and shake it lightly. Nothing should slip and nothing should rattle. Note that there is some springiness inherent in the metal and the rubber leg tips—it should not be excessive.
3. With the legs open to about half their widest spread, give the tripod head a

light push—enough to lift one leg off the floor. It should not fall over or fold.

4. With pressure on the head, try to slide the open tripod across the floor. The rubber tips should prevent this from happening.

5. Twist the head from side to side—there should be no wobble in the legs.

6. Examine the locks. They should not slip under pressure, and too much effort should not be exerted in tightening or releasing. Locks should permit partial tightening or loosening in order to make adjustments.

Using the Tripod

Once a tripod has passed the test within reasonable bounds, the camera can be placed upon it. Always try to keep one leg directly under the lens (unless extremely wide-angle lenses are being used). With view cameras or long lenses, be sure that they are balanced on the platform. Long lenses usually have their own tripod sockets, and view cameras can be moved forward or back to establish good balance.

By attaching the camera, the tripod's center of gravity is raised, and consequently its stability is diminished. The center of gravity can be lowered by attaching weight below the center post. Simply hang a camera bag there, if it is heavy enough. Or fill a bag with sand or water and hang it under the tripod. It is best to do this after the tripod is set up and most of the adjustments are completed.

Whenever setting up on uneven terrain, a slanted surface, or a stairway, place two legs on the "downhill" side of the camera.

• *See also:* CAMERA SUPPORTS; PANORAMIC PHOTOGRAPHY.

Tropical Photography

The advice given in this article applies to any part of the world where hot and humid or hot and dry conditions prevail for long periods. In many places within the tropics, heat coupled with high humidity is constant throughout the year. In other places, conditions may be extremely hot and dry; then dust becomes a major problem for the photographer. As

a rule, the tourist need take only elementary precautions to protect equipment and materials, but the photographer whose stay in the tropics will be much longer must protect photographic goods against heat, humidity, dust, and the growth of fungus or mildew.

Moderately high temperature in itself is not detrimental to cameras and auxiliary equipment, but it hastens the natural deterioration of sensitized materials, particularly color films and papers. However, high temperature and high relative humidity together promote corrosion of metal, growth of fungus, and moisture damage to packaging materials. Moreover, high temperature and high relative humidity greatly accelerate changes in the sensitometric characteristics of films and photographic papers. Abrasive dust is a serious threat to the glass surfaces of lenses and other optical equipment, as well as being a nuisance in processing.

The following instructions are intended for photographers who work in tropical climates either as residents or on location for a considerable time. The precautions may or may not be necessary depending on the particular climate and on the facilities available. Today, many buildings in the tropics are air-conditioned, and such appliances as humidifiers, dehumidifiers, and refrigerators—portable or otherwise—are either available locally or they can be shipped in and used where electricity is supplied.

Care of Photographic Equipment

Avoid subjecting cameras and accessories to intense heat, except for those times when the equipment is in actual use. When high temperature is coupled with high humidity, the growth of fungus on bellows, camera cases, fabrics, and even lenses is a certainty.

Do not leave cameras and accessories in hot sunshine for longer than is necessary. Also avoid leaving them in enclosed spaces, such as the glove compartment or the trunk of a car that is standing in the sun. Remember that a white surface reflects heat as well as light. For that reason, a white-painted enclosure remains cooler in sunshine than a dark-colored one.

Abrasive dust is a major problem in many tropical climates. There are few enclosures that can exclude it altogether. Enclosing the camera and auxiliary lenses in plastic bags is helpful, but in a humid atmosphere the stagnant air in the bags promotes the rapid growth of fungus. Equipment should not be kept enclosed in this way for longer than a few hours.

Constant cleaning of the camera parts before and after use is a necessary procedure. Special care must be taken with lenses. The abrasive action of gritty dust is a serious threat to the glass surfaces, and consequently, to the photographic image. Clean lenses by gently brushing or blowing off dust. Any wiping or cleaning with fluid or tissue must be done with the greatest care and as infrequently as possible. Keep both ends of lenses capped when not in use.

Some photographers mount a haze filter or a piece of optical glass permanently on the lens as protection against abrasion by dust. A scratched filter can be renewed at moderate cost if necessary. A haze filter has no appreciable effect on exposures.

Storage of Photographic Materials

Sensitized photographic materials are perishable products under practically any conditions. Proper storage is therefore important at all times. Deterioration is particularly rapid in a hot and humid atmosphere.

Black-and-white materials withstand moderate heat without serious changes in their characteristics. Color materials, however, must be kept at temperatures below 10 C (55 F) in order to retard undesirable changes. Storage at -18 to -23 C (0 to -10 F) is recommended if color materials are stored for a considerable time.

Extremes of relative humidity are a serious threat to all photographic materials, even at moderate temperatures. At high temperatures, the effects of humidity are greatly accelerated. Not only are the material's sensitometric characteristics impaired, but physical damage occurs as well. Sheets of film may stick together or become glazed in patches where they touch one another. Rolls of film may "block" or stick so that they cannot be unwound, or the outside edges of the roll may be affected more than the inside so that the film buckles. Moreover, cardboard cartons swell and break open, labels drop off, and cans rust. These effects can be expected if the relative humidity remains above 60 percent. Extremely low relative humidity, on the other hand, is not quite so serious; however, if it falls below 15

percent for a considerable time, an electric humidifier should be installed and set to maintain a relative humidity of 40 to 50 percent in the storage area. (*See:* Storage of Sensitized Materials and Processing Solutions.)

Care of Exposed Films

When a film has been removed from its moisture-resistant envelope, it is immediately subject to deterioration in a hot and humid climate. When the film has been exposed, the latent image will also deteriorate. Color films are particularly susceptible in this respect. Consequently, all films should be processed as soon as possible after exposure. If processing facilities are not available in the near vicinity, mail the film to the most convenient processing station immediately. If this is not possible, enclose the films in an airtight jar or a can together with a desiccant, and place them in a refrigerator. Exposed films can be kept for several days in this way.

Exposure

Although it has often been said that less exposure is needed in the tropics, this is not necessarily so. Measurements made in various parts of the world have shown that when atmospheric conditions are similar and when the sun is at the same elevation in the sky, the intensity of illumination is practically the same regardless of geographical location. Since the sun reaches a higher elevation in the tropics than elsewhere, the light intensity is extremely high when the sun is at its zenith. This in itself is not a difficulty—exposure can easily be adjusted for the higher light intensity; but when the atmosphere is clear and the sky cloudless, the lighting contrast is also extremely high. In these conditions, shadows tend to lack detail even though the highlights are correctly exposed or perhaps overexposed.

In color photography, little can be done about the above effect except to wait until lighting conditions are more favorable. In black-and-white work, extra exposure can be given to get more shadow detail, and then the development of the film can be reduced to lower the highlight density. Another effect of taking photographs when the sun is directly overhead occurs in landscapes without high trees or buildings. The absence of shadow then yields a very flat, uninteresting picture. The only way to avoid this result is to photograph the subject either earlier or later in the day when shadows are longer.

Processing Films

If processing is carried out in an air-conditioned building, tropical temperatures will not be a problem. If the building is not air-conditioned, install a room air conditioner in the darkroom to avoid the difficulties associated with high-temperature processing. Color processes are carried out at relatively high temperatures, but in any case, it is not recommended that color processing be undertaken under primitive conditions.

If for some reason you are forced to process black-and-white films when temperature control is impossible, follow this procedure:

1. Use a prehardening bath, such as Kodak prehardener SH-5, before development. This hardens the emulsion enough to permit processing at temperatures up to 38 C (100 F).
2. To avoid reticulation of gelatin coatings on the negatives, keep the temperature of all solutions, including the wash water, within 3 C (5 F) of each other.
3. Fix the film in a fresh hardening fixer, such as Kodak rapid fixer or Kodak Ektaflo fixer.
4. Rinse the negatives for 30 seconds in fresh water and then bathe them in a hypo eliminator, such as Kodak hypo clearing agent, for 2 minutes with agitation. Wash for 5 minutes in running water or in several complete changes of fresh water. Washing for longer than 10 to 15 minutes at high temperature softens the gelatin and should be avoided.
5. In a dusty atmosphere, grit and sand find their way into processing solutions and wash water. To avoid scratching the films, rinse them well but do not wipe them before drying. Use a wetting agent, such as fresh Kodak Photo-Flo solution, to help drain off surplus water, and hang the films to dry in a dust-free place.

High-Temperature Processing. Whenever possible, hold the temperature of the processing solutions at 18 to 24 C (65 to 75 F). When this is not practical, take special precautions to avoid excessive swelling and softening.

At higher temperatures, use a prehardener before development to allow use of normal solutions and processing procedure, even at temperatures as high as 43 C (110 F). See the prehardener formula in the article HARDENING BATHS for full instructions on its use, including adjustment of developing time for various temperatures. See the article HIGH-TEMPERATURE PROCESSING for details on processing film at high temperatures.

Processing Black-and-White Papers

In general, black-and-white printing is not particularly troublesome in tropical climates unless the temperature in the darkroom is extremely high. Remember, however, unless prints are properly fixed and thoroughly washed, they discolor and fade when conditions are hot and humid all the time.

The following hints will be helpful if prints must be made when conditions are difficult:

1. At high temperatures, development will be very much shorter than the normal recommended time. Do not force development beyond the point where the print does not appear to be getting darker. Overdevelopment results in fog and yellow stain, as well as in softening of the paper.
2. Change the developer as soon as it becomes discolored. Oxidation takes place rapidly in a hot atmosphere.
3. Use a less energetic developer, such as Kodak Selectol instead of Kodak Dektol developer. This permits a slightly longer developing time.
4. The addition of a chemical agent, such as Kodak anti-fog, no. 1, to the developer helps to prevent stain and fog on papers that have been improperly stored.
5. To prevent stain and swelling of the gelatin, use a fresh stop bath and agitate the prints thoroughly, particularly during the first few seconds of immersion.
6. Use the two-bath fixing system and keep the baths fresh to provide the best hardening and the most permanent

prints. Improperly fixed prints will stain and fade rapidly in a hot, moist atmosphere.

7. Reduce washing time to the minimum by using a hypo clearing agent.

Processing Color Films and Papers

It would appear that processing color films and papers under tropical conditions would be easier than handling black-and-white films, inasmuch as almost all modern color materials are designed for processing at temperatures of from 31 to 39 C (88 to 102 F). It is important, however, to remember that if temperature and humidity in the darkroom are excessively high, damage can occur to color materials before processing actually begins. Strict temperature control during processing is just as necessary at high room temperatures. And, most of all, humidity control is essential during the drying of the films or papers to avoid damage.

A portable room air conditioner that has a 4400 BTU capacity is probably adequate for a small darkroom, but it should be allowed to run for several hours before work begins. This is to allow the machine to reduce the humidity, as well as the temperature, to more adequate levels. If adequate conditions are not available, then no attempt should be made to process color films in the tropics. It is better to dehydrate the film and pack it for shipment to a regular laboratory.

Avoid improvised room cooling with ice. While it can reduce temperatures to tolerable levels, it does nothing to reduce the humidity, and under some circumstances, may in fact increase it.

Preservation of Negatives

Because deterioration caused by residual chemicals in the emulsion takes place rapidly in a hot and humid atmosphere, always fix and wash films thoroughly. In handling negatives, wear cotton gloves to avoid finger marks. When the negatives are not in actual use, keep them in clean envelopes, because any greasy residue deposited on the surface by indoor atmosphere promotes the rapid growth of fungus, which eventually destroys the gelatin coating on the film.

The most important consideration in storing negatives in a humid climate is to keep them dry. That is to say, maintain a relative humidity of be-

tween 40 and 50 percent in the storage area. If a building is properly air-conditioned, the relative humidity will not be higher than this. However, if it exceeds 55 percent for any considerable period, install an electric dehumidifier. If other means of keeping negatives dry are not available, they can be stored in a heated cabinet as described later in this article. Alternatively, they can be enclosed in a metal box with a desiccant.

For the best storage conditions, negative envelopes should conform to ANSI Standard PH4.20, "Photographic Filing Enclosures for Storing Processed Photographic Films, Plates, and Papers." In a tropical climate, however, negatives should not be stored for a long time without inspecting their condition. Do this at regular intervals so that any deterioration that might have taken place can be remedied and more suitable storage conditions can be arranged.

Preservation of Prints

In general, the same remarks apply to preserving prints as to preserving negatives. Careful processing and storage in a dry place are the principal requirements.

When black-and-white prints are used for decoration or display, hypo-alum toning has been found helpful in preserving the prints from atmospheric effects and from attack by fungus. Color prints should be lacquered so that they can be wiped clean occasionally.

Prints should always be dry-mounted; many pastes and gums are hygroscopic, and they attract insects and fungus. Use photographic-quality mounting board—impurities in ordinary cardboards may discolor the prints in a short time. This applies also to interleaving paper and album leaves.

At relative humidities below 60 percent, prints keep well in an album if the pages are large enough to allow a 3½-inch border on all four sides of the prints. The closed album then gives a measure of protection against atmospheric effects and attack by insects or fungus, particularly when the prints have been treated with a fungicide such as Hyamine. Instructions for using Hyamine are given later in this article. Note that fungicides cannot be used with color prints.

If the relative humidity is above 60 percent, pack the prints or the album in a sealed container together with a desiccant. Single prints, whether mounted or unmounted, should be interleaved with good-quality paper. To be sure that deterioration is not taking place, inspect valuable material periodically and renew the interleaving paper or any other packing material at these times.

Fungus

Airborne spores of fungus are everywhere, and they exist in immense variety. Mold and mildew are the familiar kinds that flourish in warm, damp places. Generally, the type of fungus troublesome to photographers in the tropics grows most readily at temperatures between 24 and 30 C (75 and 85 F). It feeds on dead organic matter such as leather, cloth, wood, paper, and gelatin, but it will spread and damage other materials—the glass of lenses in cameras and binoculars, for example.

Moisture is essential to the growth of practically all varieties of fungus, and they thrive in darkness. In a hot damp atmosphere, cameras, sensitized materials, negatives and prints, as well as clothing and other fabrics, will be attacked. The only really practical way to prevent the attack of fungus is to keep the articles as dry and clean as possible.

A heated box or a cabinet in which an electric light bulb or a small electric heater element is kept switched on can be used to keep cameras and other equipment dry. Adjust the temperature in this type of enclosure so that it is about 5 C (10 F) higher than the room temperature. Also, allow air to circulate through ventilation holes in the top and bottom of

This spotted effect is not uncommon in tropical photography. Growth of fungus on unexposed film is the cause. Fungus often occurs when film in a partially opened envelope is exposed to a warm, damp atmosphere.

the box or cabinet. Do not keep films or photographic papers in enclosures such as those described above.

The best way to reduce the relative humidity in a room is by using a refrigeration-type dehumidifier. Then the heated enclosure is not necessary. In this connection, remember that although a room-type air conditioner reduces the temperature, in so doing, it may increase the relative humidity. Some units are more efficient in dissipating moisture than others. In a properly air-conditioned building, however, the difficulty will not arise.

Fungicides

These chemicals are not generally useful in protecting photographic goods from fungus. Many fungicides are poisonous and most of them have a detrimental effect on color materials. However, they can be used to retard the growth of fungus on processed black-and-white negatives and prints.

Treating Black-and-White Negatives. When the negatives have been washed, bathe them in a 1 percent solution of zinc fluosilicate and water, and dry them without wiping. To promote uniform drying, add 1 part wetting agent, such as Kodak Photo-Flo solution, to 200 parts zinc fluosilicate solution. Any residue that remains on the base side of unbacked films, such as 35 mm, motion-picture, and aero films, can be removed with a damp sponge. *Remember to wash the sponge thoroughly afterwards.*

WARNING: Zinc fluosilicate is an extremely poisonous chemical; its use as described above should be confined to photographic workrooms. It can be fatal if swallowed, even in a dilute solution. Wash the hands and everything else that has been in contact with zinc fluosilicate thoroughly after each use. Place clearly recognizable poison labels on all containers of the chemical. On no account should zinc fluosilicate, or negatives that have been treated with it, be stored in areas to which children have access.

Treating Black-and-White Prints. Since both gelatin and paper are feeding grounds for fungus, protection against such growth is necessary for prints that are displayed or stored for long periods in tropical climates. Although there is no known method that affords complete protection, the following procedure coupled with proper processing and

washing will protect prints against deterioration for several years. Immerse the well-washed prints in a 1 percent solution of Hyamine 1622* for 3 to 5 minutes with occasional agitation. The solution temperature should not be lower than 21 C (70 F). White-base papers may show a very slight discoloration due to the Hyamine solution, but this is less objectionable than the damage caused by fungus.

At present, there is no treatment similar to the above that can be used for color prints. However, spraying the prints with lacquer gives some protection. Print lacquer is not immune to attack by fungus, but the lacquered surface can be wiped clean at frequent intervals. Take care not to finger-mark the surface, because the oils from the skin provide excellent fare for airborne spores of fungus.

Removal of Fungus. Because the growth of fungus causes gelatin to become soluble in water, negatives and prints that have been attacked by a fungus growth must not be washed with water. Generally, the damage done by fungus is irreversible, but if the growth is slight, it can be removed by wiping the surface with a piece of cotton moistened with film cleaner.

Remove the cardboard mounts from slides before cleaning and remount them afterwards. Place negatives in fresh sleeves or envelopes, and discard any folders or interleaving paper used for packing prints. Replace the folders or interleaving paper with clean, dry material. Refer to the previous section "Preservation of Prints" in this article for further information on this subject.

Using a Desiccant

As stated earlier in this article, humidity is probably the worst enemy of photographic goods in tropical climates. If materials are enclosed in an airtight container when the atmosphere is humid, the situation is not altered—conditions in the container are similar to those in which it was loaded and sealed. However, if a desiccant such as silica gel is enclosed in the container with the goods, the desiccant absorbs moisture and protects them from the effects of excessive high humidity. In this connection, remember that the relative humidity is usually high in a refrigerator, and it may be extreme if the relative humidity of the surrounding air is high.

*Supplied by Rohm and Haas Company, Independence Mall West, Philadelphia, Pa. 19105.

Silica gel resembles coarse, white sand in appearance; each grain is porous, and like a sponge, it absorbs moisture in considerable quantity. Silica gel is odorless and tasteless, as well as nonreactive with most common materials. It is obtainable in its natural form or colored with an indicator dye that changes from deep blue to pink when saturated with moisture. It can then be dried in a hot oven for a few hours and used again. The colored silica gel is dry when the color returns to blue.

• *See also:* COLOR FILM PROCESSING; FORMULAS FOR BLACK-AND-WHITE PROCESSING; FUNGUS ON FILM; HARDENING BATHS; HIGH-TEMPERATURE PROCESSING; STORAGE OF SENSITIZED MATERIALS AND PROCESSING SOLUTIONS.

Further Reading: Time-Life Books, eds. *Caring for Photographs.* New York, NY: Time-Life Books, 1972; Phillips, Van and Owen Thomas. *Travellers' Book of Colour Photography.* Garden City, NY: Amphoto, 1973.

T-Stop

The *f*-stop settings of lenses are calculated from the relationship between the size of the aperture and the focal length. While geometrically correct, the calculation assumes 100 percent transmission of the light entering the aperture; actually, no lens gives such perfect performance.

In modern lenses, highly efficient coatings reduce light losses to an insignificant point for almost all photographic uses. But uncoated lenses have a significant light loss owing to reflection at each air-to-glass surface. Each uncoated glass-air surface reflects about 5 percent of the light; thus, a three-element lens with six surfaces might have a light loss of 30 percent. More complex lenses had losses of over 50 percent before the coating of elements became common. As a result, a simple few-element lens set at, for example, *f*/8 would transmit more light than a more complex many-element lens also set at *f*/8.

This problem was especially serious for professional motion-picture photographers, who not only needed to use a variety of focal lengths but also needed exactly matched exposures so that shots taken with different lenses could be intercut without changes in the tonal scale of the scene.

The solution was to calibrate lenses not in terms of geometrical *f*-stops, but in terms of the actual transmittance at each aperture. This produced a series of T-stops, or T-numbers. Some manufacturers supplied lenses marked in T-stops, and most professional camera operators had the transmittance of their *f*-numbered lenses measured so they could determine the equivalent T-numbers.

Calculating T-Stops

T-values are related to transmittance (T), which is the numerical ratio between the amount of light a lens transmits and the amount of light incident upon it. For example, if a lens transmits three-quarters of the light, its transmittance is $75 \div 100 = 0.75$. (Transmission is the percentage expression of the same information. That is, transmission = transmittance $\times$ 100. And, of course, transmittance = transmission $\div$ 100.)

For a perfect lens with a transmittance of 1 (or 100 percent transmission), T-values and *f*-values are identical. For actual lenses, the relationship is:

$$\text{T-number} = \textit{f}\text{-number} \div \sqrt{\text{Transmittance}}$$

For example, in a lens with 70 percent transmission, $T = 0.7$ and the T-value of the *f*/8 setting is:

$$T = 8 \div \sqrt{0.7} = 8 \div 0.84 = 9.5$$

Thus, in objective terms the lens is about one-half stop slower than its marked value. If all lenses have the same degree of loss, this is not a serious problem. However, since many lenses had significantly different transmittances, it was useful to know their T-values so that they could be set at apertures that transmitted equal amounts of light even though the *f*-numbers of the settings might have differed.

Obsolescence of T-Stops

Modern lens coatings have virtually eliminated the need for T-stops because transmission is commonly 90 percent or better. For example, compare the T-values of *f*/8 in two lenses, one with 90 percent transmission (T=0.9) or a 10 percent loss, and one with 96 percent transmission (T=0.96) or a 4 percent loss:

$$8 \div \sqrt{0.9} = 8 \div 0.95 = 8.4$$
$$8 \div \sqrt{0.96} = 8 \div 0.98 = 8.2$$

In each case, the T-value is less than one-sixth of a stop different from the *f*-value, so there is no advantage in T-stop calibration.

In addition, depth of field cannot be calculated from T-numbers, because it depends on optical geometry—as utilized in calculating *f*-numbers—and not on transmittance characteristics.

T-values are useful in determining settings for apertures that are not circular. Many simple automatic-exposure cameras use adjustable plates to create diamond-shaped or other noncircular apertures for mechanical simplicity. The T-values of various-size openings may be computed in designing the control system, but they are not marked on the camera and are of no concern to the photographer. An alternate approach is to use the diameter of a circle whose area equals the area of the odd-shaped opening to calculate the *f*-number.

Thus, the T-stop system now has only very specialized relevance. Never widely used, it is now virtually obsolete; it is very rare to encounter a lens marked with T-numbers.

• *See also:* DEPTH OF FIELD; DIAPHRAGM; *f*-NUMBER; *f*-STOP.

Tungsten-Halogen Lamp

The tungsten-halogen lamp is a form of incandescent lamp containing a tungsten filament in an envelope made of quartz or high-silica glass and having a small amount of iodine or bromine vapor in place of air within the envelope. The best known lamp, the quartz-iodine lamp, is a specific type of tungsten-halogen lamp.

The halogen vapor in the lamp prevents tungsten evaporated from the heated filament from being deposited on the inside of the lamp walls. This prevents darkening with age so that the lamp has an output of nearly constant color temperature throughout its life. Fused quartz or a form of heat-resistant glass is required for the envelope because the filament is operated at a very high temperature.

Compared with conventional incandescent lamps, tungsten-halogen lamps provide very light weight and small size, greater efficiency, and ex-

tended usefulness in color photography because of unchanging color temperature. However, they offer little improvement in total burning hours.

• *See also:* HALOGEN LAMP; LIGHTING; QUARTZ-IODINE LAMP.

Twin-Lens Reflex Cameras

A twin-lens reflex (TLR) camera is a camera in which one lens is used to form the image to be recorded on the film, and a second lens of matched focal length is used for viewing and focusing. The TLR concept originated in the nineteenth century, but was of limited use with glass plates and sheet films. The first successful twin-lens reflex camera, the Rolleiflex, was introduced in 1928, thirty years after the invention of modern roll film. It established the design that has dominated the field ever since.

Modern Twin-Lens Reflex Cameras

Today, almost all TLR cameras use 120/220 roll film to produce images measuring 6 × 6 cm (2¼″ × 2¼″) or 6 × 4.5 cm (2¼″ × 1¾″). (There is one TLR studio camera, the Gowlandflex, designed to use 4″ × 5″ sheet film.)

The normal lens for 120/220 TLR cameras has a focal length of 75–80 mm, and usually has a built-in shutter. The viewing lens, mounted directly above on the same lens board, must have exactly the same focal length for accurate focusing, but it may have a wider aperture to provide as bright an image as possible and to minimize depth of field as an aid to adjusting focus precisely.

Most TLR cameras do not have interchangeable lenses. Wide-angle and telephoto focal lengths are obtained by adding matched attachments in front of both lenses, or by focusing through an attachment which is then moved to the lower lens to take the picture. In those cameras that do have interchangeable lenses, the entire lens board is replaced with another which carries a pair of lenses of the desired focal length. This requires that the camera have an auxiliary shutter at the focal plane to protect the film when lenses are changed at midroll.

Many cameras have a folding crank on the side, which simultaneously advances the film and cocks

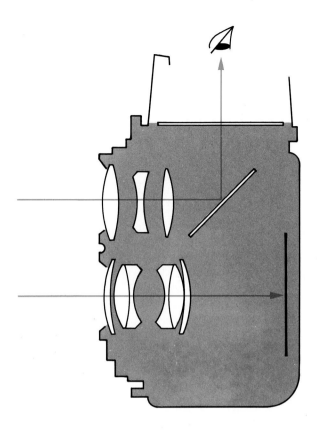

A twin-lens reflex camera is in a sense two cameras in a single housing. The optical distance from the viewing lens, mirror, and viewing screen must equal that from the lower lens to the film. The viewing and taking lenses move as a unit in focusing. The pop-up focusing magnifier folds down to permit full-screen viewing.

the shutter with a single, full turn, or which advances the film with a half-turn forward and cocks the shutter with a half-turn back. The least expensive models have a knob to advance the film and a separate lever to cock the shutter. A frame counter is coupled to the advance mechanism. Some cameras have built-in meters, which may be coupled to either an automatic or semiautomatic exposure control system.

Twin-Lens Reflex Viewing

The image from the viewing lens is reflected by a mirror upward to a viewing screen. The image is upright, but reversed right-for-left. The mirror does not move, which eliminates the vibration, noise, and image blackout at the moment of exposure that are unavoidable with a single-lens reflex camera. A folding hood shields the screen from stray light; it usually has a built-in pop-up magnifier to aid in critical focusing.

Because the hood is open at the top, the image must be viewed from above the camera. This leads to a characteristic chest- or waist-level point of view which may not be suitable for all subjects—for example, portraits—but which makes low-angle photography especially easy. Eye-level viewing may be accomplished by various methods. In the simplest method, a panel in the front of the hood is pushed down to cover the screen and permit straight-through viewing from an eyehole in the rear hood panel. This sports-finder viewing requires that the camera be either focused on infinity or zone-focused by means of the distance scale located around the focus control knob or along the lens-board track.

A second method of eye-level viewing uses a mirror in the hood, which is lowered to an angled position to reflect the screen image to the rear panel eyehole. The most versatile and accurate method uses an accessory prism viewer that replaces the hood above the screen.

TLR Parallax

Because the two lenses of a TLR camera are separated by 50 mm or more (2 or more inches), parallax can have a significant effect on the accuracy of viewing and framing, especially at close distances. In some cameras, a coupling mechanism tilts the viewing lens downward to compensate as close distances are focused; in others, it moves a mask in the viewfinder. The simplest cameras provide only reference lines on the viewing screen by which the actual top of the picture can be judged, but the bottom of the picture is off the screen. Although these methods permit more accurate framing, they cannot correct for the different angle from which the two lenses see the subject. This can be overcome by the somewhat cumbersome expedient of using a tripod with an adjustable center post, or an accessory telescoping tube support. After focusing, the camera is raised to place the lower lens exactly in the position occupied by the viewing lens in order to take the picture.

• *See also:* CAMERAS; FOCUSING SYSTEMS; PARALLAX; SINGLE-LENS REFLEX CAMERAS; VIEWING AND FOCUSING.

Ultraviolet and Fluorescence Photography

Ultraviolet cannot be seen by the normal human eye and is often termed "invisible," as are all other electromagnetic radiations except those in the short visible range. Photographic emulsions, however, are inherently sensitive to most wavelengths of ultraviolet. By using a filter that absorbs all visible light but passes ultraviolet, it is possible to make a photographic exposure with just ultraviolet. This technique is called "ultraviolet photography."

Ultraviolet Photography

The main purpose of ultraviolet photography is to provide information about an object or material that cannot be obtained by other photographic methods. Obviously, if differentiation between two substances is produced in photography with visible light or infrared radiation, there is little need to resort to ultraviolet photography. If the first two methods fail, however, there is always the possibility that the third method might succeed. In many cases, it is worth a try.

Ultraviolet photography is usually accomplished by reflected radiation and depends upon the premise that two or more elements of an object will reflect or absorb ultraviolet to different degrees. Techniques in visible and in infrared photography operate on essentially the same principle—except, of course, that in most visible-light photography the elements of an object may show color contrast.

Some materials will absorb ultraviolet, while others will reflect these radiations. Some have partial absorption and partial reflection. These effects can be recorded photographically by using ultraviolet radiation.

Ultraviolet Radiation

The complete range of electromagnetic radiation extends from the extremely short wavelengths of gamma and x-rays to the extremely long wavelengths that comprise the radio bands. The visible spectrum is included in this range and contains a narrow band of radiations from about 400 to 700 nanometres in wavelength. These are the radiations used in normal photography with either color or black-and-white film. Another narrow band of radiations is also included in the complete spectrum and is comprised of shorter wavelengths than the visible. This is the band of ultraviolet radiation, extending from about 10 nanometres in wavelength to 400 nanometres, the lower limit of the spectrum.

Kinds of Ultraviolet

For practical photographic purposes the ultraviolet spectrum is arbitrarily divided into three very narrow bands: long-wave ultraviolet, middle ultraviolet, and short-wave ultraviolet. Another band, called "vacuum ultraviolet," also exists but is not usable in photography.

Long-Wave Ultraviolet. Long-wave ultraviolet is considered to extend from about 320 to 400 nanometres. This is the range of ultraviolet transmitted by regular optical glass, of which most photographic lenses are made. This range, therefore, is of most practical value in ultraviolet photography.

Middle Ultraviolet. This includes radiations from about 280 to 320 nanometres. Part of this band of ultraviolet rays (295–320) is included in sunlight, and is noted for its tanning action on human skin, sometimes causing sunburn. These rays are also emitted from sunlamps used indoors for tanning effects. Middle ultraviolet radiations are not transmitted by regular photographic lenses. A lens made of quartz, however, will transmit these rays and could therefore produce an image using them. Quartz lenses transmit the long-wave ultraviolet.

Short-Wave Ultraviolet. Short-wave ultraviolet extends from about 200 to 280 nanometres in wavelength. This band is sometimes called "far ultraviolet," since it is farthest from the visible range. It is notable for its germicidal effects, but will also cause sunburn of unprotected eyes or skin. For this reason, you should never look directly at a source of short-wave ultraviolet radiation. A quartz lens will transmit most wavelengths of short ultraviolet.

Vacuum Ultraviolet. This includes wavelengths shorter than 200 nanometres, and down to about 10 nanometres, the upper limit of x-rays. These radiations are transmitted only through a vacuum, and thus are of no practical value in photography. They exist in sunlight, but are detectable only in outer space. In the laboratory, they might be produced from an artificial source in a vacuum.

Radiation Sources

There are many light sources that emit ultraviolet radiation, but not all of them are suitable for all types of ultraviolet photography.

Sunlight. Sunlight is probably the most common source of long-wave ultraviolet radiation. Although the long and some middle waves of ultraviolet pass rather freely through the atmosphere, the short waves are attenuated by scattering and by absorption due to moisture and gases in the atmosphere. A sufficient amount of long-wave ultraviolet is usually present, and bright sunlight could be used to illuminate rather large areas with ultraviolet radiation, particularly on a dry day. For ultraviolet photography with sunlight, a filter is placed over the camera lens. This filter should transmit long-wave ultraviolet freely, and absorb *all* visible light. The filter should be closely fitted to the camera lens so that no visible light enters the lens.

Fluorescent Tubes. These are often used in the photographic studio to provide visual illumination over a large area. Special tubes of this type can be used to furnish ultraviolet radiation for photography. Ultraviolet is produced in such tubes by a discharge of electricity through a carrier gas, such as argon.

The glass of the tube is usually opaque to most visible light but freely transmits the long-wave ultraviolet. Tubes of this type are often called "black light" tubes, since they appear black visually. They can be obtained in several lengths, up to 48 inches long, so they can be used to illuminate large areas with ultraviolet light. They can be operated in standard fluorescent light fixtures, with the standard starter coil and ballast. Tubes of this type are called "low pressure" mercury vapor lamps.

Mercury Vapor Lamps. Mercury vapor lamps of "high pressure" consist of small tubular quartz envelopes in which mercury vapor is produced under a pressure of several atmospheres. These lamps require high electrical current for operation, with a considerable output of long-wave ultraviolet. They also, however, emit some middle-wave and short-wave ultraviolet. They are of particular advantage in illuminating reasonably small areas with high ultraviolet brightness. Special mercury vapor lamps of this type, and of high wattage, are of particular interest in both ultraviolet photomicrography and ultraviolet spectrography. Mercury vapor lamps produce extremely bright spectral lines, in both the ultraviolet and the visible range. (See the accompanying graph.) Special transformers are usually required for operation, and a warm-up period of several minutes is necessary for highest brightness.

Arc Lamps. These are also used on occasion to produce very intense ultraviolet radiation, either medium-wave or long-wave. The cored carbon arc is probably the most well-known lamp of this type. An arc is produced by impressing electricity across two electrodes of carbon in close proximity, and in air. Since the carbon is consumed in the process, a mechanical means is necessary to maintain a constant separation between the electrodes. In a similar manner, electrodes of cadmium can be used to produce an extremely bright line at 275 nanometres. The xenon arc is enclosed in a small glass tube containing metal electrodes in a high-pressure atmosphere of xenon gas. Although this arc lamp emits some long-wave ultraviolet, its primary use is in visual-light photography and photomicrography. A continuous spectrum is produced in the ultraviolet, visible, and infrared spectral ranges.

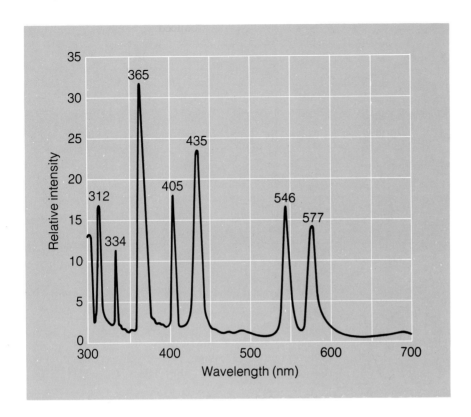

The special lines of high-pressure mercury arc lamps emit considerable long-wave ultraviolet radiation; note that there is some middle-wave and short-wave ultraviolet emission as well.

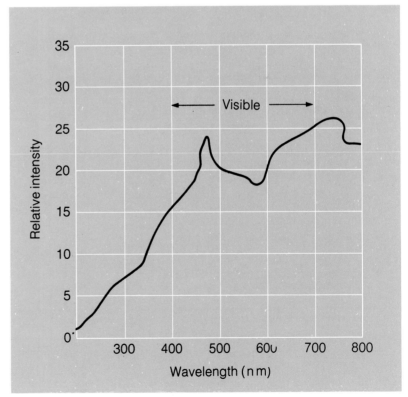

The average emission spectrum of high-pressure xenon arc light is more suited to visual light and photomacrography; some ultraviolet light is emitted.

Ultraviolet and Fluorescence Photography

Electronic Flash Lamps. These lamps vary considerably in ultraviolet output, depending to some extent on the type of gas contained within the tubes. A tube containing a high percentage of krypton or argon emits more blue and long-wave ultraviolet than one in which xenon predominates. All electronic flash lamps, however, emit some long-wave ultraviolet and can be used in reflected ultraviolet photography. Those lamps in which the tube and envelope are composed of quartz also emit some shorter wavelengths of ultraviolet.

Wire-Filled Flash Lamps. This type of lamp is also suitable for reflected ultraviolet photography, since these light sources, either blue-coated or clear, emit enough long-wave ultraviolet for instantaneous exposures at near subject distances.

Photographic Considerations

In order to photograph an object by reflected ultraviolet radiation, the following steps are necessary:

1. Illuminate the object by means of a radiation source that emits ultraviolet.
2. Exclude all visible light from the camera by placing over the lens a filter that transmits *only* ultraviolet.
3. Record the image in the camera on a suitable photographic material (film or plate).

Illumination. The selection of a source for ultraviolet photography depends primarily upon certain factors such as availability, cost, convenience, object size, and source emission. Sunlight, of course, is most readily available, costs nothing, and provides a broad source of illumination. On the other hand, the intensity of ultraviolet available is quite variable due to changes in light conditions and by attenuation of ultraviolet by scatter and absorption in the atmosphere. A bright, sunny, dry day is best.

To control illumination conditions more satisfactorily, ultraviolet photography is usually accomplished indoors. The most readily available ultraviolet source is the "black light" fluorescent tube. Tubes of this type can be obtained from all major electrical supply firms (General Electric, Sylvania, Westinghouse). These tubes can be fitted to, and used in, regular fluorescent light fixtures, can be obtained in short or long lengths to suit the size of object to be illuminated, and are reasonably inexpensive. Since the glass of which each tube is made contains a visibly opaque filter element, it is usually necessary to illuminate the subject temporarily with an auxiliary light source (such as a tungsten floodlamp) for framing the picture and focusing the lens. Long tubes of this type are excellent for ultraviolet illumination of large areas, as in the photography of paintings or large documents.

Mercury vapor lamps of the "high pressure" type are usually small and are most suitable for illuminating small objects in close-up photography, in photomicrography, and in spectrography. The xenon arc can be used for long-wave ultraviolet photography by filtering the visible emission.

Electronic flash lamps provide a broad source of visual illumination, with some ultraviolet emission. The efficiency of ultraviolet illumination is limited, however, by the type of gas contained in the tubes, and by the percentage reflection of ultraviolet from the reflector. An aluminum reflector provides a high percentage of ultraviolet reflection. Enough ultraviolet is emitted from any electronic flash, however, to permit instantaneous exposures with a hand-held camera, provided that the subject distance is not too great.

Wire-filled flash lamps are probably the least expensive and most convenient long-wave ultraviolet sources of all. They are available in a wide variety of sizes, representing various light intensities, can be easily procured, and can be used with most any camera. Even the smallest lamp (AG-1, AG-1B, or Flashcube) provides a high enough ultraviolet brightness for instantaneous exposure with a hand-held camera at a subject distance of about 2 metres (6 feet) or closer. Lamps of this type, however, could not be used for medium-wave and short-wave ultraviolet photography, since these radiations are not transmitted through the glass envelope.

Filters (Long-Wave Ultraviolet). Regardless of the source of illumination, a filter must be placed over the camera lens. This filter should have a high transmittance of ultraviolet, and should not pass any visible light. Exposure by ultraviolet only is the aim point of ultraviolet photography. Ultraviolet-transmitting filters are usually made of glass in which coloring agents are contained to control transmittance. Most types of glass will transmit long-wave ultraviolet, but will absorb all medium-wave and short-wave ultraviolet. This is not a disadvantage in general ultraviolet photography, since lenses used in cameras are made of optical glass, whose transmittance is also limited to long-wave ultraviolet. There are no gelatin filters suitable for this type of photography.

The Kodak Wratten ultraviolet filter No. 18A is a glass filter with high percentage transmittance of long-wave ultraviolet, particularly the 365 nanometre line of the mercury spectrum. This filter or its equivalent is highly recommended for long-wave ultraviolet photography.

Ultraviolet-transmitting filters can also be procured from other filter manufacturers. It is suggested, however, that filter transmittance curves be obtained and examined for efficiency of both ultraviolet transmittance and visible light absorption. Filters for this purpose should have no visible light transmittance.

Interference Filters and Quartz Lenses. If ultraviolet photography is to be accomplished with medium-wave and short-wave ultraviolet, a quartz lens must be obtained for the camera. Also, a filter

that transmits these radiations must be used over the lens. Quartz lenses are available on special order from some firms.

Filters for medium-wave and short-wave ultraviolet transmittance are usually of the interference type—that is, evaporative coatings of suitable materials on an appropriate substrate (transmitting medium).

A radiation source for this purpose should emit both medium-wave and short-wave ultraviolet. A mercury vapor lamp is probably most appropriate. If specific spectral lines in either the medium-wave or short-wave region are desired, a monochromator containing a suitable radiation source and equipped with a diffraction grating may suffice.

Photographic Materials. All photographic emulsions contain silver halide, which is inherently sensitive to blue and ultraviolet. Sensitivity in the ultraviolet actually extends far into this region, but the response of a film or plate is somewhat limited, due to absorption of ultraviolet by gelatin, the medium in which silver halide crystals are suspended. For long-wave ultraviolet photography, most any film or plate can be used to record an image; the choice is almost unlimited. Only black-and-white films need be considered, since color film has no advantage.

Images formed with ultraviolet usually present low contrast. Therefore, if a high-contrast film is not used, medium- to high-contrast development should be practiced for best effect.

Special Ultraviolet-Sensitive Materials. When higher sensitivity to ultraviolet is needed, or when sensitivity is desirable in the medium-wave and short-wave regions of the ultraviolet, it may be necessary to resort to special emulsions. Photomicrography and spectrography are two applications that require such emulsions. Eastman Kodak Company can supply Kodak SWR (short wave radiation) plates and films or Kodak spectroscopic plates and films in various sizes.

The Problem of Focus. Although a camera lens is specified as having a definite focal length, this characteristic pertains to visible light only. When infrared is used to form an image, the focal length of the lens is longer than specified; when ultraviolet is used, it is shorter. An image in sharp focus visually may be quite unsharp in a photo taken by ultraviolet. For ultraviolet photography, a good tech-

Setup for reflected UV photography. A No. 18A filter over the lens absorbs visible light and permits only reflected ultraviolet light to reach the film.

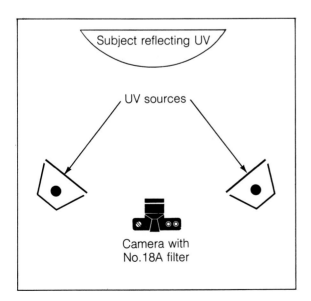

Subject reflecting UV

UV sources

Camera with
No. 18A filter

nique is to achieve focus visually and then to decrease the lens aperture to obtain more depth of field. The amount of aperture decrease is a function of normal focal length. Lenses of short focal length inherently have more depth of field and will require less aperture decrease than those of long focal length. In 35 mm photography, lenses usually have short focal lengths (38 mm, 45 mm, 50 mm, and so forth). A lens-aperture decrease of at least 2 stops below wide-open will usually suffice. Test exposures at various apertures, however, will definitely establish the largest aperture for sharp focus in reflected-ultraviolet photography.

Exposure Determination. The methods by which exposure can be determined in reflected-ultraviolet photography are using an exposure meter, making test exposures, or establishing a guide number when flash lamps are used.

Most conventional exposure meters have some sensitivity to ultraviolet. The incident-light type of meter, however, is the most convenient. If the cell can be covered with a Kodak Wratten ultraviolet filter No. 18A (or the equivalent) to exclude all visible light, the meter will give an indication of ultraviolet intensity. The intensity will vary, of course, as the distance from radiation source to subject is varied. The source should be positioned so that the entire area to be photographed is well illuminated. If a mercury vapor lamp is used, no filter is necessary in front of the lamp, and the visible light emitted will ascertain efficiency of illumination. If the lamp contains an ultraviolet transmitting filter that cannot be removed, the coverage and evenness of illumination must be determined by ultraviolet intensity alone.

Rated Speed. The rated speed for any film is determined for visible light and does not apply for ultraviolet. An arbitrary ultraviolet film speed can be obtained by test exposures; this speed rating can then be applied in setting the meter to indicate exposure to ultraviolet. The ultraviolet speed will be considerably lower than the visible-light speed.

A specially designed meter from Ultra-Violet Products, Inc., San Gabriel, California, 91778 measures ultraviolet intensity. It is called Blak-Ray® ultraviolet intensity meter and is a hand-held device for measuring the intensity of emission from ultraviolet sources and the radiation incident on a surface from a source. Visible light has no effect on the meter. Two sensors are available, one for long-wave ultraviolet and another for short-wave. Meter readings are in microwatts per square centimetre, which can be correlated to exposure time in ultraviolet photography. The meter requires no batteries, electrical supply, or other source of power.

If an exposure meter is not available, or not adequate, exposure must be determined by a series of test exposures. In general, exposure time will be considerably longer than if visible light were used (for one aperture setting). A test series could, therefore, be made at a small *f*-number, with variations in exposure time over a wide range—starting with a short exposure time and increasing by a factor of two.

Flash Exposure. The determination of exposure with flash lamps is simplified, since a guide number can be determined from one test exposure series. The duration of a flash is fairly constant, so a fixed shutter speed (1/25 or 1/30 sec.) can be used for the series. All exposures in the series should be made at the same lamp-to-subject distance. The test series should include exposures at all available lens-aperture settings.

Applications of Ultraviolet Photography

Although the practical applications of ultraviolet photography appear to be few in number, the ultraviolet technique can present a definite advantage in some instances. In the examination of questioned documents, for example, suspected alterations or additions might be made visible only by the use of ultraviolet. Also, faded documents can often be made more legible by reflected-ultraviolet photography, since the faded ink may be brought out in contrast to the paper or other base on which the writing appears. Applications have been recorded in the field of dermatology, where ultraviolet photography has revealed differences in skin conditions. A primary example of ultraviolet photography occurs in photomicrography, where it can be used either to show absolute differences in ultraviolet absorption with unstained specimens or to obtain better sharpness and resolution in the micro-image than is possible with visible light.

Fluorescence Photography

When certain materials (solids, liquids, or gases) are subjected to short-wave electromagnetic radiation, they will emit another radiation, of longer wavelength and very often in the visible spectrum.

The exciting radiations may be x-rays, gamma rays, electrons, ultraviolet, or even some visible wavelengths. This phenomenon of induced light emission is called luminescence and there are two distinct types, known as fluorescence and phosphorescence.

Fluorescence. If the luminescence ceases within a very short time (10^{-8} seconds) after the exciting radiation is removed, the phenomenon is called *fluorescence.* Although fluorescence is commonly produced by excitation with ultraviolet energy, other radiations can also be used in some applications. Certain materials, for example, will fluoresce under the stimulus of x-rays. This is evidenced by the use of fluorescing screens in the production of radiographs. Some materials will fluoresce with electron beam excitation. For example, the image in an electron microscope can only be seen on a fluorescent screen. It is also possible to stimulate fluorescence with some visible wavelengths. Blue light, for example, stimulates green fluorescence in some compounds.

When a material does fluoresce, the action is often called *autofluorescence.* Some materials, however, do not fluoresce under any stimulation, but they can be impregnated with other materials that will fluoresce. This action is often called *secondary fluorescence.* This technique is commonly used in fluorescence microscopy, where a nonfluorescent material is stained with a *fluorochrome,* a dye that will fluoresce.

There are many thousands of materials that exhibit the phenomenon of fluorescence, and fluorescence photography has numerous applications because it will provide information that cannot be obtained by other photographic methods.

Just the fact that a substance will fluoresce is an important characteristic. The particular radiation that excites fluorescence and the specific position of that fluorescence in the visible spectrum can be clues to the identity of a substance. Also, contrast between the elements of a material can often be produced by fluorescence, even when they appear similar otherwise.

Phosphorescence. Although fluorescence ceases almost immediately after the exciting radiation is removed, there are some substances that continue to emit luminescence for some time, even hours, after removal of the exciting stimulus. This phenomenon is called *phosphorescence* and is produced in compounds called *phosphors.* Phosphorescence, like fluorescence, is stimulated by many radiations, but in fewer substances. The image on a television screen, for example, is produced by phosphorescence. An electron beam sweeps across the

Fluorescence is a response to stimulation by specific wavelengths. (Left) An absorption cell containing a dilute solution of sodium fluorescein as it appears under the mixed wavelengths composing white light. (Right) The same cell fluoresces green when irradiated with blue light.

television screen and excites persistent luminescence in phosphors coated on the inside of the tube. Three different phosphors are present on the screen of a color television set, and they emit red, green, and blue light to form colored images.

Oscilloscopes and radar screens also employ phosphors to produce images by electron-beam excitation. These screens, as well as television screens, are often photographed in order to record the images.

Excitation Sources

The most common radiations used to excite fluorescence are the long ultraviolet wavelengths, and many of the radiation sources used for ultraviolet photography or micrography can also be used for fluorescence recording. Short- and medium-wave ultraviolet are sometimes applicable, such as in photographing chromatograms or certain minerals. Some shorter visible wavelengths are used occasionally to produce fluorescence, either at longer visible wavelengths, or in the infrared.

Photographic Technique

When fluorescence is stimulated either with ultraviolet or visible wavelengths, there are several

The setup for fluorescence photography must be made in a darkroom. No. 18A filters permit only ultraviolet light to illuminate the subject, causing fluorescence. A No. 2B filter absorbs ultraviolet light, so that only visible wavelengths from the subject reach the film.

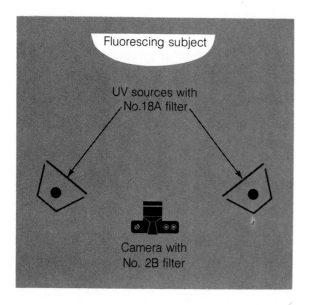

factors that must be considered for efficient photography. The subject must be illuminated with the exciting stimulus, and this is accomplished by selecting a suitable source that emits the necessary radiation. A filter is used with the source to screen out other radiations and to transmit the exciting radiation. Another filter, usually placed between the subject and camera, absorbs any residual exciting radiation and transmits the fluorescence. The fluorescence is then recorded on a suitable photographic material. (See the accompanying diagram.)

Illumination. One of the main factors influencing the brightness of fluorescence is the intensity of the exciting radiation. Fluorescence brightness is generally of very low order compared with image brightness in other types of photography. It is important, therefore, that the radiation source be as close to the subject as possible, while furnishing even illumination over the area to be photographed.

The size of the subject must be considered in selecting an appropriate source of illumination. When a large subject is to be photographed, the source should cover a large area with as bright an illumination as possible. The long fluorescent tubes (low-pressure mercury vapor lamps) are quite suitable. High-pressure mercury arcs are also useful, but are small sources. If they are used to illuminate a large area, there may be a sacrifice in fluorescence brightness, resulting in extremely long exposure times. If the long tubes are selected, two or more (in suitable reflectors) can be placed on each side of the subject to provide a considerable quantity of exciting radiation. If the subject is large and flat, such as a painting or large document, the tubes should be placed so that the incident illumination angle is less than 45 degrees. Make sure, however, that no direct light from the source is "seen" by the camera. The lamp reflectors can be oriented so that this condition does not occur.

High-pressure mercury-vapor lamps are excellent for illuminating small objects or small areas. One lamp, however, is usually not adequate, since illumination is then provided from one side only. At least two lamps should be used, one on each side of the subject, especially when the subject is three-dimensional.

Electronic flash lamps are especially useful when living subjects that exhibit fluorescence are to be photographed, since instantaneous exposures are possible. Although one lamp may be sufficient, two lamps (one on each side of the subject) will provide twice as much light and will allow smaller lens apertures for increased depth of field.

The illumination of the subject should consist only of the radiations needed to excite fluorescence. All ambient illumination (room lights) and all other illumination from the source must be excluded from the subject. Fluorescence photography is most often accomplished either in a darkened room or in a lighttight enclosure.

Filters

At least two distinct types of filters are used in a fluorescence photography system. The first, called an *exciter filter,* is placed between the subject and the radiation source. It transmits the radiation needed to excite fluorescence. The second, a *barrier filter,* is placed in front of the camera lens (or somewhere behind the objective lens in a microscope) to remove any residual exciting radiation and to transmit the fluorescence.

Other filters, such as color compensating filters, can be used occasionally along with the barrier filter for special effects, particularly when color films are to be exposed.

Exciter Filter. The filter used with the radiation source is called an exciter filter, and its purpose is to transmit the exciting radiation efficiently and absorb all, or almost all, of the other radiations emitted from the source. When ultraviolet is the radiation used to excite fluorescence, the exciter filter should pass a high percentage of the ultraviolet radiated from the source. If visible blue or blue-green light is used to excite fluorescence, then the exciter filter for this purpose should transmit either of these radiations freely and absorb all others.

Some ultraviolet sources intended for fluorescence work include exciter filters, either incorporated as a coloring agent in the glass envelope or attached to the reflector or the lamphouse. This filter must be used, even when some visible blue light is transmitted. If the illuminator is not equipped with a filter, however, then a more efficient one can be selected. For example, if a high-pressure mercury arc is used to provide long-wave ultraviolet, either a Kodak Wratten ultraviolet filter No. 18A or Corning Glass No. 5840 (filter No. CS 7–60), mounted in front of the source, will screen out all radiations except the long-wave ultraviolet. These filters have very similar transmittance, passing about 70 percent of incident ultraviolet at 365 nanometres. Similar filters are also available from other firms.

Barrier Filter. The exciter filter in front of the light source transmits the radiation necessary to excite fluorescence. Not all of this radiation is used, however, and some residual radiation still exists—reflected from, or transmitted through, the subject. If this residual radiation is not removed, it will record on film. Since it is usually of higher brightness than the fluorescence, it will cause more exposure than the fluorescence. Another filter must be used, usually in front of the camera lens, to prevent the residual exciting radiation from causing exposure. This filter acts as a barrier to the exciting radiation, and is logically called a *barrier filter.* An efficient barrier filter absorbs all radiation transmitted by the exciter filter and transmits only the wavelengths of light evident as fluorescence. If ultraviolet is used to excite fluorescence, then the barrier filter must absorb ultraviolet. If the exciter filter passes both ultraviolet and some short visual blue, then the barrier filter must absorb both ultraviolet and blue.

Barrier Filter Selection. The selection of a barrier filter also can depend upon the fluorescence wavelengths produced. If blue fluorescence is achieved in the subject, the barrier filter should transmit this blue light. This situation can present a problem if the wavelength of the blue fluorescence is the same as, or similar to, the wavelength of the blue light transmitted by the exciter filter. The only solution is to substitute an exciter filter that has no blue transmittance. If, however, the exciter filter transmits blue up to about 420 nanometres and blue fluorescence occurs at a longer wavelength in the blue, then a pale-yellow barrier filter is necessary to absorb all wavelengths below about 425 nanometres and to transmit all longer wavelengths. If no blue fluorescence occurs, then the problem is simplified. Any yellow filter that absorbs ultraviolet can be used, if fluorescence wavelengths are transmitted.

Another problem that can occur, however, is fluorescence of the barrier filter itself. The coloring material in the filter may show a bright fluorescence when irradiated with ultraviolet. Some yellow filters exhibit this effect. The result can be a fogging of the film; the desired fluorescence record may be degraded and can appear hazy. There are two possible solutions to this problem: (1) A filter that absorbs only ultraviolet—such as a Kodak Wratten filter No. 2B or 2A (or the equivalent)—can be placed in front of the existing barrier filter to prevent its fluorescence; (2) Another barrier filter can be selected, one that does not fluoresce but has similar absorption. The possible fluorescence of a proposed barrier filter can be determined beforehand by holding it in the beam of a filtered source that emits ultraviolet light. If the barrier filter does fluoresce, it will appear to glow.

Color Films

All photographic emulsions are inherently sensitive to blue and ultraviolet. This is why all blue and ultraviolet transmitted by the exciter filter must be absorbed by the barrier filter. Otherwise, the film will be exposed to these radiations, which may cause greater photographic effect than the fluorescence. If a color film is used, any ultraviolet reaching the film will record as blue, seriously degrading the record of fluorescence colors. Similarly, any unwanted blue light passing through the barrier filter will degrade the fluorescence record.

Color film, of course, presents the greatest advantage in recording fluorescence colors. Daylight-type color film is especially recommended because of its balanced sensitivity to the blue, green, and red regions of the visible spectrum. Color film balanced for tungsten illumination is seldom recommended, since it has higher blue sensitivity than the daylight type. It could, however, be used efficiently for recording blue fluorescence only.

Since fluorescence colors are usually of low brightness, a high-speed color film is especially recommended in order to minimize exposure time.

Applications of Fluorescence Photography

Like any type of photography, the photography of fluorescence is practiced to supply information that cannot be obtained by other means. Just the fact that a substance does fluoresce is enough to differentiate it from one that does not. When two substances both fluoresce, they may differ in fluorescence color, or their fluorescence may occur in distinctly different portions of the spectrum—visible or invisible.

Questioned Documents. An outstanding application of fluorescence photography is in the field of law enforcement—most particularly in the examination of questioned documents. When other photographic methods fail to reveal suspected alterations in, or additions to, a document (check, letter, will, and so forth), it is always possible that a fluorescence

Fluorescence is useful in determining the composition of specimens such as this ore sample, seen at left under white light. Fluorescent light produced with short-wave ultraviolet irradiation reveals calcite (red) and Willemite (green) in the ore (right).

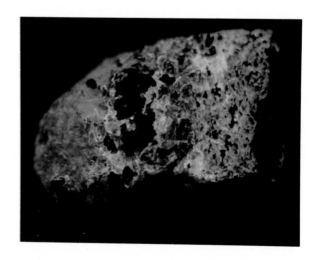

technique will provide fruitful results. Many inks may show a difference in visible fluorescence. The effects of bleaching or erasures can also often be detected by this means. Most papers on which documents are written or printed contain cellulose fibers. These fibers often fluoresce brightly when the paper is illuminated with ultraviolet in a darkened room. Erasures will alter this fluorescence; the effect can be recorded and enhanced on a high-contrast black-and-white film. If inks have been bleached, as with an "ink eradicator," the bleach material still in the paper may show a typical fluorescence color. If it does, the effect can be recorded on either black-and-white or color film.

Paintings. Very often, before any attempt is made to clean, repair, or restore a painting, photographs are made by several techniques to obtain all possible information about its condition. One of these techniques is to illuminate the surface of the painting with ultraviolet and to photograph the resultant fluorescence. A permanent record is thereby obtained which provides information about any past retouchings, overpainting, and restorations. After a painting has been cleaned and the old varnish completely removed, a fluorescence photograph is often made of the painting before revarnishing. This photograph will show the surface condition of the painting itself without the varnish barrier. Since varnish will absorb ultraviolet and may produce a typical yellow-green fluorescence, its presence on the painting would obscure any fluorescence of the pigments in the painting. Occasionally, of course, repair or restorations are accomplished with the varnish in place.

Minerals. Ultraviolet radiation has often been used to excite fluorescence in minerals in both field and laboratory. Both long-wave and short-wave ultraviolet sources can be used, since many minerals may fluoresce strongly with one wavelength but very weakly, or not at all, with the other. Some forms of calcite, for example, look almost white under visual light, but when excited with short-wave ultraviolet in a darkened room stand out with an intense red color. Another mineral, called "Willemite," fluoresces an intense green with short-wave ultraviolet excitation.

• *See also:* BLACK-LIGHT PHOTOGRAPHY; DOCUMENT EXAMINATION BY PHOTOGRAPHY; FLUORESCENCE; INFRARED PHOTOGRAPHY.

Umbrella Lighting

Photographic umbrellas are devices used to reflect light in a controllable way. They consist of a shaft with a bracket to hold a light, and a collapsible frame covered with fabric. While everyday umbrellas are always curved to let the rain run off, lighting umbrellas may be curved (usually) or flat (sometimes). The inside of the lighting umbrella is used to reflect light.

While photographic umbrellas can be employed with incandescent or flashbulb light, they are almost always used with electronic flash. They vary in size from about 1m (3 ft) up to 2 m (6 ft) in diameter. The smaller ones are generally used with small, portable electronic flash units, while the larger ones are generally used in studios with high-powered electronic flash units.

In practice, the umbrella handle is fastened to a light stand, and the flash unit is attached to a bracket on the handle, aimed at the inside of the umbrella fabric. The bracket can be moved up and down along the handle, varying the area of the light spread reflected toward the subject from the fabric. When the flashtube is closer to the fabric than the focal point, the light spread is great. As the flash is moved farther down the handle away from the fabric, the light on the subject gets more concentrated. In a sense, an umbrella is a form of controllable bounce lighting.

Quality of Light on Fabric Surface

Foil-Covered Fabric. Direct electronic flash produces a hard light with narrow shadows. The foil-covered fabric produces a hard light similar to that of direct flash, but creates broader shadow lines somewhat similar to an undiffused floodlight. Some photographers consider this type of umbrella more suitable for commercial or illustration photography than for portraits or fashion pictures.

Aluminum-Painted Surface. The aluminum painted surface produces a light that is somewhat less harsh than that provided by the foil type. It is considered suitable for portraits of men, or character studies, as well as for still-life setups.

Satin White Surface. The satin finish is the general-purpose umbrella, producing a pleasing,

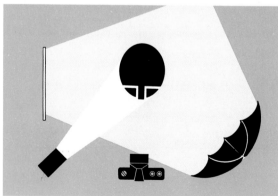

Umbrella lighting is often used for studio portraiture; both satin-finish and matte-surface umbrellas produce the diffuse type of lighting evident in this photograph. To make this picture, electronic flash mounted on a large umbrella at the camera's right was used as the main light; fill light was provided by a reflector at left. The highlights in the model's hair were achieved by placing a narrow-beam spotlight high over the camera and slightly to the camera's left. Photo courtesy of Hasselblad Corp.

This simple, uncluttered setup is typical of umbrella lighting in a studio using a high-powered electronic flash unit.

has an advantage and a disadvantage. The advantage is that the umbrella light has less fall-off with distance than direct flash, and covers a greater depth with even illumination. The disadvantage is that exposure must be found by trial and error, or by the use of a flash meter. Once an acceptable *f*-number is found for a given film speed, it is effective over a fairly wide working distance for a given placement of the flash on the umbrella handle. When the flash unit is moved along the handle toward the fabric, the light is spread over a wider area; hence, it is less intense on the subject. When moved away from the fabric, it grows more intense, but over a smaller area. A good practice is to have several flash positions, one *f*-stop apart, marked on the handle.

Silver and white umbrella surfaces reflect light without changing its color temperature. Gold and bluish umbrella surfaces that warm the light (lower its color temperature) or cool it down (raise the color temperature) are available. These are rarely used, and then only for special purposes. The degree of color change has to be found experimentally.

• *See also:* FLASH PHOTOGRAPHY; LIGHTING.

Underdevelopment

In black-and-white negative processing, correct negative development is usually considered to be the amount of development that gives negative density ranges that can be printed to make quality prints on a particular enlarger or printer, usually on a normal-contrast grade of paper. Any development less than this, which results in a lower density range, is considered to be underdevelopment.

There are a number of factors that affect photographic contrast, one of the important ones being the luminance range of the subject. It is quite possible to have correctly developed and underdeveloped negatives on a roll of film developed in one process. Negatives of normal subjects may have a good density range, while negatives of flat subjects (low-luminance-range subjects) may be underdeveloped because they have a negative range too low to make good prints. If a compromise development time is chosen so that the normal-subject negatives can be printed on a low-contrast grade of paper, and the low-contrast-subject negatives can be printed on a

semi-diffuse light suitable for many purposes. Some satin-finish umbrellas are opaque, while others are made of a thin, translucent fabric. The thin type can be used in the regular reflective manner, but can also be used as a direct, diffused light source. In this case, the umbrella is aimed toward the subject and the light from the flash is diffused through the fabric onto the subject. It is usually used quite close to the subject both to get enough light and to provide a relatively broad source. Flat umbrellas of this type are particularly useful.

Matte-White Surface. Light bounced off the matte-white surface is very diffuse and is useful for portraits because it minimizes skin blemishes, thus reducing the amount of retouching required.

Exposure

Distance and *f*-numbers are interrelated by guide numbers when direct electronic flash is used. Exposures found by guide numbers are fairly accurate because the tubes on electronic flash are relatively small compared to the light-to-subject distance. However, the guide-number principle fails when the diameter of the source becomes relatively large compared to the flash-to-subject distance. This

higher grade of paper, the development is considered normal for the conditions. See the article CONTRAST for a discussion of developing times.

Color materials have rigidly specified development times and temperatures. If color negatives are underdeveloped, the prints will appear flat, with poor highlights and shadows. There is also likely to be a color shift from highlights to shadows because underdevelopment usually causes crossed curves in the three color negative layers.

There are two developments in the processing of transparency materials. The first development is a black-and-white development, which controls the contrast and density, while the second development, the color development, produces the positive color image. Underdevelopment in the first development results in transparencies that are dark and low in contrast, and shadow detail may be entirely lost.

Underdevelopment in the color developer will result in poor blacks (low maximum density), weak colors, and color shift from dark to light.

Reversal color prints made from transparencies are also developed twice—in a first black-and-white developer and a second color developer. The effects of underdevelopment are similar to those of transparency materials.

Black-and-white prints usually must be underdeveloped when they have been overexposed. They are "pulled," which means they are given a shortened development time to keep them from getting too dark. Some photographic papers have a wide development latitude and do not show too much change with this treatment unless it is extreme. Other papers must be developed fully, or they will have uneven densities and muddy highlights.

Color prints made from negatives show poor maximum density, low contrast, and poor blacks when they are underdeveloped.

• *See also:* CONTRAST; DEVELOPMENT.

Underexposure

The correct or normal exposure of a photographic film (black-and-white or color, negative or reversal) is usually considered to be the minimum exposure that will produce a satisfactory image when the film is processed. Underexposure is any exposure less

Some underexposure of black-and-white films can be compensated for in the developing process. Column at left represents several exposure variations: (top) underexposure and overdevelopment; (center) underexposure and normal development; (bottom) underexposure and underdevelopment. Column at right shows the resulting positive prints.

than the normal exposure that begins to show a lessening in quality.

With negative materials, the judgment must come on the basis of prints made from the negative. An underexposed negative will look thinner (have less density) than a normal negative and will have less detail in shadow areas. Prints made from underexposed negatives generally have poorly separated tones overall, and poor maximum blacks with practically no detail in the shadow areas.

Technically, in continuous-tone negatives of conventional subjects, a negative is considered to be correctly exposed if tones that should be reproduced as just lighter than black have a density of 0.10 greater than that of the film base. Negatives that have less than this value are considered underexposed.

Underexposure in transparency materials is more difficult to define because, due to the lack of a printing step, it shows up in all the tonal regions. Shadow areas are black with little or no detail, mid-tone areas are darker than normal, and highlight areas are "muddy." Highlight reproduction is usually very important in transparencies, so that, technically, underexposure can best be measured in that part of the tonal scale. With a normal, full-scale subject, a correctly exposed transparency should have specular highlights whose density comes close to that of the film's gross fog level, while diffuse highlights should have a density about 0.10 greater than that.

Prints made from negatives are underexposed when they are too light overall for the lighting conditions in which they will be viewed. Reversal prints made from transparencies are underexposed when they are too dark overall .

Underexposure in special photographic processes shows up in a number of ways. For example, aerial films are exposed so that the darkest subject tone is exposed just above the toe on the characteristic curve. This is to get maximum tonal separation because of the contrast lowering effect of the moisture content of even clear air.

• *See also:* AERIAL PHOTOGRAPHY; EXPOSURE.

Underwater Photography

As with any specialized branch of photography, there are numerous aspects of underwater photography and many areas of specialization. Photographs can be taken underwater at almost any depth with manned vehicles, unmanned vehicles, or platforms anchored to the ocean floor. This article, however, will deal with the photography that can be done by divers using simple sport diving equipment.* Infor-

*Diving with self-contained underwater breathing apparatus (SCUBA) requires special training through nationally recognized certification courses. Dive shops, the YMCA, and *Skin Diver* magazine can provide details on diving courses in your area.

mation will also be provided for the non-diver, who can take pictures near the surface with little more than a protected camera and a mask and snorkel.

Equipment

In general, all photographic equipment can be used underwater, provided it is adequately protected. Equipment for use underwater should be quite sturdy. It will be subjected to seawater (an especially corrosive liquid), it will receive hard bumps (almost unavoidable while getting into and out of boats), and it will spend considerable time in hot sun (again, almost unavoidable on boats and beaches). Underwater photographic equipment must be tough; Lexan ®, polyethylene plastics, cast and extruded aluminum, and stainless steel are the principal materials used in its construction. The materials partially account for the high cost of equipment.

It is possible to buy protective housings for almost every type of photographic equipment needed underwater. As off-the-shelf items, reliable housings are available for simple cameras, 35 mm cameras (rangefinder and SLR), roll-film cameras (TLR and SLR), movie cameras, instant-film cameras, exposure meters, and electronic flash units.

Providing housing for in-air photographic equipment is not the only way the diving photographer can take what is needed underwater. There are also extensive lines of self-contained underwater photo gear available. With these units the outer shell of the device itself protects the inner workings from the intrusion of water. This design makes for more compact, and therefore less buoyant and easier-to-handle equipment. Electronic flash units of various sizes and exposure meters are available in such a self-contained design. But the prime example of this type of equipment is the Nikonos camera (also known as the Calypso/Nikkor).

The Nikonos. The Nikonos is a self-contained underwater 35 mm camera that needs no housing to protect it from exposure to water. It is compact and easy to use, and it has become the standard against which all other underwater equipment is measured. It has four interchangeable lenses (they can only be changed in air), and numerous accessories are manufactured for exclusive use with it. These accessories include flash units, viewfinders, close-up lenses, extension tubes, plus an assortment of brackets and connectors to hold the equipment together and link it electrically.

As functional as the Nikonos is, there are times when an in-air camera in a housing may be more effective. Two reasons make this true. First, with the Nikonos, viewing is not done through the lens. Viewing is done through the small built-in viewfinder or through an auxiliary viewfinder mounted on top of the camera. Parallax is a problem. Second, focusing is not done visually. To focus the lens, estimate the distance to the subject and then set that estimate distance on the lens.

Camera Housings. The biggest advantage gained by housing a camera is that the camera used can be a single-lens reflex. The advantages of using a single-lens reflex camera underwater are the same ones gained by employing that type of camera in air,

the two most important being that you view the subject and focus unit through the camera lens. This is the case no matter what lens is on the camera. Viewing the subject through the lens eliminates parallax, and visual focusing rather than estimating the distance to the subject eliminates guessing subject distance. Being able to focus visually becomes increasingly important the closer you get to the subject, since accurate focusing is critical for close-up photography.

Cameras in housings can also use a wider variety of lenses than are available for the Nikonos: Most modern housings are equipped with interchangeable ports; standard ports make it possible to use normal and wide-angle lenses, and with special-purpose ports, macro, fisheye, and telephoto lenses can be used. Cameras in housings can also be equipped with motor drives.

A typical, self-contained, underwater 35 mm camera system usually includes a number of components. (A) Optical viewfinder; (B) exposure meter and bracket; (C) handle and camera tray; (D) Nikonos camera and lens; (E) sync cable connectors; (F) adjustable flash arm; (G) Subsea Mark 150 electronic flash unit. Photo courtesy Subsea.

A conventional single-lens reflex camera and an in-air electronic flash unit can be taken below when suitably housed. This system includes: (A) electronic flash housing; (B) adjustable flash arm; (C) sync cable; (D) camera housing; (E) dome port; (F) light-sensor port for use with auto-flash units; (G) housing handle. Photo courtesy Oceanic Products.

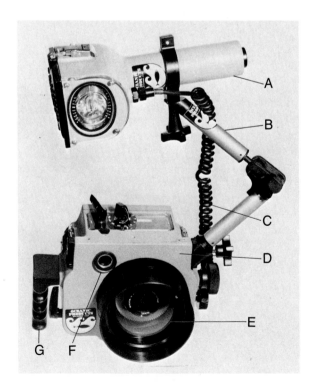

Finally, most modern housings are designed to permit the use of action finders. These special-purpose viewfinders give the diving photographer a large, bright area on which to compose and focus. The image the viewfinder provides is erect and unreversed, and the whole image can be seen when the eye is positioned 6 cm (2½ inches) from the screen —about the distance your eye will be from the screen when the camera is in a housing and you are wearing a face mask. In the overall dimness generally encountered underwater, focusing is difficult at best; the advantage of having a bright image is very important.

Selecting a Housing

The first function of a housing is to protect the camera within it. Most commercially available housings do that, but one housing may be better than another for various reasons. Consider how many features of the in-air camera are lost when it is enclosed in the housing. The housing should limit the camera's normal functions as little as possible, and all the controls should be as easy to operate underwater as in air.

Both metal and plastic housings are widely used by amateur and professional photographers, and each type more than adequately serves the first function of a housing: to keep the camera within dry. Most of the advantages of metal housings over plastic ones are matters of strength and convenience. Whether those advantages are worth the extra cost of metal housings over plastic ones (four times as expensive) is for the photographer to decide.

Lens Ports. There are two types of lens ports available for most modern housings: flat ports and dome ports.

Flat Ports and Refraction. Flat ports are the type that have been used in housings since cameras were first taken underwater, and many fine underwater housings employ glass or optical-plastic flat ports. Flat ports certainly have a place in modern underwater photography, but they do cause light rays to refract. Refraction is the bending of light rays as they pass from one medium to another. As light rays pass from water to air—as they do when light rays from a subject underwater pass through the flat port on a camera housing and into the air between the lens and the inside of the port—the rays are bent. (The rays are actually bent twice: once as

they leave the air and enter the glass, and again as they leave the glass and enter the air. In this discussion, the double bending is discounted for simplification as its effect is negligible.)

At the flat port, rays entering from the water are bent away from the "normal"—the normal simply being a line perpendicular to the flat port. The reason for the bending has to do with the fact that light travels faster in air than in water, but the important thing to keep in mind is that this bending of light rays causes the following:

1. Objects appear closer (larger) than they actually are. Objects appear to be about three-quarters of the distance they actually are from the observer.
2. Angles of coverage of lenses behind flat ports change; the angle of coverage of a lens behind a flat port will be about three-quarters of its angle of coverage in air.
3. Peripheral distortion begins to take place. Around the edges of pictures taken through flat ports, blurring and color shifts are sometimes visible. This becomes more apparent as wider-angle lenses are used.

Most flat-port distortion occurs when wide-angle lenses are used because the light-ray bending at the periphery of the port is greatest, as the following illustration shows. This causes the light rays to break up into their component colors. (*See:* ABERRATION.) The least amount of distortion occurs when lenses longer than 35 mm are used behind a flat port, because with such lenses the least amount of severe light-ray bending takes place. With telephoto lenses, the distortion is not noticeable, and the apparent shortening of distance and reduced angle of acceptance is advantageous. In the illustration, note that the ray entering the flat port at a 90-degree angle is not bent. No distortion is produced there.

Dome Ports. Dome ports are also called corrected ports because they correct (actually eliminate) the distortion associated with flat ports. Because dome ports are spherical, all light rays entering the port do so at a (theoretical) 90-degree angle. None of the distortion associated with flat ports occurs because there is no light-ray bending.

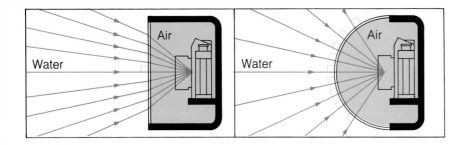

(Left) Light rays entering a camera housing with a flat port are refracted least at the center of the port and most at its periphery. (Right) Light rays are not significantly refracted as they enter a dome port. For best results, flat ports should not be used with wide-angle lenses.

Even at the periphery of the port, when super-wide-angle and fisheye lenses are used, no light rays are bent. Dome ports make it possible to use these lenses underwater and to get sharpness and color fidelity impossible with flat ports.

NOTE: In water, a dome acts as a lens and produces an apparent, or virtual image that is much closer to the dome than the actual distance to the object. When focusing, you actually focus on the virtual image. This will not be confusing because you will not be aware it is happening; you will be focusing visually, and will not normally be consulting the distance scale on your camera lens. If you could see the camera's distance scale (in most housings you cannot), it might confuse you because the scale would give a distance much closer than the distance you would estimate the actual subject distance to be. Because the virtual image is formed close to the dome, the particular lens you are using must be capable of focusing that close. With some dome housings, it will be necessary to attach close-up lenses to certain camera lenses to permit focusing on the close, virtual image. The manufacturers of housings always include specific information concerning any close-up lenses needed to get good results.

Environment

Any piece of photo equipment that is taken below the surface of the water is not only subjected to the wetness of the medium, but also to the pressure created by the weight of the water.

On the surface, atmospheric pressure is one atmosphere (14.7 psi). This pressure is exerted because the weight of a column of air over a specific area creates a downward force. Underwater, the same principle applies, but the downward force is greater because water weighs considerably more than air. The accompanying table shows how quickly pressure builds as the divers and equipment go deeper underwater.

Equipment being taken underwater must be protected from the pressure differential created as the equipment goes deeper. In most instances, camera housings and other equipment cases are fully sealed against the external pressure by a device called an o-ring. These simple rings of rubber actually create a better seal as they are subjected to increasing pressures. (See the accompanying illustrations.)

Most underwater equipment can withstand pressure of about 7 atmospheres (102 psi) and can

PRESSURE INCREASES AS DEPTH INCREASES			
Depth		**Pressure**	
Metres	**Feet**	**Atmospheres**	**psi**
0	0	1	14.7
10	33	2	29.4
20	66	3	44.1
30	99	4	58.8
40	132	5	73.5
50	165	6	88.2
60	198	7	102.9

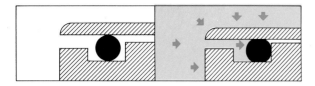

(Left) Before being subjected to pressure, the cross-section of the o-ring is round. (Right) As the equipment housing is subjected to pressure, the o-ring deforms and creates a seal through which moisture cannot pass.

be taken to depths of 60 m (200 ft), the practical limit for safe sport diving.

Behavior of Light Underwater

Underwater, available light (also referred to as ambient or natural light) is the light from the sun that reaches a subject after passing through the atmosphere, the surface of the water, and finally the water itself. Since water is approximately 800 times more dense than air, light traveling through it behaves differently from light traveling through air. There is always much less light underwater than on the surface at any given time, and the quality of the light is soft and diffused. This is because of the combined effects of the reflection, refraction, scattering, and absorption of light.

Reflection. When the sun is directly overhead, little light is reflected off the surface of the water. The best light penetration occurs during the hours around noon. When the sun is closer to the horizon,

some of its light does not penetrate the water because it is reflected off the surface. Surface conditions as well as the angle of the sun also affect how much light is reflected. When the sea is calm, little light is reflected; but when the sea is choppy, many small surfaces that reflect light are formed. The least amount of light will be lost to reflection on bright, calm days between the hours of 10 A.M. and 2 P.M., so this will be the best time for picturetaking.

Refraction. Light that is not reflected off the surface of the water passes down into it, but as it does, it is refracted. Refraction is the bending of light rays as they pass from one medium to another. The least amount of light-ray bending occurs when the sun is directly overhead, but as the sun approaches the horizon, light-ray bending increases. This causes light rays to travel farther to reach a given depth, and the increased distance the light must travel reduces its intensity. Light lost to refraction will be least around noon.

In-air techniques need not be left at the surface. Panning the camera isolated this spotted goatfish from the background very effectively. Photo by Herb Taylor.

(Above) Schooling blue tangs are a difficult underwater subject because of their dark coloring. Additional exposure is desirable, and some source of artificial light is extremely helpful. (Left) Good conditions for photography can be found in the waters of the Northeastern states on days when the light is good and the water clear. Photos by Herb Taylor.

Scattering. The number of suspended particles and minute organisms in a body of water will vary greatly with geographic location, time of year, weather, and other factors. Light passing through a medium filled with floating debris is scattered and diffused as it makes its way through the mixture. In addition to reducing the overall amount of light, suspended particles also greatly affect flash photography underwater. To know when suspended particles will be at their lowest concentrations, you must learn about the weather and biological activity in the bodies of water in which you will be taking pictures.

Absorption. When doing available-light color photography, one of the first things you will notice is that your pictures will have an overall blue or green cast. This is because of the selective absorption of sunlight by the water. Light coming from the sun consists of all the colors of the spectrum, but the colors are mixed and the light appears white. Water acts as a filter and selectively absorbs some of the colors that make up "white light." Most of the red wavelengths in white light are absorbed by the time they reach 20 m (60 ft); only the blue and green components of white light penetrate the water to any appreciable depth (see the accompanying diagram). To maintain all the colors that are present, do your photography close to the surface, or add auxiliary lighting.

Combined Effect. The combined effects of all the above factors point the way to one of the most important things you can learn about underwater photography: The key to consistently good underwater pictures is to keep the distance between the camera and the subject to the very minimum. This reduces the amount of water through which light from the subject must travel to record on the film. Even in the clearest water, these four factors—reflection, refraction, scattering, and absorption—act,

(Above) This is a rather dramatic example of the color shift to blue in underwater photography at depths greater than 20 m (60 ft). This photo was taken at 30 m (90 ft). Shallow-water photography will maintain most colors reasonably well. Photo by Herb Taylor.

(Right) Water acts like a filter that selectively absorbs the colors of the spectrum. Selective absorption varies in different bodies of water. In clear water, yellow may be seen as deep as 15 m (45 ft), while in murky water yellow may be seen only to about 7 m (20 ft). The ◀ symbol shows penetration in murky water. Recording full color underwater almost always requires auxiliary lighting. However, there is one exception to the correlation of loss of warm colors with increasing depth: Materials treated with fluorescent dyes retain their normal hues regardless of depth.

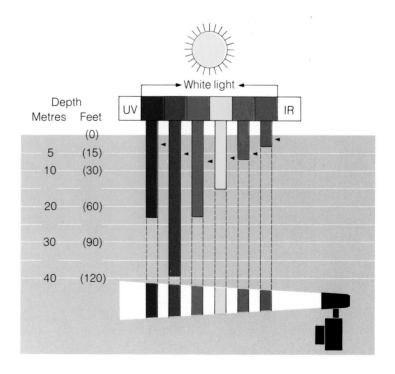

to a degree, and make it difficult to record sharp images with good contrast and detail. To get good contrast and detail, stay as close as possible to the subject for the particular kind of picture you want.

Working Distance. A general rule of thumb for underwater photography is: Do most of your picture-taking at distances within one-fifth of the limits of visibility (clearness of the water). If the visibility is 30 m (100 ft), work between 0 and 6 m (0 and 20 ft); if the visibility is 3 m (10 ft), work between 0 and 0.6 m (0 and 2 ft).

This is the reason why wide-angle lenses are the best choice for general-purpose underwater photography. With lenses that range from 28 mm to 15 mm you can get close to the subject and thus reduce the amount of water between you and it. With wide-angle lenses much of the scene will be encompassed in view, plus the greater depth of field associated with these lenses will be gained. Adequate depth of field is often a problem underwater because low light levels often force you to use large *f*-stops.

Refraction and Working Distance. One problem to contend with when establishing a working distance is refraction. Refraction is the phenomenon that makes objects underwater appear closer (larger) than they actually are. Because objects underwater appear closer (larger), correctly estimating distances underwater takes practice and it can sometimes cause confusion when setting distance scales on cameras without rangefinders or focusing screens. If you are using such a camera, you can:

Estimate the distance and set that estimated distance on the scale, *or* measure the distance and then multiply by ¾ and set the calculated distance. For example, if the measured camera-to-subject distance is 4 m (13 ft), set the distance scale at 3 m (9 ft).

$$4 \times \tfrac{3}{4} = 3 \text{ m} (12 \times \tfrac{3}{4} = 9 \text{ ft})$$

You should use one method or the other. Using both methods alternately only creates confusion.

Exposure

Once the working distance is established, proper exposure should then be determined. In properly exposed pictures, the intensity of the light in the image closely resembles the intensity observed in the original scene. For most purposes, properly exposed pictures are those that are pleasing to you and to most of the people who see them. (*See:* EXPOSURE.)

Estimating Exposure. Estimating how much light is present in any given scene in air is difficult; underwater, it is even more so. In bright daylight, in air, exposures can be estimated by using the one-over-ASA method. Simply set the aperture at *f*/16 and set the shutter speed to the reciprocal (1/50 is the reciprocal of 50) of the ASA of the film you are using. For example, in bright sunlight, in air, with an ASA 64 film set the aperture at *f*/16 and the shutter speed at 1/60 sec.

With wide-angle lenses, a photographer can get close to a subject and thus limit the amount of water between it and the camera. Large angles of acceptance and great depth of field make wide-angle lenses ideal for most general-purpose underwater photography. Photo by Herb Taylor.

A school of grunts photographed in shallow water. Photo by Herb Taylor.

This method of exposure determination may yield an adequately exposed photograph, but by no means is it a way to get accurate exposures consistently. The method only works in bright daylight. When taking pictures on cloudy days or in open shade, be sure to make exposure adjustments. To determine the exact adjustments with any regularity is nearly impossible. Underwater, using the above method and making adjustments for depth and all the other factors that subdue light underwater reduces the accuracy of estimating the exposure still further.

Measuring Exposure. Using an exposure meter is essential for getting accurate exposures consistently on land and underwater. The basic technique for using any reflection-type exposure meter (the type most often used underwater) is by simply setting the appropriate film speed on the meter, pointing the meter at the subject, and then aligning a dial or pointer with the indicator needle. With this method, you will have a selection of shutter-speed and *f*-stop combinations that will yield the correct exposures.

Near the Surface. When measuring the light reflected off subjects near the surface, the meter needle may waver over a range of readings because of surface ripples or chop. For good exposure, average the readings and use the average setting or a setting between the average and lowest light level.

Deeper. As you go deeper, the amount of light will stabilize, but it will still change should passing clouds block the sun. Deeper still, exposures will not vary with fast-changing surface conditions, but light values will fall as the sun approaches the horizon.

For accurate exposures, meter the portion of the total picture that is most important. Get as close to the subject as possible for metering, set the appropriate shutter speed and *f*-stop on the camera, then move back to compose and take the picture.

Whenever you are measuring the light of an overall scene, measure the most important parts and try to avoid having the meter influenced by a sandy bottom or the bright surface of the water. Try to be aware of the angle of acceptance of the exposure meter and aim it to measure the area desired.

When you cannot get close to your subject, use a substitute metering technique. For example, you can meter the reflectance of your hand if photographing people in bathing suits, but you cannot expect to get good exposures if you measure the light from a bright object near the surface and then photograph dark subjects 9.1 m (30 ft) below the surface. Getting close to the subject and measuring the light coming off it is the best way to get accurate exposures. Bracketing will help you get perfect exposures consistently.

Mounting Exposure Meters. The best place for an exposure meter while you are diving is to attach it firmly to your other photographic equipment. Special pieces of hardware designed to hold different exposure meters are available commercially and are a good investment. Attached with a bracket, you will always know where your meter is. Attached to

An underwater housing enables you to make movies with an in-air camera. As with any underwater photography, the photographer should be braced against unwanted movement. Photo by Neil Montanus.

the end of a line, a negatively buoyant meter will be bumping into your other equipment or dragging along the bottom. On the end of a line, buoyant exposure meters usually wind up pointing toward the surface for long periods of time. A CdS meter, may give a false reading when you use it because such meters "remember" the bright reading of the surface.

Though the exposure meter will give a range of *f*-stops and shutter speeds, generally you will have only one or two combinations to choose from, depending on the type of film being used and the level of illumination. The choice will be further limited by shutter-speed selection.

For practical purposes, because of current, wave surge, and your own buoyancy, avoid shutter speeds slower than 1/60 sec. Even using 1/60 sec. requires good breath control and a steady hand. Often it may be necessary to brace or wedge yourself into the bottom terrain for steadiness.

Films and Filters

In addition to proper exposure, try to attain proper color balance when using color films. Proper

color balance in a picture means that the color values approximate the actual color values in the scene photographed. Underwater, daylight-type films are the kind most commonly used because they do not require filters even though natural light underwater is more blue than the natural surface light for which they are balanced.

Black-and-White Film. Using black-and-white film underwater with available light can yield results that closely approximate what is seen. The blues and greens usually encountered lend themselves to representation on the gray scale of black-and-white film.

Filters. As mentioned earlier, the water you dive in acts as a filter. It passes more light of its own color to the film than any of the other colors that make up white light. In water that is essentially blue, more blue light will reach the film than any of the other components of white light. Filters can help in underwater photography by creating contrast and improving color balance.

Filters and Color Film. Near the surface, you can restore to color films some of the reds lost through absorption by using a red filter. The CC30R filter is the type most commonly recommended, but any of the CC (color compensating) red filters can be used, depending upon the amount of correction desired. If you go deeper underwater, a magenta-yellow correction filter will create a pleasing color balance. Color photography illuminated by electronic flash can be improved with a warming filter, such as an 81A.

Filters and Black-and-White Film. With black-and-white films, filters can be used to create the contrast that is lost because of diffusion and absorption underwater. Near the surface, contrast can be created by using a red or an orange filter. This will cause the red or orange portions of the subject to be lighter on the final prints than if no filter were used. Going deep with these filters diminishes their effect, since no natural red or orange light is present to pass to the film.

Yellow filters can create contrast deeper underwater in much the same way they create contrast in air. By passing yellow light and holding back blue light, contrast is created. In the final print, light-colored subjects will stand out against darker backgrounds. In air, blue skies can be darkened with yellow filters; underwater, blue water backgrounds can also be darkened with these filters. Blue filters work opposite to the way the yellow filters do. By passing the blue light of water backgrounds and holding back light from brighter-colored subjects, prints will show a lightened background against which a darkened subject will appear.

Using Filters. When using filters, you must think about the effect they will have. On a typical dive, you could easily encounter situations that would call for different filters; no one filter is good in all situations.

Almost every filter will reduce the amount of light that reaches the film. For proper exposure, you will have to know exactly how much light is lost because of the filter, and then make an equivalent exposure increase by selecting a wider aperture or slower shutter speed, or both. Filter manufacturers supply exposure-increase information with their products. (*See:* FILTERS.)

Auxiliary Lighting

Excellent photographs can be obtained by using only available light, but at some point the need for auxiliary lighting is necessary. Light may not always be present in the quantities needed. But the most important factor about auxiliary lighting is its effect on color. Because colors are partially absorbed as light passes through water, blues and greens will be the predominant colors the film will record unless you add light. From a practical standpoint, an underwater still photographer can add light to a scene with either flashbulbs or electronic flash. The accompanying table illustrates the advantages and disadvantages of electronic flash units versus flashbulbs. The choice is a matter of specific needs. Here are some questions you should answer when trying to decide whether to use bulbs or electronic flash.

This sequence shows how the same underwater scene can be rendered differently. (Left) The photograph is illuminated by available light only; many would find it quite acceptable. (Center) With fill-in flash, much more color and detail are visible. (Right) Fill-in flash and a warming filter are combined to provide natural skin tones and bright colors. Photos by Neil Montanus.

ELECTRONIC FLASH versus FLASHBULBS

Electronic Flash Advantages	Flashbulbs Advantages
1. No flashbulbs to carry or change underwater. 2. No flashbulbs to dispose of. 3. More space when traveling (enough FP bulbs for ten 36-exposure-roll dives take a great deal of space).	1. The low initial cost of a unit. 2. The ability to vary light output by bulb selection. 3. Exposure control through shutter-speed selection (with FP bulbs). 4. Color control through clear or blue flashbulb selection. 5. High light output per unit of weight. 6. The units are compact and simple.
Disadvantages	**Disadvantages**
1. The initial cost of a large electronic flash unit is high. 2. Only one, or at best two, shutter speeds can be used with electronic flash. 3. The more light you require, the bulkier the units become. The difference between AG-1 and FP6 flashbulbs is negligible, but the difference between moving through the water with a small strobe in a housing versus a large, self-contained unit is considerable.	1. The continuing high cost of flashbulbs. 2. Slow loading and unloading of bulbs underwater. 3. The bulkiness of many bulbs while traveling and diving. 4. Bulb disposal problems.

How serious are you about underwater photography?

How many flash pictures will you be taking?

How much money do you have for an initial outlay?

If you expect the majority of your work to be available-light photography, or if you have a limited amount of money to invest in underwater lighting, flashbulbs are probably the best bet. If you are dabbling in underwater photography, you definitely should choose flashbulbs.

When compared with other underwater lighting equipment, flashbulbs and flash cubes are unbeatable in terms of weight of equipment and amount of light produced. Photo by Neil Montanus.

Flashbulbs. Should you decide on flashbulbs, you will find that comparing weight of equipment with amount of light produced, a bulb is unbeatable. Tiny AG bulbs create enough light for close-up photography, and big FP bulbs deliver the most light a diver can easily use underwater.

Blue versus Clear. If you prefer the use of flashbulbs, you will also have to decide whether to select clear or blue bulbs. In air, blue-coated bulbs are intended for use with daylight film because the light they yield is similar to daylight. In air, clear flashbulbs are balanced for use with indoor film, and since indoor lighting is generally more red than daylight, clear flashbulbs emit light that is redder than the light from blue flashbulbs. Underwater, the extra red of the clear bulbs tends to add red to photos on daylight film taken at distances of 1.3 to 2.8 m (4 to 8 ft). When clear bulbs are used closer, the extra redness adds an overall cast that looks false—this is especially so in green water. For close shooting, blue bulbs will yield proper color balance with daylight film. At longer distances, it is generally agreed that the clear flashbulbs produce more pleasing results, although the consequent color balance might be considered improper.

Electronic Flash. For the serious diving photographer, electronic flash units are really the most practical solution for adding light to underwater photography. Two important reasons make this so: money and time.

Though the initial cost is high for most self-contained electronic flash units, the continuing expense for flashbulbs over a given period of time will eventually exceed that initial investment. You must determine how much flash photography you plan to do, and over what period of time, and then measure that against the cost of the specific pieces of equipment being considered.

Time is an important factor because with electronic flash units you can take 36 exposures on a dive due to the fast recycling times of most units. It is important to realize that film is the least expensive part of a photo dive, so completing a dive with unexposed film left in the camera is not economical. With flashbulbs, you simply cannot change bulbs, compose a picture, and make an exposure within a minute, and that is what you would be trying to do if you wanted to expose 36 frames on one average dive.

Comparing Units. Electronic flash units for underwater use can be broken down into two general categories: self-contained units and housed units. Whether you decide on a unit designed and built exclusively for use underwater or choose to house a unit designed for use in air is again a matter of need for the kind of photography you intend to do. Whether or not you already own a strobe unit probably will influence your decision.

(Above) This lone yellowtail snapper was separated from the background by the judicious use of artificial light. (Left) Catching a subject in a natural activity is a useful approach underwater, as it is in air. This parrot fish is about to graze on the algae on the adjacent coral heads. Photos by Herb Taylor.

Exposure with Flash. The universally accepted method for determining accurate flash exposure in air is by using the guide-number method. A guide number is simply a number assigned to a particular combination of film and light source. This number, when divided by the flash-to-subject distance, yields an f-number that will provide an acceptable exposure. (*See:* GUIDE NUMBERS.)

Film speed (ASA) and light source are, of course, the two most important factors that govern proper exposure, but other factors should be considered too—especially underwater.

Because of the many variables in underwater photography, normal flash guide numbers cannot be used. Alternate guide numbers and actual exposure settings supplied by underwater equipment manufacturers can only give a starting point from which to determine exposure information. You will have to make a comprehensive test with your own camera and lighing unit in the water where you will be doing most of your work. But when you move to significantly different conditions, you will have to make new tests. Once you establish your own personal exposure information for each situation, you will be on your way to consistently accurate exposures.

The Test Roll. With one roll of film on one dive you will be able to make a test that will give exposure information that should help you with all your future underwater photography. To make a meaningful test, though, you must keep an accurate record of exposures. Information such as surface light conditions, water clarity, film, and flashbulb type (or electronic flash unit) can be recorded in a notebook or log. It is a very good idea to keep a log of tests for ready reference when photographing under conditions similar to previous encounters. Information that will vary over the course of the test-roll dive should be recorded in the actual test frame. This can be accomplished by including in the frame a grease-pencil slate with flash-to-subject distance, f-stop, and depth. If you are using FP flashbulbs and varying shutter speeds, the shutter speeds should also be noted. If you are using an electronic flash unit with different power settings, the power setting should be noted.

Ideally, the test frame will also include a color chart and a gray scale. Good examples of both are made by Kodak, but they are of cardboard. A test chart made by Seacor Inc. (P.O. Box 22126, San Diego, Calif. 92122) includes all of the above and provides an area in which to write variables, and it can be taken underwater.

Including a diver in the test frames is a good idea, too, to see how flesh tones are rendered. It is best to use transparency (slide) film for the test because of its narrow latitude.

To begin the test, record the constants (film, light source, sea conditions, and so on) in the log; and then mark on the slate the depth, flash-to-subject distance, and the first f-stop (also record other variables if necessary). Start with the widest aperture and make exposures at one-stop intervals to the smallest aperture. Be sure to record the change in f-stops on the slate as you go. Make a series of exposures near the surface, a series at about 10 m (30 ft) and another series at about 20 m (60 ft). When the film is processed, evaluate the results carefully.

Exposure calculations and color evaluations for underwater photography are best calculated by making the test described in the text. Use a submersible color chart. Including a diver in the test exposures is helpful in judging skin tones. Photos by Neil Montanus.

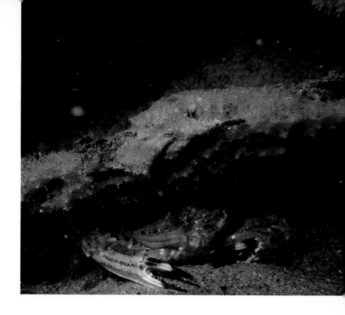

Backscatter is commonly encountered in underwater pictures made with flash. It is evident in this photograph. The spotting over the crab is caused by artificial light reflecting off suspended particles of sediment. Photo by Herb Taylor.

(The pictures that please you can be considered accurately exposed unless you are thinking about doing professional shooting; in which case, you should seek professional advice.) Based on the results, establish your own personal guide number.

Backscatter. This is a problem frequently encountered in underwater flash photography. (It is a problem encountered in air only when taking flash pictures in a snowstorm.) Backscatter is characterized by bright spots of light that cover a scene and obscure the subject. Underwater, the spotting is caused by light from the flash reflecting off suspended particles into the lens. Particles, suspended debris, or living planktonic creatures are always present in all bodies of water. The number of particles will vary with season and surface conditions and also with the type of bottom and the number of divers in the area.

To avoid backscatter, it is necessary to keep the light source away from the camera and to light the subject at an angle. Usually a distance of 45 cm (18 inches) and an angle of 45 degrees are sufficient to limit backscatter. Avoid direct frontal lighting. Lighting the subject from above and at an angle of 45 degrees to the side also creates natural-looking

You can further minimize backscatter by not disturbing bottom sediment in the area where you are taking pictures. If you know you will be working in an area where the bottom is easily roiled, you should move very slowly. You might consider removing your fins.

Backscatter is more of a problem with flashbulbs than with electronic flash for two reasons. First, most electronic flash units have narrower angles of coverage than flashbulbs; therefore fewer particles are illuminated. Second, the duration of flash is much shorter with electronic flash units than with flashbulbs; therefore the particles are illuminated for a shorter period of time. If the particles are lit for a long period of time, they appear larger because of their movement during the exposure.

Diving with Cameras

Diving with someone you know and trust is important on any dive, but on a photo dive, a good partner is invaluable. Taking pictures underwater can be much easier if you have a concerned partner who becomes, in addition to a dive buddy, an assistant photographer and model.

Difficult entries into the water can be easier if you have a good diving partner to pass valuable equipment to. The last thing you want to do is jump into the water with cameras in your hands. Underwater photographic equipment is tough, but there is no reason to subject it to undue shock. It receives enough rough handling in the normal course of events.

Before you leave the surface with your cameras, check your equipment carefully—personal gear and photo gear. Make sure everything is tight and in place. Inspect equipment thoroughly, looking for leaks or anything out of the ordinary.

During the Dive. Once underwater, a good partner will keep track of position and air supplies to avoid a tiring surface swim after the dive. A good partner will also be aware of potential dangers and keep you from settling into stinging corals or spiny sea urchins while focusing on something else.

As an assistant photographer, your partner will know what kind of pictures you are after before the dive and be able to help you find what you want or guide fish your way. In addition to carrying your extra camera, a good partner can help transfer your electronic flash unit to it when you have finished the film in the first camera—a maneuver that always requires extra hands.

Taking a friend along as a model is one way to lend interest to an otherwise routine image. The model may also be called upon to act as an assistant to the photographer. Photo by Herb Taylor.

As a model, your partner will pose patiently in the coldest of waters and will feed fish or invertebrates to help you get a picture. You can make your partner a better model by providing brightly colored gloves, hood, and suit stripes, and by explaining that better pictures can be had if equipment gauges and straps are not dangling.

Diving at night for pictures is almost impossible without a good assistant. You simply do not have enough hands to operate a camera, flash unit, and flashlight easily. A good partner will know when to point a light at a potential subject to facilitate focusing and to point it at your camera to help you make adjustments. A good partner, too, will know enough to keep the light out of your eyes.

Diving in a wetsuit that covers your legs and arms is useful for the diving photographer, even in the tropics. With a full suit, you will be able to forget about the minor annoyances encountered while diving. Abrasions, stinging corals, and jellyfish will be less of a problem for the protected diver. Thus attired, you can settle to the bottom (after looking for major annoyances like moray eels, stingrays, and stonefish) and concentrate on photography.

Maintenance

All equipment used underwater needs special care, especially if it is used in salt water. Salt water, when left to evaporate on cameras and housings, leaves mineral deposits around delicate controls and switches that can play havoc with your equipment. Do all you can to prevent this from happening.

After a dive, thoroughly soak and then rinse all your equipment in clean fresh water. Be sure to flush any areas where salt water could accumulate—for instance, the flashbulb sockets and the areas around the controls.

When the equipment has been thoroughly rinsed, let it air dry, or blot it dry with a soft towel. Never use hot air to dry equipment, and never leave it to dry in the sun. The lens ports of your equipment should always be blotted dry to prevent the formation of waterspots. When drying ports of acrylic plastic (most dome ports are of this material), be especially careful not to scratch the ports' surfaces. Scratches are extremely difficult to remove, and although small ones probably will not affect the quality of your photos, large ones can.

When thoroughly dry, housings can be opened and flash units separated. Do this in an area where you have plenty of room to spread out your equipment. When you begin this phase, you should have within reach all tools and accessories you will need to break down your equipment for thorough cleaning and lubrication. You should also have handy the film you will use for your next dive. This will save you the trouble and extra work of opening the housing and loading film at the dive site.

O-ring Care. After opening your equipment, inspect for signs of leakage. Look for moisture that may have worked its way past the main o-rings. Often the "outside" of o-rings will have droplets of moisture on them. If any wetness or salt deposits are detected "inside" the o-rings, replace them. If not, the o-rings can be wiped dry and relubricated with silicone grease. An annual change of o-rings is a good maintenance procedure.

This photograph of orange Caribbean coral is a striking example of underwater close-ups, obtainable by the use of extension tubes or supplementary lenses. Divers frequently confuse this coral with sea anemones; actual size of the polyp is about 3 cm. Photo by Herb Taylor. ▶

Underwater Photography

Flooding

Nothing can match the unfortunate experience of having a very expensive piece of photographic equipment flood with seawater. Should it happen, you must immediately try to salvage what you can.

Step 1. If your camera floods, remove the film and any batteries that might be in it. If the flooded item is an electronic flash unit, turn it off, open it to let the water drain away from batteries, and then carefully remove the batteries to avoid shock.

Step 2. As quickly as you can, get the flooded item into clean fresh water. Salt water begins its corrosive action in very short time—a few hours can make the difference between a relatively easy (major, but easy) repair job and a difficult and costly one. Soak the flooded item in a large container filled with tap water and then hold it under flowing tap water. The item should be immersed for at least half an hour. While the unit is in the tap water, operate the controls. Operate switches, levers, the shutter—all the controls. The idea is to drive away all the salt water from pockets where it might accumulate, and also to drive it away from the tiny gears and springs that salt water attacks quickly.

Step 3. Use a gentle stream of compressed air to remove as much moisture as possible from the working mechanisms of the equipment.

Step 4. Soak the item in alcohol, and again activate all the controls for at least half an hour. Now the idea is to drive away the moisture from the inner workings of the camera. The alcohol does this as it absorbs the water and evaporates quickly. As the alcohol removes the moisture, though, it also removes most of the camera's lubricating fluids.

Step 5. Use more compressed air to drive out remaining moisture and help the alcohol evaporate.

Step 6. Pack the equipment with a desiccant, and then ship it to the manufacturer. Whenever you return equipment to the manufacturer, be sure to include details about the flooding and the steps you took immediately afterward.

Flooding a camera in a lake or river is not the worst thing that can happen to a camera, but flooding one in seawater really is. Nothing short of complete stripping, cleaning, and reassembly of the camera—a virtual rebuilding—can ever get it back into anywhere near its original condition. Only a fully qualified repair technician can provide the care that equipment needs after exposure to salt water.

2524

(Above) These grunts were photographed in a Florida freshwater spring. While their normal habitat is the Gulf of Mexico, grunts take refuge in warmer freshwater environs when the Gulf begins to turn cold. Photo by Herb Taylor. (Facing Page) Tube worms, photographed (top) at 3-to-1 reproduction ratio, and (bottom) at 1-to-1, or actual size. A peculiarity of these creatures is that they will withdraw instantly into their shells if the photographer unwittingly blocks the light of the sun. Photos by Neil Montanus.

Flood Prevention

Most floodings occur because of carelessness or rushing to assemble equipment, or a combination of the two. Check equipment as many times as you can before you dive with it. Check it the night before you dive (when it should be assembled and prepared to go); check it at the dive site before you enter the water; and check it one more time on the surface before you go down. If at all possible, avoid on-site loading and unloading film. The last place you want to open your camera is on a crowded boat or a sandy shore, unless absolutely necessary.

Safety

Diving itself is a strenuous activity, and you must be in peak physical condition to dive. Pushing a camera before you as you swim underwater makes diving even more strenuous. Because the hydrodynamics of most underwater equipment is bad, moving through the water with them is difficult. Since the water does not flow smoothly around equipment, drag is created, and you consume more air and burn more energy than divers without cameras (all other factors that make good divers being equal).

Know your limits. Safe diving should always be first and foremost in your mind. Do not hesitate for a second to abandon your photo gear if that will improve the situation. Equipment can always be replaced.

• *See also:* ABERRATION; ELECTRONIC FLASH; EXPOSURE; FLASH PHOTOGRAPHY FILTERS; GUIDE NUMBERS; REFRACTION.

Uranyl Nitrate

Uranium oxynitrate

A metal salt, used in toning baths for brown to red tones. It is also used in intensifiers for negatives, and as a dye mordant in certain toning baths.
Formula: $UO_2(NO_3)_2 \cdot 6H_2O$
Molecular Weight: 502.18

Greenish-yellow crystals, somewhat efflorescent. Very soluble in acetic acid, water, alcohol, and ethyl ether.
CAUTION: Poison; radioactive substance.

U.S. Stops

This system of lens stops was used mainly on old rapid rectilinear lenses. The abbreviation "U.S." stands for "Uniform System," and not for "United States."

In the Uniform System, each stop produced either double or half the exposure of the following or preceding stop. The numbers were inversely proportional to the exposure produced. The base of the system was an aperture that was just one quarter of the focal length (in the f-system, it would would be $f/4.0$); this aperture was called U.S. 1. The numbers then doubled at each stop; thus, the U.S. numbers corresponded to f-stops as follows:

U.S. 1 = $f/4$		U.S. 32 = $f/22$	
U.S. 2 = $f/5.6$		U.S. 64 = $f/45$	
U.S. 4 = $f/8$		U.S. 128 = $f/64$	
U.S. 8 = $f/11$		U.S. 256 = $f/90$	
U.S. 16 = $f/16$		U.S. 512 = $f/128$	

• *See also:* f-NUMBER; f-STOP.

Variable Contrast

The contrast of black-and-white negatives can be varied to a considerable extent by controlled changes in development time, temperature, or formula. (*See:* CONTRAST) Contrast in printing is varied primarily by the choice of a paper contrast grade. The desire to increase convenience and flexibility in printing led to the production of selective or "variable" contrast papers. Attempts to achieve contrast control through variable print development are generally less successful. With some modern papers a slight to moderate degree of contrast change can be obtained by various combinations of developers with different characteristics.

Selective-Contrast Papers

A number of papers are available that can produce a range of contrasts equivalent to about three-and-a-half or four numbered contrast grades. Although called variable-contrast papers, the term "selective contrast" is more accurately descriptive.

A selective-contrast paper acts as though it has two emulsion layers: a low-contrast layer that is sensitive to green wavelengths and a high-contrast layer that is sensitive to blue wavelengths. They are designed for exposure with a standard (3200 K) enlarging bulb. A particular degree of contrast is selected by using a filter in the enlarger head or under the lens to color the light so that exposure affects one emulsion layer or the other, or is divided in various degrees between the two layers.

The density range dial in Kodak publication No. R-20, KODAK Darkroom DATAGUIDE, is a useful tool for comparing the contrasts of current Kodak selective-contrast papers with negative density ranges. A comparison can also be made with single-contrast papers that are name-graded or number-graded.

The lowest contrast is obtained with a yellow filter, which absorbs all blue wavelengths but passes red and green wavelengths from the exposing light. The red wavelengths have no effect, but the green wavelengths register the exposure totally in the low-contrast emulsion layer. Maximum contrast is obtained with a magenta filter, which absorbs green but passes blue and red wavelengths. In this case, the exposure is registered entirely in the high-contrast emulsion layer. Intermediate contrasts are obtained with filters of other colors that pass various proportions of both green and blue wavelengths.

A particular advantage of a selective-contrast paper is that it permits making a print with two different degrees of local contrast—something that is not possible with graded contrast papers. Most commonly, this feature is exploited in the following way. The print is exposed through a high-contrast filter to achieve maximum separation of dark-area detail. It usually is not necessary to dodge the highlights during this exposure, because less light is coming through those denser areas of the negative. A low-contrast filter is then used to print in the highlight areas. The shadow areas must be protected from additional exposure during the printing-in process. This is an excellent way to achieve balanced prints of scenes with a very long brightness range—for example, dark details in shadowed foreground areas with a background of bright clouds in the sky.

Selective-contrast papers are available on both conventional bases and water-resistant bases, and

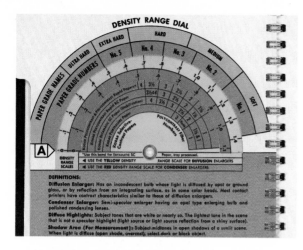

with emulsions designed for conventional, stabilization, or activation processing. They make it practical to stock only one paper in a darkroom, which provides initial economy and avoids the long-term expense of having to discard stocks of little-used contrast grades that may have spoiled with age.

Graded Papers

A certain amount of contrast variation can be achieved in printing on a high-contrast grade of paper by giving it an overall flashing, or fogging, exposure before making the image exposure. Some photographers have worked out methods of achieving specific degrees of contrast by flashing, but the procedures are relatively cumbersome, and they tend to limit rather than expand expressive control in printing. Further, there is a real danger of reducing highlight contrast. Flashing exposures after the image is exposed may be used to eliminate details in specific areas by covering them with undifferentiated dark tones; this is sometimes a useful method of local contrast reduction. For additional details, see the article FLASHING.

Variable-Contrast Paper Development

Many attempts have been made to obtain different degrees of contrast with a single paper grade by varying the developer formula. The most widely used formulation was the Beers two-solution developer. The formulas are included here largely for historical interest and experimentation. Most modern papers will show no change when processed in the various combinations. However, the rebirth of

interest in interpretive black-and-white printing has led to new investigation of these and related formulas. Some photographers have reported definite changes in contrast when using the Beers developer with slow, warm-tone papers, but the maximum change is less than a single contrast grade.

Beers Two-Solution Developer for Papers
Solution A

Water	750.0 ml
Metol	8.0 g
Sodium sulfite, desiccated	23.0 g
Sodium carbonate, desiccated	20.0 g
Potassium bromide, 10 percent solution*	11.0 ml
Water to make	1.0 litre

Solution B

Water	750.0 ml
Hydroquinone	8.0 g
Sodium sulfite, desiccated	23.0 g
Sodium carbonate, desiccated	27.0 g
Potassium bromide, 10 percent solution*	22.0 ml
Water to make	1.0 litre

To use the Beers developer, combine solutions A and B and water as shown in the accompanying table.

*To make a 10 percent solution, dissolve 10 grams of potassium bromide in water to total 100 ml of solution.

Variable Contrast

USING BEERS DEVELOPER

To make one	Take Sol. A	+	Sol. B	+	Water	
Litre	125 ml		875 ml		0	Higher
Quart	4 oz		28 oz		0	
Litre	188 ml		312 ml		500 ml	
Quart	6 oz		10 oz		16 oz	
Litre	250 ml		250 ml		500 ml	
Quart	8 oz		8 oz		16 oz	
Litre	312 ml		188 ml		500 ml	Medium contrast
Quart	10 oz		6 oz		16 oz	
Litre	375 ml		125 ml		500 ml	
Quart	12 oz		4 oz		16 oz	
Litre	438 ml		62 ml		500 ml	
Quart	14 oz		2 oz		16 oz	
Litre	500 ml		0		500 ml	Lower
Quart	16 oz		0		16 oz	

EXPERIMENTAL VARIABLE-CONTRAST PAPER DEVELOPER

(Use stock solutions. Normal developer: *Kodak* Dektol; D-72; or equivalent. Soft developer: *Kodak* Selectol-Soft; D-52; or equivalent.)

To make one	Take Normal developer	+	Soft developer	+	Water	
Litre	1000 ml		0		0	Higher
Quart	32 oz		0		0	
Litre	375 ml		125 ml		500 ml	
Quart	12 oz		4 oz		16 oz	
Litre	250 ml		250 ml		500 ml	Medium contrast
Quart	8 oz		8 oz		16 oz	
Litre	125 ml		375 ml		500 ml	
Quart	4 oz		12 oz		16 oz	
Litre	500 ml		0		500 ml	Lower
Quart	16 oz		0		16 oz	

A more useful adaptation of the two-solution idea is to mix various proportions of two standard developers that have different characteristics. One is a normal cold-tone developer such as Kodak Dektol or D-72 developer. The other is a soft-working formula such as Kodak developer D-52, or the softer —and thus more useful—Kodak Selectol-Soft developer. The accompanying table for an experimental variable-contrast developer suggests some proportional combinations. There will be no significant variation in cold-tone papers, but warm-tone enlarging papers such as Kodak Ektalure paper and some contact papers may show contrast variations of about a half grade, or a bit more. (Formulas for D-72 and D-52 are included in the article DEVELOPERS AND DEVELOPING.)

Variable Contrast

This approach to contrast control should be considered experimental—results cannot be predicted except on the basis of testing and experience. However, in some cases the method will meet the need for a "grade 3¾" paper, or one of some other intermediate step, to achieve a particular expressiveness in a print.

• *See also:* BLACK-AND-WHITE PRINTING; CONTRAST; DEVELOPERS AND DEVELOPING; FLASHING; FORMULAS FOR BLACK-AND-WHITE

View Camera

The term "view camera" is generally taken to mean a medium-to-large-format camera; the terms "technical camera" and "stand camera" are also encountered. Studio cameras for formal portraiture are of the large-format type, but they are generally mounted on a heavy, wheeled stand for limited movement within a studio. View cameras are practically always used mounted on a tripod or some other kind of rigid stand.

The principal features that set the view camera apart from others are the availability of the adjustments, and the method of focusing and composing the image by means of a ground-glass screen at the back of the camera.

The large formats in general use are from 4″×5″ to 8″ × 10″. Cameras that take 11″ × 14″ film are available for special purposes. View cameras that take 2¼″ × 3¼″ film are also available, but again these are special-purpose instruments. Serious large-format work is generally undertaken with cameras whose minimum format is 4″ × 5″, because it is somewhat difficult to assess the results of camera adjustments on a smaller format. If negatives smaller than 4″ × 5″ are desirable, they can be made on a larger camera by using interchangeable camera backs or roll-film adapters.

Types of View Cameras

Although the main concept of the view camera has not changed much since the early days of photography, many refinements and improvements have taken place. Lenses have been improved in both speed and quality, and more different types of lenses

are available. The standard, flat-bed view camera is still available in various sizes. However, one modern trend is towards the monorail design, which has inherently greater versatility. As the term monorail implies, these cameras have a base consisting of a single member, which may be of tubular or square section. This design employs interchangeable components, such as lens standards, camera backs, bellows, and base or rail lengths. Thus, a monorail view camera constitutes a system that allows the photographer to put together the components for a camera that best suits his or her immediate requirements.

Another modern trend is toward the lightweight field cameras. They are a modification of the flat-bed type, but have been refined so that they weigh as little as 2½ pounds in the 4″ × 5″ size.

Choosing a View Camera

Clearly, the choice of a camera must be based on your own particular circumstances. If all you intend to do is an occasional large-format job, as might be the case in a small studio, it would be uneconomical to invest in a camera system such as that described in the preceding section. In this situation, a reasonably priced 4″ × 5″ camera with several lenses of different focal length would enable you to undertake most of the assignments that call for the use of a large format. In this connection, remember that a camera having a normal-length bellows cannot always be used with an ultra-wide-angle lens, because the bellows cannot be compressed sufficiently to give the necessarily short lens-to-film distance. Sometimes, the difficulty can be overcome by resorting to a recessed lensboard that brings the lens closer to the film. However, cameras with special bellows for wide-angle work are obtainable, and in some cases, separate wide-angle bellows are sold as an accessory.

If you propose to undertake a wide variety of large-format work to include product photography of all kinds, architectural work, interiors of buildings, a variety of industrial photography, as well as close-up work, a more versatile camera system with a good selection of lenses will be needed. Assignments of this kind often call for the high quality of 8″ × 10″ color transparencies.

Then, consider the cost. Clearly, it would be uneconomical to buy an expensive camera if you were to use it only once a month, for example. In this

Variable Contrast

situation, if an inexpensive model is not adequate for your purpose, consider renting the camera you prefer for those assignments on which it is needed.

Determine the size of negative or transparency you will need to make. If you often have to carry the outfit, choose the lightest and smallest one that will do the work adequately. Otherwise, do not restrict yourself to the smallest format, because different sizes of camera back can be used on an 8″ × 10″ camera. Remember, however, that the larger the format the more expensive, less plentiful, and heavier are the lenses that cover it. Moreover, the size of the negative is felt throughout your processing and printing system. For example, if you produce 8″ × 10″ negatives, you need a similar size enlarger to accommodate them.

Another factor that enters into using the larger formats is exposure time. The depth of field with the long-focal-length lenses needed to cover, for instance, an 8″ × 10″ film is shallow. In stopping the lens down to increase the depth of field, a correspondingly longer exposure is needed. In some situations, this limitation might cause difficulty when you photograph moving parts of machinery, operators at work, or anything else that requires fast shutter speed. Since jobs of this kind are often photographed on location, you may or may not have adequate light to get sufficient exposure.

Do not invest in an 8″ × 10″ camera and a battery of expensive lenses to go with it unless you are certain that the limited, but essential, advantages of this format will be required by the work you are going to do. In general, the work that requires an 8″ × 10″ negative or transparency is in some high-quality advertising photography, catalog work where transparencies are made with specified image sizes for the "cut and butt" technique, and the highest quality portraiture. Almost without exception, this work will be in color. There is little, if any, reason to use the largest negatives in black-and-white photography unless your intention is to make contact prints of usable size. A 4″ × 5″ black-and-white negative properly made will yield results adequate for practically all photographic purposes. Moreover, there are many advantages to be gained by using this size negative, among which are cost of lenses and material, portability, length of exposure, availability of suitable lenses, and the greater depth of field given by lenses that cover this format.

Two exceptions to the foregoing remarks are in high-quality portraiture where the large negative is easier to retouch without the work becoming visible on an enlargement, and in mural work where the largest negative is desirable, but not essential. Probably there are other situations in which an 8″ × 10″ negative would be necessary, but the decision can be made only when all the details of the particular job are known. (*See:* PORTRAITURE.)

Shutters

The shutters generally used with view cameras are either those situated between the elements of the lens or as a separate unit behind the lens. As far as efficiency is concerned, there is little to choose between the two types, but for ease of setting the behind-the-lens type is preferable. Moreover, if several lenses are used, a single shutter behind the lens eliminates any possible variations that might exist among several between-the-lens types.
(*See:* SHUTTERS.)

The Camera

The camera shown in the following illustration is typical of most view cameras. Its principal parts are:

1. *Monorail, or track.* This serves as the basic support structure for the rest of the components.
2. *Front lens standard.* A U-shaped frame mounted on the monorail, which can be moved and locked into any position on the rail. The lensboard is mounted between the upright arms of the "U."
3. *Back (rear) standard.* This is exactly like the front lens standard except that the camera back is mounted on it.
4. *Bellows.* A flexible lighttight tube mounted between the lens and back standards. This permits the two standards to be moved closer or farther apart for focusing or to accommodate different focal-length lenses while maintaining the lighttight integrity between the lens and the camera back.
5. *Tripod-mounting head.* This holds the monorail on top of the tripod.

A modern view camera, the Omega View 45F, has a full complement of camera movements with tilts of ±30 degrees, swings of ±20 degrees, lateral shifts of ±32 mm, and 90 mm rising front and back. Standard parts are: (A) tripod head; (B) back standard; (C) locking levers; (D) camera back; (E) bellows; (F) lensboard; (G) lens; (H) front standard; (I) monorail.

6. *Lens.* The appropriate focal-length lens is mounted on a flat plate attached to the front lens standard.

7. *Ground-glass back.* A piece of ground glass mounted on the camera's rear standard. The image projected by the lens is brought into focus and composed on this glass. The image will be upside down and reversed from side to side.

View Camera Movements

In approaching the use of the view camera, it is important to realize that there are only four basic individual movements.

1. The lens can be pivoted around its optical center.
2. The lens can be moved from side to side or up or down in relation to the film.
3. The ground glass can be pivoted.
4. The ground glass can be moved from side to side or up and down.

These movements are not necessarily just vertical or horizontal, but can be any place in between as well. This means that the lens, film, and subject relationship have an infinite number of potential positions. However, if the primary movements and what they accomplish are understood, then mastery of the view camera is well within your reach.

Keep one basic rule in mind at all times: In order to have control over what you are doing, it is necessary to have a starting place from which you can work. This starting place is the neutral, or zero, position. That is, all swings, tilts, and slides are centered and in the neutral, or zero, position. The shutter should be open and the diaphragm at its widest opening.

View cameras are commonly used for product and tabletop photography. The extendable bellows and swing and tilt adjustments make this an ideal camera for focusing fairly close up while maintaining acceptable depth of field.

Another thing to be aware of is that for every correction you make, it will be necessary to make either focusing or positioning adjustments. In other words, every time you swing or tilt either the back or the lens, you will have to refocus or slide either the lens or back from one side to the other, or raise or lower one or the other to recenter the image.

The reason for this is that any time there is a manipulation of either the swings or tilts, there will be a change in the relationship between the ground glass and the optical center of the lens. These changes will be greater with cameras having bottom swings than with those with swings located at the center of the lensboard and back, but changes will nevertheless occur with both types of camera.

Keep in mind that the image on the ground glass is upside down and backward. This is perhaps one of the most difficult aspects of working with the view camera. You can get around this problem by using a reflex viewing back, which can be mounted on the camera in place of the normal ground glass. Many cameras now have such an accessory.

Definitions. The following are definitions of the view camera movements.

1. Rise. Rise occurs when the camera back or lensboard is raised vertically from the centered, or neutral, position.
2. Fall. When either the camera lens board or back is lowered vertically from the centered, or neutral, position fall occurs.
3. Slide. Slide occurs when either the camera lensboard or back is moved hori-

zontally from the centered, or neutral, position.

4. Swing. When either the camera lens or back is rotated around its vertical axis, swing occurs. Swinging the camera back is discussed in terms of the film emulsion.

5. Tilt. Tilt occurs when either the camera lensboard or back is rotated around its horizontal axis.

Sequence of View Camera Operations

The following is the step-by-step process of setting up the camera, framing the subject, focusing the camera, and exposing the film.

1. Perspective. Position yourself so that the size relationships of the front and back parts of the subject give you the size relationships you will need in your completed photograph. This is the position where you should set up the camera.

2. Frame the Subject. Center the image on the ground glass.

3. Focus the camera. You will find it useful that a view camera can be focused from either the front or the rear. By moving the back instead of the lensboard, the lens-subject relationship remains constant and the image size on the ground glass remains the same. This is particularly useful when doing close-ups, where even a small movement of the lens can make a marked difference in subject size.

4. Check for Coverage. With the camera positioned for the proper perspective, make certain that the lens covers enough of the subject from side to side and from top to bottom. And check to see if there is so much coverage that the needed part of the subject occupies only a small segment of the negative. If your framing is not what is needed, then change lenses for a focal length that will give you the proper coverage.

5. Refocus. If you changed to a different lens, then refocus.

6. Adjust Image Size. At this point, it generally will be necessary to make slight adjustments in image size. This calls for moving the camera either closer to or farther from the subject. If a major adjustment is needed, it will be necessary to move the entire tripod. For minor adjustments, it is possible to slip the camera rail backward or forward in its tripod mount. This moves the entire camera

without the problems caused by repositioning the tripod.

7. Make Corrections. If distortion is to be corrected, swing or tilt the camera back.

8. Recenter the Image. Use the camera back slides or rises to recenter the image.

9. Adjust Sharpness Wedge. If depth is insufficient, swing the lens to position the main wedge of sharpness through the important points of the subject.

10. Additional Sharpness Adjustment. If distortion is no problem and it is not possible to swing the lens enough to precisely position the wedge of sharpness, the back may also be swung to aid in this positioning.

11. Reposition Sharpness Wedge. Refocus the camera back to more precisely position the wedge of sharpness.

12. Exposure Increase. Calculate the exposure increase needed because of the bellows factor.

13. Check Depth. Stop the diaphragm down while checking the ground glass to make certain there is sufficient depth of field.

14. Check Picture Area. If a compendium bellows is being used, check the four corners of the ground glass to be certain the bellows does not intrude into the picture area. Also check to make sure that nothing extraneous to the picture is visible on the ground glass. If it is, remove it.

15. Set Shutter Speed and Cock. Close the shutter. Set the shutter speed appropriate to that which will give you the correct exposure based on the preselected diaphragm setting. Cock the shutter. Keep in mind that in situations where subject movement calls for a high shutter speed, either more light must be provided on the subject or a compromise must be made in the depth by using a larger diaphragm opening.

16. Insert Holder. Pull back the spring-mounted ground glass and slide in either the cut-film or roll-film holder. Be certain all camera and tripod screws are firmly engaged or you might shift the focus when pulling out the spring back.

17. Remove Slide. Check the lens to be certain it has been closed, then pull the dark slide from the holder.

18. Stop. Wait until any vibrations or movements of the camera have had a chance to subside.

19. Make the Exposure. Always use a cable release to fire the shutter. Pressing the shutter-release button by hand could generate enough movement to dull the razor-edge sharpness possible with this type of camera.

20. Replace Dark Slide. More than one piece of film has been ruined because the holder was pulled out of the camera before the dark slide was replaced.

21. Lock It. Turn the latches on the end of the holder to make certain the slide is not accidentally pulled out.

22. Check Slide. In replacing the slide, be certain it has been turned so that the *black side is facing out.* This indicates that the film has been exposed. It is easy to become confused and make a second picture on the same piece of film if this procedure is neglected.

23. Advance Film. When using a roll-film holder, *advance the film immediately* after the exposure has been made so there is no danger of making a second exposure on top of the first one.

24. Check Focus. Remove the holder, open the camera shutter and diaphragm, and recheck the focus to make certain it did not shift while you were manipulating the camera.

Focusing the Camera

One of the objects in using a large-format camera is to get negatives of the greatest possible sharpness so that detail can be recorded to the best advantage in the photograph. Focusing the camera, therefore, should be done carefully. When you have composed the picture on the ground-glass screen and have made any necessary corrections or adjustments to the image, pause for a moment to rest your eyes, and then check the focus again, preferably with a focusing magnifier. Then, stop the lens down to an aperture that will yield the depth of field that you consider adequate for the particular shot, but remember that the image on the ground glass usually appears to be sharper than it will appear to be in the negative. You will become accustomed to this effect after some experience in using view cameras.

Before assuming that the image is as sharp as possible after focusing and stopping the lens down, you should be aware that with some otherwise excellent lenses the point of sharpest focus shifts as the aperture is changed. If you suspect that this is a characteristic of a lens, make one test negative with the lens focused at full aperture and another focused at the aperture you intend to use; then compare the

two images to see if there is a difference in sharpness.

Always mount your camera on a good, solid tripod or other type of stand. A large camera with a heavy lens is always prone to vibrate. Probably, more unsharpness is due to camera movement or shake than is due to improper focusing or inferior optical quality of lenses. Before making the exposure, pause to allow any possible vibration to die out. On a windy day, try to expose between gusts. Allow heavy vehicles, railway trains, and the like, to pass before making the exposure.

Other Factors That Affect Sharpness. Large-format cameras are generally used to produce photographs that convey information of some kind to the observer. The precision of modern view cameras, the performance of high-quality lenses, and the high definition of present-day sensitized materials are somewhat academic unless they are realized in the form of clear, sharp prints with a minimum of graininess. To obtain such results, every significant element in your photographic system must receive the same careful attention you give to composing and focusing the picture on the ground-glass screen of the camera. Here are some points to consider:

1. Make sure that your camera lenses are clean and free from dust or finger marks. Otherwise, your negatives will lack contrast and critical sharpness, and the resolution of fine detail will suffer accordingly.

2. To minimize the effect of flare caused by reflection of light from the interior of the camera, be sure that the interior is painted matte black. Flare is non-image-forming light that affects the negative by adding density to the shadows. Thus, shadow detail is reduced in contrast and the overall density range is lowered.

3. Because overexposure causes increased graininess and loss of definition, give only sufficient exposure to obtain satisfactory shadow detail.

4. Do not develop negatives much longer than the time recommended in the instruction sheet packaged with the film, because overdevelopment results in high contrast and increased graininess.

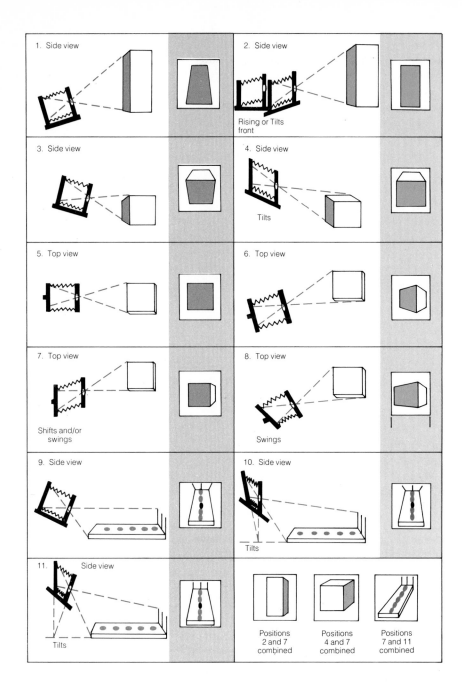

The following labels appear within the illustration:

1. Side view
2. Side view — Rising or Tilts front
3. Side view
4. Side view — Tilts
5. Top view
6. Top view
7. Top view — Shifts and/or swings
8. Top view — Swings
9. Side view
10. Side view — Tilts
11. Side view — Tilts

Positions 2 and 7 combined
Positions 4 and 7 combined
Positions 7 and 11 combined

These drawings illustrate the relationship between the front and back of a view camera and their effect on perspective. The shaded areas in the drawings illustrate the change achieved by manipulating the camera. Drawings 9 and 10 show the way a view camera can be used to control depth of field. Drawing 11 sketches the way to achieve parallel verticals with increased depth of field.

The accompanying drawings show the concept of view camera perspective.

• *See also:* ARCHITECTURAL PHOTOGRAPHY; CAMERA MOVEMENTS; CAMERAS; CAMERA SUPPORTS; ENLARGERS AND ENLARGING; LARGE COLOR PRINTS AND TRANSPARENCIES; LENS MOUNTS; NOTCH CODES; PERSPECTIVE; PORTRAITURE; SHUTTERS; VIGNETTING; VISION.

Further Reading: Eastman Kodak Co. *Kodak Professional Photoguide,* pub. No. R-28. Rochester, NY: Eastman Kodak Co., 1977; _____. *Photography with Large-Format Cameras,* pub. No. 0-18. Rochester, NY: Eastman Kodak Co., 1973; Shaman, Harvey. *The View Camera: Operations and Techniques.* Garden City, NY: Amphoto, 1977; Stroebel, Leslie. *View Camera Technique,* 3rd., rev. ed. New York, NY: Hastings House, 1976.

Viewing and Focusing

Viewing is the process of using a viewfinder or a framing device to select the angle and distance from which the camera will view a subject, and to determine where the boundaries of the picture shall be. Focusing is the major step in ensuring that those details which ought to be sharp in the final image will be, in fact, registered sharply on the film. (Such factors as vibrations, dirt on the lens, and film lying out of the focal plane will also affect sharpness.)

Taken together, viewing and focusing are the visual part of actually taking a photograph, in which a great many interpretative or creative decisions are made, often almost unconsciously. Some of the material presented here is covered in greater detail in the more specific entries listed in the cross-references.

Viewing Devices

The simplest viewfinders are frames or cut-out masks that mark off the field taken in by a camera lens, usually the normal lens for the format. The wire-frame type is often called a sports finder—it shows the picture area but does not interfere with seeing the surrounding area, so action moving into the field of view can be seen and anticipated. Masks are openings cut into opaque plates. Many cameras have wire frames or masks that fold flat against the body when not in use.

It is often convenient, especially in large-format photography, to use a separate framing device to explore a subject from many different points of view without having to set up the camera at each location. A mask can be cut quickly and easily from a piece of cardboard of suitable size, $8'' \times 10''$, for example. The opening is in the same proportions as the film format, but should be two or more times larger for formats smaller than $4'' \times 5''$. For instance, a 35 mm film frame is 24×36 mm ($1'' \times 1\frac{1}{2}''$); a convenient mask opening is four times larger, 100×150 mm ($4'' \times 6''$). The frame can be used to show the field of any lens. If it is the same size as the negative, hold it in front of the eye a distance equal to the focal length of the lens to be used; if it is larger, multiply the focal length by the enlargement factor of the frame dimensions to find the proper viewing distance. The example frame is four times

larger than the format, so it should be held a distance of $4 \times$ focal length in front of the eye. More detailed instructions for making and using this kind of viewing frame are included in the article LANDSCAPE PHOTOGRAPHY.

Wire focal frames that mark off the area covered and establish proper distance for close-ups are especially useful with cameras that do not have through-the-lens viewing. Their construction is explained in CLOSE-UP PHOTOGRAPHY.

The next step after an open-frame viewfinder is a simple optical finder, which usually has a negative finder lens and a positive eye lens. Such a finder may incorporate lines indicating the field of view of one or more camera lenses within a larger mask opening. It may also have one or more markings to indicate one or two edges of the field of view at close distances to compensate for camera parallax.

Using Simple Viewers

Direct viewfinders provide the brightest possible image of the subject, but of course give no indication of focus adjustment. The most important limitation, however, is parallax. The problems arising from the fact that the viewfinder axis and the camera lens axis are separated are discussed in other articles. There is also parallax when the eye is not properly aligned with the viewfinder axis.

If the eye is off-axis, it will see a different field than is outlined by the frame. To ensure proper eye alignment, most viewers incorporate a rear frame, mask, or eye post that can be related to the front frame, or to cross hairs or reference marks. Three types are illustrated.

When an eyepiece mask is used, the eye must be the correct distance behind it to see the field of view accurately. If too far away, the rear mask restricts the field to less than it should be; if too close, the eye sees a wider field. The illustrations explain this problem. To achieve proper viewing, first hold the camera a greater-than-normal distance from the eye, with the eye centered on the viewfinder. Move the eye closer until all four edges of the front frame or mask are just visible through the rear opening. Maintain that distance as you move the camera for various viewpoints and it will soon become habitual.

Rangefinder Cameras

Most cameras that use rangefinder focusing combine it with an optical viewfinder consisting of

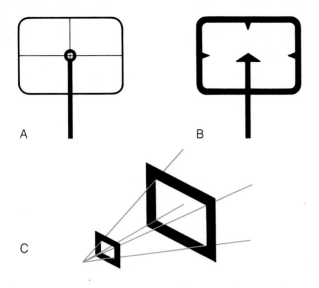

Unless the eye is aligned along the axis of the viewing mask or frame, perception of the field will be incorrect. Eye-viewfinder parallax can be corrected by: (A) alignment of a peep-sight with crosshairs in the front frame and (B) alignment of the arrowhead of the eyepost with index marks on the front mask. (C) Concentric masks delineate the exact field when their edges coincide with the frame of the smaller (eyepiece) mask.

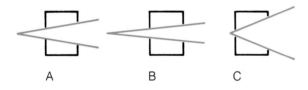

Eye distance is critical when using a direct viewfinder. (A) At the proper distance, the eye will just see the edges of the front mask aligned with those of the rear mask. (B) If the eye is too far away, the smaller mask narrows the field of view excessively. (C) If the eye is too close, the small mask does not have a limiting effect, and the eye will see a field of view that is too wide.

a negative (finder) lens, an eyepiece lens, and projected bright frame lines for various lenses. While the optical quality of the viewing lenses in rangefinder cameras may be superior to that of simpler cameras, the viewfinder design itself is just the same. The limitations of such systems are lens-viewfinder parallax, and the number of different fields of view that can be shown practically in a single finder. Usually the limit is four fields in a 35 mm camera—typically, those for 35 mm, 50 mm, 90 mm, and 135 mm lenses.

Through-the-Lens Viewing

View cameras and single-lens reflex cameras provide the most accurate indication of what will be recorded on the film because they eliminate parallax. There may, however, be some inaccuracy in the field of view they indicate; the field may include more or less than what is recorded on the film, or it may not be centered with the eventual image. The problem is usually slight, and a method of determining any difference is given in the article TESTING. More importantly, no other system simultaneously shows field of view, focus, and the effect of the lens focal length on depth perspective. So long as there is sufficient light from the subject (even at maximum aperture, all lenses reduce image brightness), this kind of viewing is usually preferred for precise work. It is essential for close-ups, and for accurate focusing at great distances with telephoto lenses.

Viewing Considerations

The viewfinder presents the whole picture, but it is a common mistake to devote attention only to the center of interest. Viewing should pay as much concern to the edges of the picture as to the center. It is easy to check whether a background element seems to be growing out of the top of a subject, or whether something in the foreground blocks the view. But what is getting cut off at the edges? An unfortunate "amputation" of a strong form or a line at a picture border can claim attention or create a sense of incompleteness. Other elements completely within the field may claim too much attention by reason of color, shape, or position. They must be noticed in viewing, and the view adjusted to subordinate them to the main subject. At first it may take a conscious effort to scan the entire image with equal attention, but eventually it becomes automatic.

Viewing is a way of checking composition, which is the arrangement and balance of picture elements. In photography outside the studio, where pictures are not set up but are selected, the most important aspect of composition is framing—shifting the picture borders to locate the main subject properly and to include only what ought to be seen in the outer picture areas. Often only a slight adjustment makes a major improvement in a picture.

The smaller the viewing image, the easier it is to judge total picture effect, because the eye can encompass everything with a minimum of scanning movement. This is one reason the 35 mm format is so practical for "decisive moment" photography, which depends on seizing the instant when the pattern of visual elements sum up the feeling or meaning of an event.

With large-format cameras, the view in the camera should continually be compared with a direct look at the subject. When the camera image is as satisfying as the direct view, the picture is ready to be taken.

The grid lines included on the viewing screen of many through-the-lens cameras are not compositional guides. They are alignment devices that are especially useful for checking horizontal and vertical elements. They quickly reveal whether the camera is tilted to one side, or whether there is distortion because the film plane is not parallel with the subject.

Focusing

The methods by which images are focused are well covered elsewhere, especially in the articles FOCUSING SYSTEMS and RANGEFINDER. Whether focusing is accomplished on ground glass or a microprism screen, with a split image, or otherwise, a comparison or "racking" technique must be used. Only by moving the image in and out of focus can the point of maximum sharpness be determined. With through-the-lens systems, this requires the brightest image and minimum depth of field, which means using the largest lens aperture.

However, it then becomes important to check whether focus shifts slightly when the lens is stopped down to a small aperture. This phenomenon is most likely to occur with large-format lenses and enlarging lenses. It may be possible to check for it by using a magnifier to observe the image, but brightness decreases as the f-stop grows smaller, and depth of field increases making the comparison with surrounding details more difficult. It is more precise to make comparison photographs, one after critically focusing at maximum aperture, the others at small apertures, changing shutter speed to adjust exposure. Try to avoid using neutral density filters for this check. Filters can shift the focus point of an image; for this reason it is important to focus with a filter in place over the lens for critical adjustment. This applies equally to the use of selective-contrast printing filters in front of an enlarger lens.

Focus shift may occur in a zoom lens. This is not a problem in still photography because the picture is focused sharply at whatever focal length is chosen. In motion-picture photography, zoom focus-shift can be especially annoying when the lens is zoomed from a wide to a telephoto view during a single shot. In that case, a small area is magnified greatly, so that any poor focus is most noticeable. Proper focusing technique is as follows. Before beginning a shot, zoom the lens to maximum telephoto focal length and focus critically at maximum aperture. Zoom back to whatever view is to be used at the beginning of the shot. Adjust the aperture setting. Begin the shot and zoom in at the appropriate time. If there is any focus shift, it will be the wide view that is slightly out of focus, where it is least noticeable, and not the telephoto view where the slightest amount of poor focus is plainly visible.

Although through-the-lens systems show depth of field, it is hard to evaluate accurately unless the camera image is the same size the print will be. If not, things that seem sharp in the camera may be enlarged enough to reveal actual unsharpness in a print. Many 35 mm cameras have a "depth of field preview" control that stops down an automatic diaphragm lens from the maximum, or focusing, aperture to the working aperture for visual inspection of the image. Some photographers feel that this feature has limited usefulness, because the final picture image is nearly always larger than the camera image.

It is often very difficult to focus precisely under very dim light conditions. One solution is to place a very small light source, such as the bare bulb of a pocket flashlight, at the subject position and focus on it as sharply as possible. The flashlight must be removed before taking the picture; even if turned off, an exposure that is sufficient for the dim light might reveal the flashlight's presence in the picture.

In very close-up work and photomacrography, it is very difficult to focus by moving the lens independently of the film plane, because a great deal of movement may be required simply to find the subject within the field of view. It is far easier to establish the lens-to-film distance required for a desired magnification, and then to move the entire camera setup to focus the image sharply. Many accessory bellows units have double rails—one to permit bellows extension, the other to permit shifting back and forth on the tripod—precisely for this purpose.

In enlarging, the image should be focused by observing the projected grain pattern; that is what carries the image in the negative. A magnifier is required. (Those that incorporate a mirror reflecting element may not be usable at the very edges of the projected field because the angle of reflection falls outside the eyepiece coverage.) An out-of-focus grain pattern has a soft appearance, somewhat like mushy oatmeal; when sharply focused, the pattern looks like distinct grains of sand, or of salt and pepper.

• *See also:* ALBADA, L.E.W. VAN; CLOSE-UP PHOTOGRAPHY; COMPOSITION; DEPTH OF FIELD; DEPTH OF FOCUS; FOCAL RANGE; FOCUSING SYSTEMS; LANDSCAPE PHOTOGRAPHY; OPTICS; PARALLAX; PRISMS; RANGEFINDER; SINGLE-LENS REFLEX CAMERA; TESTING; TWIN-LENS REFLEX CAMERA.

Further Reading: Evans, Ralph M. *Eye, Film, and Camera in Color Photography.* New York, NY: John Wiley & Sons, 1959; Graham, Clarence H., et al, eds. *Vision and Visual Perception.* New York, NY: John Wiley & Sons, 1965; Ivins, Willima M., Jr. *Prints and Visual Communication.* Cambridge, MA: M.I.T. Press, 1969; Pirenne, M.H. *Optics, Painting, and Photography.* New Rochelle, NY: Cambridge Univ. Press, 1970.

  Vignetting

Vignetting can mean three things in photography. First, it can refer to an effect created by a design defect in a lens-camera system. Second, it can refer to a darkroom technique for producing images that fade gradually toward the print's outside edges. Third, it can refer to an in-camera technique for creating photographs with light-toned edges.

Lens-Camera Defect

Technically, vignetting is the progressive change in the cross-sectional area of a beam of light passing through a lens as the beam assumes an increasingly oblique angle to the lens axis caused by thickness diameter factors of the lens mount. The cross section of an oblique beam passing through a lens is always different from the cross section of an axial beam taken in the same plane. Vignetting causes the oblique rays to be cut off; at extreme oblique angles, the light is cut off entirely, but this is nearly always beyond the format coverage.

Vignetting is usually diminished or eliminated when the lens is stopped down from its largest aperture, but in rare cases, it may show up as a complete loss of illumination of the image in the corners of the format when the lens is stopped all the way down. (*See:* LENSES; OPTICS.)

Darkroom Technique

Vignetting is also a printing technique used to eliminate distracting or unwanted background. This technique is primarily used for enlargements of people, and it is popular for printing high-key portraits that are made up mostly of light tones.

You can easily vignette a print by projecting the image from the negative through a hole in an opaque cardboard. Cut the hole in the cardboard the same shape as the area you want to print. The hole should be the size that will give you the effect you want when you hold the cardboard halfway between the enlarger lens and the paper. Cut the edges of the hole in a sawtooth pattern so that the image fades gradually into the white paper. In vignetting, keep the vignetter in continuous motion during the print exposure. (*See:* ENLARGERS AND ENLARGING.)

A printing vignetter may be made from cardboard or plastic with an opening cut in the center. It is held in front of the enlarging lens during printing.

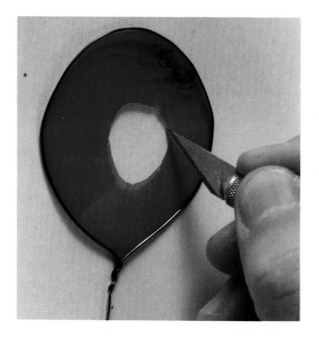

A conventionally printed portrait is often enhanced by vignetting. The technique, illustrated at right, is particularly effective with high key portraits. Photo by Emiel Blaakman.

Printing Several Images with Vignetting. You can use the vignetting technique to print portraits from more than one negative on a single sheet of enlarging paper. Assume you want to print from three negatives. Decide where you want each image to appear on the final print, and draw circles on a sheet of white paper on the enlarger easel to indicate the location of each image. Put the first negative in the enlarger, and adjust it so that the image you want fills a circle. Remove the white sheet of paper, and make your exposure test for the first negative. It is not necessary to use the vignetting technique for your exposure test. Now, using the vignetting technique, make the first exposure on the enlarging paper that will be your final print. (It is a good idea to put a small "X" in one corner on the back of the enlarging paper to help keep it properly oriented.) After you make the exposure, put the paper with the circles on it back in the easel and adjust the enlarger and easel position for the second picture. Follow the same procedure you did for the first negative. After you have exposed the second negative, follow this same procedure for the third negative. Then, process the print.

In-Camera Technique

Vignetting is also done with a camera accessory, the matte box. This is simply an extended lens hood that terminates in one or more slots capable of holding masks, filters, and/or a vignetter.

The most widely used form of camera vignetter is a sheet of translucent plastic with a serrated oval opening. This is held in position a short distance in front of the lens (distance about equal to 1–2 times the lens focal length).

Its purpose is to obliterate or obscure the detail surrounding the subject, and by so doing, to focus attention on the center of interest. If used correctly, the vignetter will produce a beautiful blend from the sharp central area to the diffused detail at the edges of the picture.

It is easy to vary the effect by smearing transparent colors on the vignetter, by vignetting only the bottom half of the scene, or by varying the translucency of the vignetting material selected.

Carefully observe the vignetted effect in your camera viewfinder to be sure it is what you wish, and modify it if necessary. View the effect at the actual aperture you will use to make the exposure. Be sure to shield the vignetter from direct rays of the sun, which could cause an undesirable flare effect. The vignetter seems to work best with a lens of about twice the normal focal length. Do not stop the lens down to a small opening, because the serrated edges of the vignetter may start to come into focus.

• *See also:* COMBINATION PRINTING; ENLARGERS AND ENLARGING; LENSES; MATTE BOX; OPTICS; SPECIAL EFFECTS.

Vision

Vision is one of the senses. It is the sense that makes use of light reflected from the surfaces of objects to provide knowledge of the environment. Through the written word, vision transmits the thoughts, ideas, and experiences of others. Through photographs, vision communicates the visual aspects of things from one place to another and from one time to another.

The Optics of Vision

Light is a form of electromagnetic radiant energy. (*See:* LIGHT.) It comes from a source and radiates. That is, it travels in all directions from the source. It travels in straight lines in rays, at a speed of over 300,000 kilometres per second (186,000 miles per second).

As it travels, it exhibits both the characteristics of wave motion and corpuscular or particle motion. Each particle is a unit of energy, a quantum called a photon. The wavelengths of light are very short—about $\frac{1}{2000}$ of a millimetre ($\frac{1}{50000}$ of an inch).

There are a number of forms of electromagnetic radiant energy. The type of energy depends on the wavelength. Light is the form that has wavelengths to which the human eye is sensitive, within a normal range of 400 to 700 nanometres. (A nanometre is a billionth of a metre.) Some eyes are slightly sensitive to wavelengths beyond this normal range. White light is a mix of all the wavelengths of light.

Visual Aspects. A source like the sun or a light bulb emits white light. Traveling in straight lines, the light illuminates objects. That is, the light travels through space and air and strikes the surfaces of objects. Some of the light is reflected by the object surfaces. Part of the light may be reflected to an observer's eyes, where it causes vision.

The nature of the object surfaces causes them to reflect light in different ways that make the surfaces look different to the observer. Their typical appearance is their visual aspect.

Although the visual aspect of an object depends largely on the way a surface reflects light, and the visual aspect therefore depends on the nature of the light reflected to the eyes, it is common practice to ascribe the visual aspect to the object itself. We say the object is colored or gray, that it is light or dark. We say it is smooth or rough, or dull or shiny.

If a surface reflects nearly all wavelengths equally, the reflection is achromatic, the visual aspect is neutral, and the color is black, gray, or white.

If a surface reflects a high percentage of the light, its visual aspect has a high brightness, and its color is light. If it is neutral and light, its color is white or light gray. On the other hand, if a surface reflects a low percentage of the light, it has a visual aspect of low brightness, and it is a dark color. If it is a neutral dark, it is dark gray or black.

If a surface reflects some wavelengths more than others, the reflection is chromatic, and the visual aspect is colored. If the light whose wavelengths are predominantly from 400 to 500 nanometres is reflected, and light whose wavelengths are from 500 to 700 nanometres is absorbed (hence not reflected), the color is a saturated blue. If the surface reflects light about the same in the 400 to 500 nanometre range, but reflects more in the 500 to 700 nanometre range, the color is a desaturated blue.

The characteristics of the surfaces of objects that are dependent on the way they reflect light are hue, brightness, and saturation. Hue is a characteristic of chromatic reflection and is determined by what wavelengths are the most reflective.

What hue a color is may be related to the spectrum; for example, a surface has a red-orange hue

These subjects illustrate many of the characteristics called visual aspects. The white house has a high, achromatic reflection. The foreground tree trunk has nearly achromatic reflectivity, but because of its lower brightness level, its visual aspect is gray. The birch trees at right are partly in the sun and faintly shadowed. Brightness constancy of vision indicates that they are white, and that their brightness variations are caused by illumination differences, not by variations in reflectivity. The man's shirt has a chromatic (red) reflectivity of high saturation and middle brightness. The woman's pink shirt has a chromatic (red) reflectivity of fairly high brightness but low saturation. Most of the surfaces reflect semi-specularly, but the rocks have nearly diffuse reflective characteristics and the bicycle handlebars reflect specularly.

that matches light with a wavelength of 610 nanometres.

Brightness depends on how much of the incident light is reflected overall. A surface that reflects 90 percent of the incident light has a very high brightness; one that reflects 20 percent of the light has a low brightness. Brightness can be ascribed to surfaces with both achromatic and chromatic reflections.

Saturation relates to the purity of a color. Spectral colors have the highest purity and are fully saturated. No surface reflects light so chromatically that it can have a spectral level of saturation. All achromatic reflections produce completely desaturated colors. Most surfaces reflect all wavelengths, but reflect some wavelengths more than others; therefore, they produce chromatic reflections that are classified as partially saturated.

Other Visual Aspects. The manner in which we see objects is also affected by characteristics such as texture, form, and outline.

Texture. If a surface is microscopically smooth, as a polished surface, it reflects light in an orderly fashion. Reflections from such surfaces are called specular. Nearly all specular reflections are achromatic and polarized. Exceptions are polished metal surfaces. If a surface is microscopically rough, so that light rays are reflected in a disorderly manner in all directions, the reflection is diffuse. Diffuse reflections are both chromatic and achromatic.

At the macro (rather than the micro) level, surfaces are smooth, textured, or rough. A textured surface has a three-dimensional nature of raised and lowered levels. Direct light casts shadows of the raised portions onto the lower levels, making the texture visible.

Form. Most objects are three-dimensional. In direct light, some parts of the surface will be lighted, while other portions will have cast shadows on them. If the objects are sunlit outdoors, the highlighted areas will have slightly warm light from the sun, while the shadowed parts will be illuminated by blue skylight, and so will be cooler in color. Such highlighting and shadow casting show the form, or three-dimensional nature, of the object.

Outline. Objects are finite in size, so they have edges. The outer edge of an object from any angle is its outline. Lines formed by edges are important visual aspects.

Emission, Interference, Transmission, and Scattering. While most objects are seen by reflected light because most objects are opaque, some are seen wholly or partially in other ways.

Light sources can be seen directly by their emitted light. If the light emitted is achromatic, they are white-light sources; their visual aspect is white. Some sources emit chromatic light; their visual aspect is colored. Some sources emit white light, but the light is filtered by colored material on the glass envelope; they are seen as colored.

Some materials cause interference in the wavelengths of light and hence cause the light to appear chromatic. Some butterflies, some bird feathers, oil on water, soap bubbles, lens coatings, and dichroic filters are examples of materials whose visual aspects are chromatic because of interference. (*See:* LIGHT.)

Some materials are transparent or translucent—light goes through them. Stained-glass windows, filters, some Christmas candy, fiber-glass panels, tinted windshields, colored glassware, and Tiffany lamps are all examples of objects whose visual aspects are affected by the way they transmit light.

Scattering is an optical phenomenon in which very small particles are stimulated by the energy of light to vibrate, and to emit light in all directions. The fine particles in air scatter the sun's light in such a way as to make the sky appear blue and sunrises and sunsets orange and red.

Forming an Image in the Eye. The eye is a physiological optical instrument. Like a camera, it has a lens that forms an image on a light-sensitive

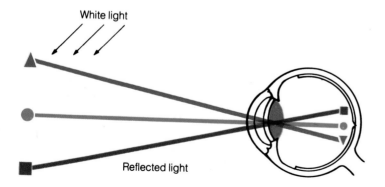

Formation of the Optical Image on the Retina

This illustration shows how the eye lens images light reflected by viewed objects to form an optical image on the retina. The optical image has the visual aspects of what is being viewed, but it is small, upside-down, and reversed as in a mirror. It is colored because the reflected light forming the image is colored. If the objects move, their images on the retina move.

surface. The formation of the image is an essential first step of vision.

Normally, a white light source illuminates the subject. Each point in each subject surface reflects light according to its nature. Some light rays reach the lens of the eye. The lens focuses the light on the retina at the back of the eye. The rays of light from each subject point come to the eye from a slightly different angle. They, therefore, fall on the retina at different points in a geometric relationship. The optical image thus formed is an upside-down image. It is relatively small, but because it is formed of light that has been modified by the reflection characteristics of the various subject surfaces, it has the visual aspects of the subject. It looks like the subject.

There are differences between the eye and a camera. A camera lens is well corrected to make a sharp image when focused on a flat film plane. The eye lens is poorly corrected; it creates a really sharp image in a field of about 2 degrees, and a reasonably sharp image out to about 5 degrees. The eye's image gets progressively worse from there on out, although it covers a field of up to 180 degrees in one direction, horizontally. It only has to cover about 150 degrees vertically. This compares with 55 degrees for a normal camera lens.

One of the worst aberrations the eye lens has is field curvature. However, nature has compensated and made the retina spherical, which places the retina close to the eye's best image all across the wide, sensitive field.

A camera lens is focused by changing its distance from the film. The eye lens focuses by changing its curvature. It is made of transparent, flexible fibers and has muscles that tighten and relax to change its shape.

There is one more important similarity between the eye and a camera. The iris of the eye is like the diaphragm on a camera. When the incident light is bright, the iris "stops down," reducing the brightness of the optical image on the retina. When the incident light is dim, the iris "opens up," brightening the optical image.

The Eye Structure. The eye is roughly spherical in shape; it is often called the eyeball. The tough membrane that holds the eye together is the sclera. At the front of the eye, the sclera is transparent, and here the sclera is called the cornea. Inside the sclera is a layer called the choroid, which contains pigment cells and blood vessels. The large part of the eyeball is filled with a jelly-like, clear material called the vitreous humor. In front of the lens, but back of the cornea, is a pocket filled with a more liquid material called the aqueous humor.

The light-sensitive surface of the eye is the retina. It is the inside layer of the eyeball and is attached to the choroid. There are a variety of tissues in the retina. The light-sensitive cells are called the rods and cones. These are connected to nerve cells. There are yellow-pigment protective cells and blood vessels to supply nutrients to the working cells.

In addition to the muscles that focus the eye lens, there are muscles that move the eye. Each eyeball is fitted in a socket. The front of the eye is open to the world, with a lid that covers the eye to protect it during sleep and to spread moisture over its surface. The nerves in the eye come together into a bundle and leave the eye at the rear. The muscles that move the eye work in balanced pairs so that the eyeball can be rotated left and right and up and down within limits. The two eyes move together so that the two images can be fused in the brain, that is, become one image with three dimensions. When there is need to see beyond the limits of the eye's turning range, the head, and perhaps the whole body, is turned.

The Light-Sensitive Retina. The light-sensitive cells in the retina are called the rods and the cones because of their shape. The rods are like panchromatic film; that is, they respond to all colors, but in the mental image they create, do not distinguish between colors. They make a black-and-white image.

Sensitivity to light means that when light falls on a rod, a chemical change takes place in the rod cell that triggers an impulse in the nerve attached to the rod. This impulse travels along the nerves to the brain, where, along with the responses from other rods and cones, it creates a visual perception. Rod responses not only indicate that there is light falling on the cell, but within limits, also indicate the intensity of the light.

The rods contain a pigment called visual purple (rhodopsin), but which is more nearly red in color. It is thought that the response of the eye to light is two-fold in a way similar to exposure and development of a film.

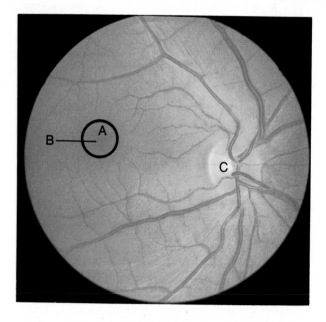

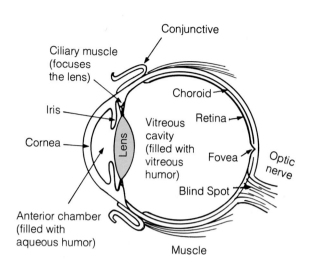

(Left) A photograph of the inside of the right eye taken through the eye lens. The blood vessels are in the retina over the light-sensitive cells. The dark red area (A), the macula, has very few blood vessels; it contains mostly cones, and the definition of vision and color of vision is high in this area. Definition of vision is highest in the fovea (B), a tiny, dimpled, yellow area in the center of the macula. The large yellow area (C) is the optic nerve, which is the terminal point for all the connecting nerves from the rods and cones. Because there are no rods or cones in this area, the eye is blind in this one spot. It is also in this area that the blood vessels enter the eyeball. (Right) The eye is spherical, filled with a watery (aqueous) humor in front of the lens and a jelly-like (vitreous) humor behind the lens. The tough membrane that forms the eyeball is the sclera. It is opaque white around the rear portion of the eye, but transparent in front of the lens, where it is called the cornea. Under the sclera is the choroid layer, which contains many blood vessels that supply nutrients to the eye. The retina is the light-sensitive inner lining of the eye. The fovea is a tiny dimple at the back of the eye on the axis of the lens. Around the fovea is an area called the macula. The rest of the retina is known as the periphery.

A small amount of light energy is required to form a latent image in a film, but a latent image cannot be seen until development expands the effect of the exposure a billion times. In a rod, the light is thought to make a slight molecular change. It is also thought that an enzyme action that causes fading of the visual purple magnifies the reaction many times to provide enough energy for the nerve signal to be sent. Rods are more sensitive to light than are the cones, and with proper dark adaption, can respond to light levels perhaps as low as a millionth of a footlambert.

There are three types of cones. They contain pigments (iodopsin) similar to visual purple, but one type contains a red pigment, one type contains a green pigment, and the other a blue pigment. These pigments can be thought of as filters. Each type of cone responds to light of the color of its pigment, and not to light of the other two colors*. The cones are much less sensitive than the rods; they cannot respond to light levels lower than a thousandth of a footlambert. The accompanying table shows the luminance levels of rod and cone sensitivities.

*The discussion of color vision presented here is based on the Young-Helmholtz theory of color vision, the first theory to explain how color is seen. There are a number of current theories that differ in some respects. The three-color cone-sensitivity theory is useful here because it makes the reproduction of color by photography easier to understand.

Relative Cone Sensitivity

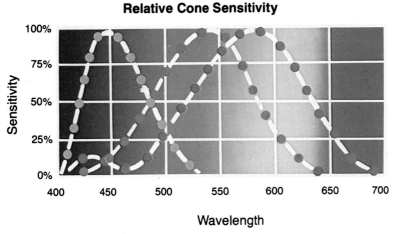

Sensitivity (%): 100%, 75%, 50%, 25%, 0%

Wavelength: 400, 450, 500, 550, 600, 650, 700

According to the three-color theory of vision, the three sets of cones have individual sensitivities to red, green, and blue light. However, as can be seen here, there is a broad overlap between sensitivities. Monochromatic light having a wavelength of about 580 nanometres would stimulate both the red- and green-sensitive cones because both are sensitive to this wavelength. When these two sets of cones are stimulated equally, the sensation is that of the color yellow. Note that the red-sensitive cones also have some sensitivity to light of very short wavelengths (400–500 nm). This is why the far end of the spectrum appears violet: both the blue- and red-sensitive cones respond to these wavelengths.

This diagram shows the sensitivity of the retina of the right eye in various areas. The small circle in the center marked F represents the fovea. The circle to the right marked B is the blind spot. The central area (darker color) is the area that is sensitive to all colors. The lighter colored area outside the central area sees blues and yellows, but not reds and greens. This difference in color sensitivity is difficult to account for with the three-color theory of vision given in the text. The gray tinted area shows where the retina is sensitive to black and white but not to color—thereby representing only rod vision. The sensitivity of the retina of the left eye is a mirror image of that of the right eye.

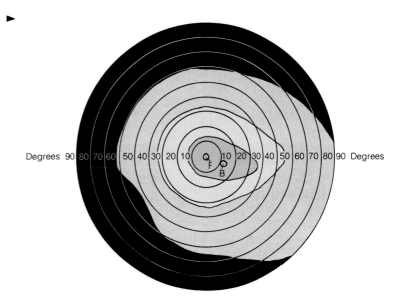

Degrees 90 80 70 60 50 40 30 20 10 | 10 20 30 40 50 60 70 80 90 Degrees

EYE SENSITIVITY LUMINANCE RANGE*

1,000,000 footlamberts	Pain level		
100,000		Cone	
10,000	White object in full sun	vision	Photopic
1,000	Normal daylight	only	vision
100			
10	Average room illumination		
1		Both	
1/10		rod and	Mesopic
1/100	Full moonlight	cone vision	vision
1/1,000		Rod	
1/10,000		vision	Scotopic
1/100,000	Starlight	only	vision
1/1,000,000	Night with no stars		

*Allowing for light and dark adaption.

The entire sensitivity range does not exist at one time. When the eye is viewing in daylight, it does not see the lower luminance ranges. When coming from daylight to lower luminance levels, it takes time for the sensitive cells to become dark adapted; it takes less than 10 minutes for the cones to reach their maximum sensitivity, while it takes nearly an hour for the rods to respond to starlight conditions.

The Nerve Connectors. The visual response to the optical image starts in the rods and cones in the retina, and visual perception occurs in the brain. It is the nerves that carry the messages that result in vision. It is believed that the message within each nerve is caused electrically, and that at junctures between nerves, the message is transmitted by a chemical change.

Each rod and cone has a receptor end and a nerve synapse, or impulse transmitting end, that connects to other nerves in a chain. Some nerves—the bipolar cells, ganglion cells, and optical nerve fibers—are cells that lead to the brain. Others, called the horizontal cells and the amacrine cells, interconnect some of the nerves from different rods and cones nearby. These perform an important function.

One of the most important aspects of a visual image is the edges of areas of various tones and colors. If a group of receptors are all giving the same kind of signal, there is no edge. If some rods or cones are given an entirely different signal than ones nearby, there is an edge. When a broad area of the same color and tone is being sensed, all the rods and cones except those near the edge can relax some and recharge their pigment.

The ganglion cells apparently act as starting and stopping cells; they detect changes in the levels of light. When the edges between two areas of unequal tone or color move across the retina, the ganglion cells respond. When this movement stops, the ganglion cells inhibit the messages. This implies that the brain is virtually unaware of uniform areas except at the edges, and only when the edges change.

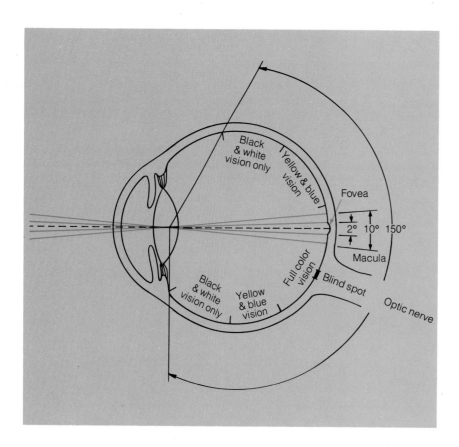

This is a top cross-sectional diagram of the eye showing the angular ranges of retinal sensitivities. This is the right eye; a diagram of the left eye would be a mirror image of this drawing. Best vision occurs in the 2-degree foveal dimple where cones are concentrated. High resolving power and full color result from the high concentration of cones in the fovea. The 10-degree macula has somewhat fewer cones and more rods. Vision here is somewhat less sharp, but still fully colored. The resolving power and saturation of color decreases gradually over the region marked "full color vision." In the area next to this, definition is poor, and only yellows and blues can be seen. In the outer zone, there are no cones, only rods, so that only black and white are seen; because the lens image is poor and because there are relatively few rods, definition is so low that only high-contrast moving objects are distinguished.

Visual Nerve Paths

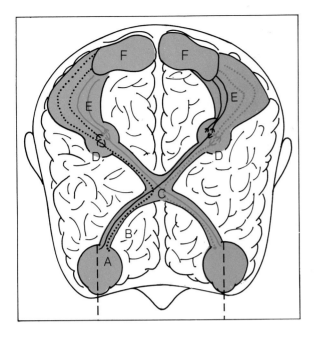

The nerve impulses from the retinas (A) travel along the axons (nerve fibers), which are grouped as they enter the optic nerves (B). In the chiasma (C) the axons cross over, those images from the left retina going to the right, and those from the right going to the left. This allows each half of the brain to compare the right and left fixed images; the primary function of this is probably stereoptic vision. Other nerve fibers go from the chiasma to the superior collicus, a lower brain center; these are thought to alert the viewer to movement of the optical image on the retinal periphery (peripheral vision). Nerve synapses in the genticulate bodies (D) connect the nerve fibers from the eyes to other nerve fibers (E) that lead from the genticulate bodies to the visual cortices (F) in the brain. It is in the visual cortices that vision takes place.

However, the vision of the field, or the mental perception of it, contains the fill-in areas. This is apparently an economical method of getting the most vision with the least impulses.

There are optical nerve fibers for each ganglion cell. They are long nerves that run across the retina to the optic disk, or blind spot, the only area in the retina that does not contain rods or cones. It is a spot, about 3 millimetres from the macula, where the nerve fibers join together and pass through the choroid to form the optic nerve, which is the bundle of nerve fibers surrounded by a protective cover.

There is one optic nerve for each eye. They converge behind the eyes and meet at a crossover called the chiasma. Here the fibers from the left and right optic nerves divide. Most of them go to the left lateral genticulate body and to the right genticulate body. Here there are synapses that convert to different nerve bundles that lead to the two halves of the visual cortex.

The visual cortexes are the part of the brain where vision takes place. There is a right and a left cortex, and they are the rear lobes of the entire cerebral cortex, which is the outer part of the cerebrum, the large part of the brain in human beings. The nerves in the visual cortex relate in a physical way to the location of the rods and cones at the other end of the nerve fibers. The visual cortex is a rough map of the retina.

While it is in the cortexes that "seeing" takes place—that is, the formation of mental images of the visual aspects that fall on the retina—vision, which is the interpretation, knowledge, and understanding of what is seen, takes place in other areas of the brain as well.

In the simplest sense, the brain cells recognize which areas are being stimulated by what color of light and of what intensity. They recognize edges and their location. Special sets of cells are stimulated by vertical lines, others by diagonal lines, and still others by horizontal lines.

Vision is Learned. A young infant probably has unfocused images on the retinas, but he or she neither sees nor has vision. The visual world is just one big, colorful chaos without meaning. In just days, the infant learns to focus and to look at things, especially the mother's face. As the infant gets to the stage of grasping things with his or her hands, he or she is beginning to learn what things are by the way they look, by their feel, their weight, how they handle, how they sound, and how they act. Vision starts when awareness of how an object (or person) looks is accompanied by knowledge of the object gained by all the senses. Recognition comes to the infant that there is *meaning* to the mental images formed in the cortexes by process of seeing.

Inherent in vision is the feeling that what is seen appears to be out in the world—not in the brain.

Each viewer has learned by long experience to interpret the mental visual images in terms of where the objects that cause the images are in relation to the self. The visual aspects of the objects causes recognition of them by knowledge of them from previous experiences. This is memory at work. Just where memory is located in the brain or how it works is not known. Recovery from memory plays a big part in vision; it is memory that turns seeing into vision. Being able to call objects by name and to describe them are ways by which it can be known that vision has taken place.

Experience also helps identify where objects are in relation to the viewer. There are many constancies in vision. One of these is size; we know how big things are. If there are two men seen, and the visual image of one is three times larger than the other, the larger one is not seen as larger, only closer, while the other one is seen as farther away. Only if all the other visual clues say that they are the same distance away are they seen as different in size.

Three-dimensional stereo vision, then, along with the depth clues, informs the viewer how far objects are from him or her. The geometry of perspective, where the images of objects fall on the retinas, informs the viewer whether the objects are in front of him or her, to the side, or above or below. This visual information lets the viewer know where he or she is in the immediate environment, and what and where the objects away are around him or her.

Normal Characteristics of Seeing. The importance of the visual aspects of physical objects—the way light reflects off their surfaces, or the way they emit or transmit light—is that these characteristics of objects modulate light that comes to the eyes and is formed into optical images on the retina. It is by these visual aspects that objects become recognizable, and by which memory is activated so that vision takes place along with seeing.

Seeing Brightness. Normally, the objects that reflect the highest percentage of light stimulate the rods and cover the greatest degree and are seen as the brightest. Those objects that reflect light the least are seen as the darkest.

However, the illumination level varies in an area being viewed, often because of the effects of light and shade. If part of an even-toned area is sunlit, and part is shaded, there is more light reflected to the eyes from the sunlit part. It is measurably brighter. However, vision has a brightness constancy so that the viewer knows that the whole area has the same tone and recognizes the light and shade effect on the surface. The effect is not seen as a variation in tone.

The eye can see a tremendous brightness range at one time, over ten times as great a luminance range as a film can photograph—about 10,000 to 1. But the luminance range in which it can see is a million-millions to one. The ability to see in this tremendous range is called brightness adaption.

Seeing Color. Color is given as one of the visual aspects of object surfaces.

If there were no eyes to see the objects, they would reflect light both achromatically and in different amounts of red, green, and blue, but they would have no color. The light would have its different wavelengths, but it would not have color.

Color exists as light with an unbalanced mix of wavelengths falls on the retina and stimulates the red-, green-, and blue-sensitive cones by different degrees. If there are wavelengths present in the 600 to 700 nanometre range, they stimulate the red-sensitive cones. Wavelengths in the 500 to 600 nanometre range stimulate the green-sensitive cones, while those in the 400 to 500 range stimulate the blue-sensitive cones.

If the wavelengths are balanced in intensity, the cones get stimulated equally, and this results in a perception of neutral. High-stimulation neutrals are whites, moderate-stimulation neutrals are gray, and low-stimulation neutrals are black. These are comparative, as indicated in the preceding section on seeing brightness, and brightness constancy helps interpret the seeing.

The amount of primary colors reflected is in direct proportion to which cones are stimulated to what degree, and thus what color is seen.

> If only one set of cones is stimulated, and the other two are not, *saturated* or very pure red, green, or blue is seen.
> If two sets of cones are stimulated equally, and the third set is not, *saturated* cyan, magenta, or yellow is seen.
> If one set of cones is fully stimulated, a second set partially stimulated, and the third set not at all, saturated colors such

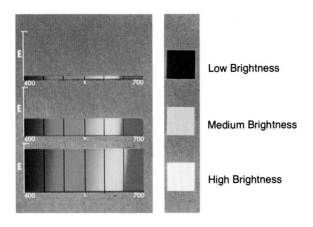

Low Brightness

Medium Brightness

High Brightness

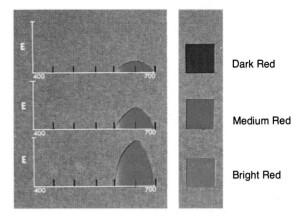

Dark Red

Medium Red

Bright Red

(Left) Achromatic light, which is often an even mix of all wavelengths, results in the seeing of neutrals. When the light level of the subject is high compared to the overall light level, the sensation is that of white. When the level is very low compared to the overall light level, the sensation is that of black. In-between levels are seen as various tones of gray. (Right) When all the energy arriving at an area of the retina is composed of long wavelengths, the resulting sensation is red; as the illuminance level varies, the sensations vary from light red to dark red. These are different brightness levels of red.

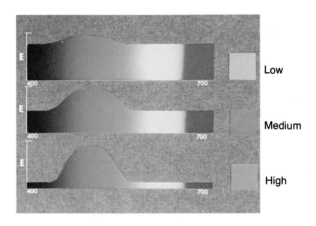

Low

Medium

High

When chromatic light falls on an area of the retina, the sensation is that of color. Shown here is light that results in the sensation of cyan or blue-green. Where there is little light of other wavelengths, the color appears saturated (bottom). As more light of all other wavelengths is added, desaturation occurs and the color sensation is that gray has been added to the color—it appears less pure. When there is only a little higher illuminance in the blue-green wavelengths than in the other wavelengths, the color appears almost completely desaturated, or "grayed out" (top).

as violets, oranges, and chartreuses are seen.

When all three sets of cones are stimulated, with one of the three at a relatively low level, the color seen becomes desaturated. This is the usual case; very few surfaces reflect light in such a manner as to create full saturation.

Boundaries between areas of different tone, color, or saturation are seen as lines. Narrow areas are seen as lines. The visual aspect of textures is seen as varying surface characteristics. Gradual changes in brightness, hue, or saturation are seen as grada-

tions, are usually caused by the light and shade effect, and offer clues to the form of objects.

The Glance Image and Visual Perception. When the eyes take one fix or glance at a section of the world, the image sensation has characteristics of the visual aspects of what is looked at, as well as characteristics of the visual system.

This brief mental image is sharp and colored at the center. The sharpest definition covers an area of about 2 degrees. Out to 10 degrees the definition lessens, but is still reasonably good. Outside of this area, the definition falls off badly. Color is fully seen out through the 10-degree area, and although the colors grow desaturated out from the center of the visual image, the viewer is not consciously aware of it. At the periphery of vision (130 degrees vertical,

180 degrees horizontal, roughly oval shaped), definition is so poor that only movement of objects that have relatively high contrast can be seen. The mental image has no color at the periphery, but the viewer is unaware of this.

The *visual perception* of the area of interest is formed of a number of sample glances. Those areas that are *visually attractive,* or that are *of interest,* are looked at directly so that they are seen in the sharp center of vision. By a number of glance images, a visual perception of what is there is formed in the mind. It does not seem to be in the mind; it seems to be out there in front, in the real world. It is accurate, because if you walk over to something, you can touch it, feel it, pick it up, or in other words, verify the visual perception by use of the other senses.

An area of the visual field is visually attractive —that is, it invites a glance—if it has visual contrast. It can be contrast of tone (brightness), hue, saturation, or texture. Saturated colors attract more than neutral tones. Bright objects, especially against a dark background, attract strongly. Warm hues such as reds and oranges attract the glance more strongly than do cool blues and greens.

Moving objects attract more than still objects, and large objects that cover a larger visual angle attract more than small objects. Photographers use the principles of visual attraction to emphasize the motifs in their pictures and to subordinate (lessen the visual attraction of) less important detail.

When the glance image indicates that there is *something of interest* to the viewer in the area outside the zone of high acuity, the viewer will move his or her eyes so that the next glance image centers on the new object of interest. All drivers find traffic signs and signals of interest for safety. This is where the storage of knowledge and understanding in the memory interacts with the new visual perceptions to become vision. Almost everyone finds a new baby or a young animal of interest. But many things are of more interest to some viewers than to others.

By a number of glances, combined with long experience of the visual aspects of many things, the viewer continually builds models in his or her mind of the surroundings, but it seems that he or she is seeing what is there.

The viewer recognizes objects from their shapes, from their textures and gradations, and from their forms. From stereoscopic vision and the depth clues, the viewer builds the model in depth, to as far away as he or she can see. As the viewer moves through the real world, this model changes to accommodate itself to changing viewpoints.

Special Aspects of Vision

Color Blindness. Color vision as presented in this article is normal vision. Some people are color blind, however, due to abnormalities in their visual systems. The most common form of color blindness is red-green blindness. In one form, called deuteranopia, greens, yellows, and reds cannot be distinguished from each other when their brightness and saturation levels are the same. Violets and blue-violets cannot be distinguished from blues. Protanopia is another form of red-green blindness. It is similar to deuteranopia, but in addition, blue-greens cannot be distinguished from grays.

Another form of color blindness is blue-yellow deficiency, where blues and yellows appear as neutrals, or as forms of reds and greens. This form is called tritanopia. In rare cases, an individual sees no color at all, but has just rod vision. This is called monochromatism.

Color Association. This is a form of visual constancy. Through experience, we learn the colors of common objects, such as blue sky, green grass and leaves, Caucasian and black skin tones, red apples, yellow bananas and lemons, red bricks, and so on almost indefinitely. Often, through reflection off a strongly colored surface nearby, the light coming from an object with a learned color (color constant) will not be that color at all. For example, a face near foliage with sun on it may have so much green in its illumination that the light reflected to the viewer's eyes is predominately green. Our minds still see the face as skin color because that is the color associated with skin. However, if a photograph is taken, and the color of the skin is shown to be greenish in the photograph, we may not accept it as natural. A photographer has to learn to see the color as it actually is, has to overcome color association by conscious effort and practice, and has to learn to produce the desired appearance in pictures.

Receding and Advancing Colors. For most people strong, saturated, warm colors (reds, oranges) are called advancing colors because objects of these colors at a distance seem closer than they are.

Strong, saturated cool colors (blues, greens), on the other hand, seem to be farther away than they actually are and are called receding colors. (For some people, advancing and receding colors are just reversed.) This may be caused by the longitudinal chromatic alteration of the eye lenses. Short-wavelength light does not focus with the same eye-lens setting as long-wavelength light. To focus red, the eye has to adjust its focus in the near direction from its neutral-color focus position, while to focus blue, it has to adjust in the far direction. The photographer can use this principle in suggesting depth by using warm-color foreground objects and cool-color backgrounds.

Lateral Effects. The hue, saturation, and brightness of a local color can be apparently changed by what color is next to it, or surrounds it.

A white object looks brighter when it is surrounded by black than it looks when it is surrounded by a gray or some light color. A black object looks blacker against a white background than it does against a gray or dark-color background. The blackest black exists only when it has a lighter surround.

When a colored object is seen against a background of a similar hue, its saturation is apparently lowered. When seen against a neutral background, its saturation is seen normally. When placed against a background whose hue is the complement of the object color, the saturation of the object color is visually increased.

When a white or light-gray object is placed before a background that is of a saturated color, the color of the object appears to be a tint of the complement of the background color. A white object against a saturated blue background, for example, appears to be a pale yellow tint. These effects are also known as simultaneous contrast effects.

A photograph edged with black will look lighter and more luminous, while a photograph on a white background looks darker and less luminous.

Optical Mixture. When small areas of different colors are seen from a distance, their colors blend to form combination colors. Color television images make use of this principle. There are red, green, and blue dots on the TV screen. When red and green dots are activated, and the blue dots remain dark, the eye mixes the red and green dots and sees yellow. All the colors are seen on the screen as additive mixtures of the dots.

Colors can be mixed by time mixture. If two colors are placed on the surface of a wheel and the wheel rotates rapidly, at 30 revolutions per minute or faster, the eye blends the colors additively. If the wheel is half red and half blue, for example, the color seen when the wheel is rotated is magenta. If the wheel surface is divided into three pie-shaped segments of red, green, and blue in the proper ratio for the illuminant used, the eye sees neutral.

Effect of Edge Gradient on Color. Colored objects in the real world are normally focused by the

(Left) Lateral brightness adaptation. The two gray squares are the same tone. The square against the white background looks darker than the one against the black background because of lateral brightness adaptation. It is also likely to appear larger. (Right) Lateral color adaptation. The two gray squares are both neutral. Most people see a tinge of the complementary color in the gray area because of lateral color adaptation. The square on the red background may appear blue-green, while the square on the yellow background may appear blue.

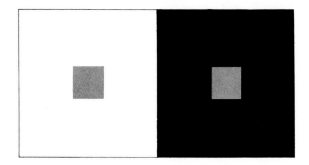

eyes and so appear sharp; we see the edges as sharp gradients. If, through some mechanism, the edges are made into gradual gradients (made fuzzy), the colors of the objects appear less saturated. This shows up frequently in the out-of-focus backgrounds of photographs or in photographs that are strongly diffused.

In these cases, there may be a double effect. Not only do the colors lose visual saturation by the gradient effect, but they actually have their color mixed optically with the colors of adjacent objects. The lens blends the colors of object edges in the optical image in all situations except that of sharp focus.

When a sharp image with steep edge gradients is diffused so that the edge gradients become gradual, there is a loss in apparent contrast even though the large areas still have the same brightness levels. Light tones appear darker, while darker tones appear lighter.

Changes That Occur with Illuminance Shifts. As the illuminance level changes, a number of visual changes take place. At very low levels of illuminance, colors become less saturated, and their hue shifts toward the blue (moonlight appears blue). This is because more of the visual response is due to rod input as the illuminance level reaches the lower level of cone sensitivity, so that most colors cannot be seen.

In addition, there is a distortion of brightness perception at very low levels of illumination. If a gray scale appears to have even steps of gray from white to black under normal illumination levels, under moonlight the black and dark grays will merge together as black, and separation will be seen only at the lighter end of the scale.

Under extremely high illumination, the tonal differences in light subjects decrease (are compressed), while the apparent brightness differences in dark tones increase (are expanded). If a photograph is to be exhibited under low or high illumination levels, the photographer can adjust the tone separation to improve the apparent tonal rendition.

After-Images. Often an observer stares fixedly at a still subject for a minute or so and then quickly changes his or her view to a plain-white or light-colored field. A negative image of the stared-at subject will appear, apparently on the plain field. This after-image will be negative in tone and color—essentially an unmasked color negative image.

A similar effect shows up if the eyes are subjected to alternate light and dark stimulation at moderate frequencies (not enough to cause flicker, or to cause blending of the images). The white will appear whiter and the black, blacker because of the quick stimulus changes. The same is true of complementary colors. If the eye is subjected to alternate red and green stimuli, the red and green both will look more saturated than if looked at normally.

Persistence of Vision and Flicker. If the lights on a scene are turned on and off at intervals of several seconds, the eyes perceive this as alternate levels of illumination. If the frequency of the switching is increased from several times a second up to about 16 times a second, the sensation of *flicker* occurs. Flicker of certain frequencies can cause discomfort. Where the greatest flicker effect is felt, vision is affected. For example, visual acuity is lowered, and even coarse details may be difficult to see clearly.

If a light is flashed on a scene for various short intervals of time, the eyes can sense the differences in time until one flash duration is less than about a tenth of a second. Shorter times are then seen as lower in intensity, but not as shorter times. This is due to persistence of vision, which is a rough measure of the time it takes for the visual apparatus to work.

When the flicker phenomenon exceeds about 16 flashes per second, the flicker effect gradually disap-

After-images. Under strong, white light (sunlight is excellent), stare at the center of the black cross in the left-hand square for 20 to 30 seconds. Then quickly look at the X in the middle of the right-hand square. A white flag with a red cross will appear shortly. The colors of an after-image are complementary to the original colors, and the tones are reversed.

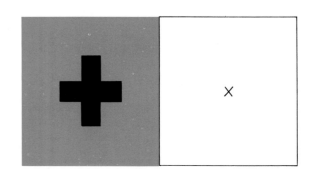

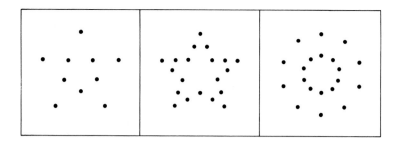

pears, and the illumination appears to be continuous. This is due to the persistence of vision. Motion pictures and television are composed of sequences of images presented to the eye fast enough so that the persistence of vision overcomes the flicker effect.

Moving Illusions. When the eyes are presented with an image that continually moves in one direction and the image ceases, objects may seem to move in the other direction. If a viewer keeps his or her eyes open and spins around several times and suddenly stops, the world will seem to go around in the opposite direction for a moment. When a waterfall is observed steadily and the eyes are gradually turned toward the edge of the waterfall, objects along the edge of the waterfall may appear to be going upward.

If you are in an automobile stopped in a line of traffic, a car is stopped next to you, and that car starts to back up slowly, your eyes may tell you that you are moving forward.

Motion Parallax. When in a moving car, objects close to the car appear to go by quickly, objects a little farther away from the car appear to move more slowly, while objects in the distance seem to stand still. The relative speed of the objects is a good depth clue as to their distance. This effect is used to create a sensation of depth in motion pictures.

Grouping. The human visual apparatus continually works toward making sense out of the visual field by the identification of objects, shapes, textures, and patterns. For example, if there is a group of similar size and shape objects in the visual field, they may be seen as connected, if they are spaced properly. If they are scattered at random and if they are widely separated, they will not be visually grouped. If they are all relatively close to each other, they may form a random-shaped group, like a clump of trees. However, if they form a row, the group will be seen as a line—a line of trees or a column of soldiers.

Three such objects equidistant from a point will be seen as a triangular grouping. Four will be seen as the corners of a square. But when there are eight or ten dots equidistant from a point, vision connects them into a circle.

When there are a great many similar forms visually close together and visually small, they group to form texture. When they are even smaller and in greater numbers, they fuse and form tone or color.

Visual Illusions. Humans try to remove the ambiguity from visual sensations by using all the visual clues to identify that which is being seen. There are instances where the clues are too few, are confusing, or are misleading, so that a judgment on what is there, how big it is, or how it is structured may be in error.

Camouflage. Certain animals, birds, and insects are colored and patterned by nature so that they visually match their normal habitat. Thus, they are difficult to see. This is protective coloration. If they live in snow, they are colored white. If they live in dead grass, they are colored tan with black streaks that look like shadows. If they live in the jungle, they have patches of tone that look like dappled shadow patches. Military uses have been made of the camouflage principle to make men, transportation, and weapons difficult for the enemy to see.

Concave-Convex Illusion. This illusion happens more in pictures than in real life. Convex bumps on a surface are typically illuminated from the top. There is a light-to-dark gradation from up to down. On the other hand, concave dents in a surface are shadowed on top, while the light brightens the lower area. There is a dark-to-light gradation from up to down. If a picture of bumps and dents is turned upside down, dents appear as bumps, and vice versa, because the light gradation direction is reversed.

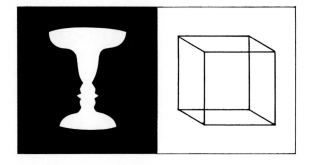

Ambiguous clues. The drawing above may represent either a goblet or two facing profiles. The perspective of the cube in the drawing on the right appears to change. Sometimes visual clues can lead to different interpretations of reality when there are not enough clues to be definitive.

This ambiguous drawing is seen sometimes as a young girl, at other times as an old woman. Drawing by E.G. Boring.

Face Illusion. Vision has a special propensity to see faces—in rocks, clouds, patterns of all sorts, and even in the moon. Illusions are drawn in which one face is obvious, and the other image is hidden. So in the head of a young lady, an old face appears. The drawing clues are made ambiguous.

Size Illusions. There are a number of visual illusions that make it difficult to assess correctly the comparative size of objects. These illusions are not usually encountered with real objects but are usually drawn to illustrate how vision makes judgments.

Two lines the same length will appear to be of different lengths if V-shaped lines are placed on their ends. On one line the V's face each other, and on the other line the V's face outward.

If a number of flat shapes of identical size are placed on a drawing with strong perspective, the ones placed near the horizon will look much larger than the ones placed on the foreground. The eye expects objects farther away to appear smaller; when they are the same size, vision says they are larger.

Form Illusion. Again, the examples of ambiguous visual clues that mislead vision as to the form of objects are usually drawings, but they illustrate how the visual clues of real objects can be misread.

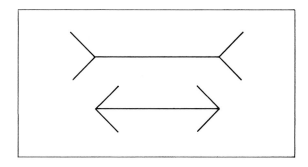

The apparent size of an object can be affected by lines in proximity to it. Both horizontal lines are the same length. The apparent difference is caused by the direction of the diagonal lines.

Direction Illusion. If straight, parallel lines are placed in context with lines at diagonals, or with radiating lines, the lines no longer seem parallel, or they no longer seem straight. Vision is constantly making comparisons to arrive at judgments; if the comparative clues are misleading, the visual judgment can be wrong.

Shimmer. When many black lines on a white background are curved and vary in width and apparent spacing, there are certain spacings that no longer appear fixed on the paper but appear to shimmer. The eyes have been found to have an extremely slight, but rapid, angular movement when they are seeing. It is thought that this helps gain resolving power because edges are imaged on neighboring

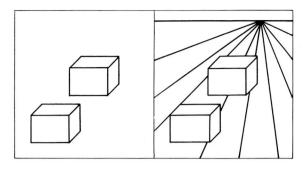 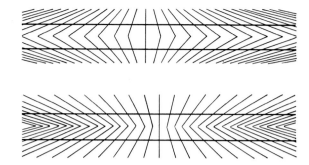

(Left) The four boxes are all the same size. In the left-hand square, they appear the same. In the right-hand square, they are in identical positions, but the upper box looks larger because perspective lines have been added. The upper box appears farther away because, in perspective, far objects normally appear smaller than near objects, unless they are considerably larger than the near objects. To appear the same size as the lower box, the upper box would have to be drawn smaller. (Right) Shapes can be affected by surrounding lines and shapes. Both pairs of horizontal lines are straight and parallel. The inward and outward bowing effects are illusions caused by the diagonal background lines.

cones, and that the movement alternately rests the cones, reducing fatigue. When the spatial frequency of a repeated pattern matches the degree of oscillation of the eyes, the shimmer appears.

• *See also:* ABERRATION; BRIGHTNESS; COLOR TEMPERATURE; COLOR THEORY; LIGHT; LIGHT: UNITS OF MEASUREMENT; OPTICS; PERSPECTIVE; RESOLVING POWER; SHARPNESS; STEREO PHOTOGRAPHY; YOUNG, THOMAS.

Vogel, Hermann Wilhelm

(1834–1898)
German chemist

Vogel was the discoverer of dye-sensitization of silver bromide emulsions, which made possible the production of orthochromatic and panchromatic emulsions, without which color photography would be impossible. With Obernetter and Perutz, he developed the first eosin-sensitized dry plate, which was the first true orthochromatic plate. In the same year (1884), he demonstrated the use of Azaline for sensitizing to green, yellow, and orange, but this dye was later superseded by the isocyanines, which conferred greater red sensitivity in panchromatic plates. He wrote *Das Handbuch der Photographie,* one of the most important textbooks on photography of the 19th century; the first edition was published in 1867, and numerous editions followed.

Voigtländer, Peter Wilhelm Friedrich

(1812–1878)
One of a family of Austrian optical manufacturers

The Voigtländer firm was founded in 1756 by an ancestor of Peter Wilhelm to manufacture mechanical instruments. The firm started to provide optical products in 1815. Shortly thereafter, it produced Wollaston meniscus lenses for camera obscuras.

Following this tradition, Peter Wilhelm Friedrich Voigtländer introduced the first portrait lens, along with an all-metal camera that took round pictures 3½ inches in diameter, in 1841. This lens was designed by Professor Joseph Petzval and, along with a newly developed method of increasing the speed of daguerreotype plates, permitted portraits to be taken with exposure times of about 1 minute.

The Petzval-Voigtländer association lasted only a few years, but Voigtländer continued to manufacture Petzval lenses for a long time. Voigtländer opened a new factory in Braunschweig (Brunswick) in 1849. He was one of the founders of the Photographic Society of Vienna.

The Voigtländer firm continues in business today. Their cameras were especially popular in the first half of this century. Their Heliar lens was considered outstanding. They introduced the first zoom lens in 1959.

Warnerke, Leon

(1837–1900)
*Engineer born in Hungary, lived most of adult life in Russia
and England*

Warnerke set up his own photographic laboratory in London in 1870. About 1880, he returned to Russia and established a photographic factory in St. Petersburg. In 1880, he invented the Warnerke sensitometer, which was probably the first device used to measure the speed of photographic emulsions. He discovered the tanning action of pyrogallic acid (Pyrogallol) on gelatin emulsions in 1881, which led to various modern relief processes such as dye transfer printing, although F. Scott Archer had discovered its use as a developing agent in 1851. He manufactured silver chloride papers from about 1889. Warnerke received the Progress Medal of the Royal Photographic Society in 1882.

Washing

In photographic processing, the purpose of washing is to remove the fixing chemicals and silver compounds that remain in the material. Washing negatives is a fairly simple operation because chemicals are not absorbed by the film base. Under suitable conditions, negatives are freed from residual chemicals after 20 to 30 minutes of washing.

Prints on water-resistant or resin-coated papers will be thoroughly washed in 4 minutes if there is adequate water flow to change the water once in that time, and if the prints are continually agitated. It is important not to overwash these papers.

Washing prints on fiber-base papers is a different problem. Chemicals are absorbed by the paper base, and to remove them completely by washing alone is difficult. Under favorable conditions, prints are washed well enough for most purposes after 1 hour. If prints are intended as permanent records, they should be treated with a hypo eliminator to remove the last traces of hypo that remain after normal washing.

Washing Apparatus

The water in any tray or tank used for washing photographic materials should change completely every 5 minutes. This rate of change should be achieved without excessive turbulence, which can damage the films or prints, and without splashing adjacent walls or floors.

A test to determine the rate of change of water in a washer can be made quite simply. Add a small quantity of potassium permanganate solution to the water in the tray or tank and observe the time the color takes to disappear. Before you make this test, however, be sure that the water in the vessel is not contaminated by hypo—weak permanganate solution is made colorless by hypo—and that the tank is free from the slimy deposit that accumulates in washers that are not cleaned frequently. Since such a deposit retains chemicals, you should clean the tank or tray before making the permanganate test. By the same token, dirty washers are a source of stains on prints, which are difficult to account for. Washing apparatus should always be kept clean by frequent wiping and rinsing. A 10 percent solution of sodium carbonate helps to remove slimy deposits from the interior surfaces of washing apparatus.

Water Supply and Conditioning

A plentiful supply of pure water is desirable in processing photographic materials for permanence. Municipal water supplies are generally satisfactory for washing negatives and prints. Water may be either hard or soft, according to the amount of calcium or magnesium salts dissolved in it. The degree of hardness has little or no effect on stability, although very soft water permits gelatin to swell excessively. Such swelling may be troublesome in some processes.

If you use water from a well or other untreated source, it may contain sulfides or dissolved vegetable matter. The presence of sulfides can be detected by an odor of hydrogen sulfide when the water is heated. A greenish color in the water indicates dissolved vegetable matter. These impurities can be removed by suitable filtration or treatment.

Solid matter must be removed by filtration. Usually a prefilter of 50 - micrometre porosity serves the main water line, and final filters of 25 micrometres protect critical processes in the typical commercial photolab. A 50-micrometre porosity filter is sufficiently fine to trap the larger particles of grit that cause mechanical damage to films and papers in processing. Filters of 25-micrometre porosity usually remove fine particles— such as clay, silt, mud, or silica—that cause turbidity.

Filters with replaceable cores are in common use in processing laboratories. The interval between periodic core changes depends upon the time it takes for a filter to clog or a reduction in water pressure across the filter to appear.

Water drawn from some wells or from other untreated sources is sometimes colored by colloidal iron or organic matter. Water in this condition can stain a photographic emulsion, but using filtration with activated charcoal will generally remove such impurities.

Generally, it is safe to assume that water is satisfactory for photographic washing if it is clear, colorless, and does not have a sulfide odor on heating.

When water is heated, gas or air bubbles come out of solution, giving the water a milky appearance. This problem most often occurs when the incoming cold water is below 10 C (50 F). If these bubbles adhere to the surface of a film or paper, they interfere with processing and washing. The remedy for this trouble is aeration of the incoming water. This procedure causes the small bubbles to combine with the larger ones that disperse easily. In sinks used for hand processing, fit aerators to the water taps; most hardware stores stock these attachments. In mechanized processing, use a ballast tank to achieve the same result. This is an open tank of suitable size in which the hot and cold water mix. Air passed through the mixed water as larger bubbles takes up the finer foam and disperses at the water surface.

In small-scale sheet processing, fluctuations in water pressure are probably no more than an inconvenience. In large-scale and in mechanized production, however, both hot and cold water lines must have a water pressure of no less than 45 psi (310 kilopascal). To provide this, sufficiently large intake pipes must lead from the mains so that the maximum demand can be drawn without a drop in pressure. If the mains themselves cannot supply the necessary pressure, you will need a booster pump to raise the pressure to the required value.

Washing with Seawater. Seawater is very efficient in removing hypo from negatives and prints. This fact may be of value to those who do processing on board ship. Remember, however, that salt is detrimental to the stability of a silver image, particularly if residual hypo is present in the material. Therefore, if you use seawater for washing films or fiber-base papers, it is imperative to remove the seawater salts by a final wash of at least 5 minutes in fresh water. Seawater offers no advantage in washing water-resistant papers.

Wash-Water Temperature. The temperature of the wash water has a definite effect on the rate of removal of hypo and silver complexes from both films and prints. Experiments have shown that a temperature of 4 C (40 F) will slow the removal of residual chemicals; a temperature of 27 C (80 F) will speed it up. When practical considerations as well as the physical characteristics of film and paper are taken into account, the most suitable range of temperature for washing is 18 to 24 C (65 to 75 F).

Washing Negatives

You can wash a small batch of films or plates in a tray, but avoid excessive turbulence, because these materials tend to scratch one another if allowed to move about too rapidly. An automatic tray siphon is an attachment that provides adequate water change in a shallow tray without the turbulence that may damage the negatives.

Large batches of negatives should be suspended in hangers and washed in a tank. With suitable hangers, both films and plates can be washed in this way. For good water circulation, place the inlet at one corner at the bottom of the tank. Allow the water to overflow at the top edges of the tank. A single outlet at the top would tend to make uniform currents that might leave certain areas in the tank comparatively stagnant, and so reduce the rate of complete water change.

To conserve water and reduce the cost of washing, do not wash negatives much longer than the recommended 20 to 30 minutes. It is also wasteful to use an unnecessarily high rate of water flow or to wash negatives in a tank much bigger than that needed to accommodate the size or quantity of material being washed.

Washing Prints

Since fiber-base paper is absorbent, it is difficult to wash the last traces of hypo and silver from prints. For most purposes, adequate washing is achieved in 1 hour if the water in the washer changes completely every 5 minutes. However, the time of washing and the rate of water flow are both meaningless if the prints are not separated constantly so that water can reach every part of each print throughout the washing time. A well-designed washer can do this fairly well with small prints up to 5″ × 7″; larger prints need frequent handling to keep them separated. A number of well-designed washers are available from photographic dealers. No washer, however, can perform satisfactorily if you wash too many prints in it at one time. Use two or more tanks and wash the minimum number of prints in each. To conserve water, you can arrange three washers in series, each one at a lower level than its predecessor. In this way, fresh water from the upper tank is used to feed the two lower tanks. Prints are moved at regular intervals from the lowest tank—where the bulk of hypo is removed—to the intermediate tank and then to the upper tank, where washing is completed by the incoming fresh water. Do not guess at the washing time; use a timer.

Water-Resistant Papers

Many black-and-white and most color papers have plastic- or resin-coated water-resistant bases. The washing instructions or recommendations supplied with these materials should be followed exactly. In general, a water-resistant print will wash clear of hypo in 4 minutes if it is continually agitated. A rate of flow sufficient to change the water once in 4 minutes is required. There is no advantage to using a washing aid to shorten washing times with such papers, and the procedure is not recommended. Do not overwash water-resistant papers, because water soak at edges could cause separation of the resin layer, described as "frilling."

Note that most color print processes do not use a final wash, but may use a stabilizer bath. Follow instructions exactly for the process you are using.

Stabilization Prints

Do not wash prints produced by stabilization processing if they are to be kept in a stabilized state. Rinsing or washing them will remove the stabilizing compounds, and the prints will become light-sensitive and begin to discolor immediately. For permanence, stabilized prints can be put through a conventional fixing bath. Then they should be washed in the same manner as conventionally processed prints.

Hypo Clearing Agent

As stated before, seawater removes hypo from photographic materials more quickly than fresh water. Investigations into this effect have shown that certain inorganic salts behave like the salt in seawater. Unlike seawater, however, they are harmless to the silver image. Kodak hypo clearing agent is a preparation of such substances. Its use reduces the washing time for both negatives and prints. At the same time, prints attain a degree of freedom from residual chemicals almost impossible to obtain by washing them with water alone. A further advantage in using Kodak hypo clearing agent is that adequate washing can be achieved with much colder water.

A number of other manufacturers also supply washing aids to increase the efficiency of thiosulfate compound removal and to shorten washing times. These do not necessarily have the same chemical composition as Kodak hypo clearing agent, and therefore may not give the same indications when washing efficiency is tested chemically. (*See:* TEST-

KODAK HYPO CLEARING AGENT

Photographic Material*	Rinse After Fixing	Hypo Clearing Agent	Wash in Running Water†	Capacity (20.3 × 25.4 cm prints per litre)	Capacity (8″ × 10″ prints per gallon)
Films	none	1–2 minutes	5 minutes	12–15 or equivalent	50–60 or equivalent
Films	1 minute	1–2 minutes	5 minutes	37–50 or equivalent	150–200 or equivalent
Single-weight prints	none	2 minutes	10 minutes	20 or equivalent	80 or equivalent
Single-weight prints	1 minute	2 minutes	10 minutes	50 or equivalent	200 or equivalent
Double-weight prints	none	3 minutes	20 minutes	20 or equivalent	80 or equivalent
Double-weight prints	1 minute	3 minutes	20 minutes	50 or equivalent	200 or equivalent

*Black-and-white films and fiber-base papers. Water-resistant and color papers should not be treated.
†Minimum washing times for prints; longer washing will not harm the print.

ING.) In each case, the manufacturer's recommendations should be followed. Note, however, that many photographers find it necessary to extend the final wash time well beyond the manufacturer's recommendations to achieve prints that test free of harmful compounds.

Films or Plates. Rinse films or plates in fresh water for 30 seconds to remove excess hypo, and then immerse them in Kodak hypo clearing agent solution for 2 minutes with agitation. Wash them for 5 minutes in a tank where the water changes completely in 5 minutes. To avoid streaks, drying marks, and the formation of water droplets on film surfaces, bathe films in a wetting agent solution for 30 seconds and then hang them up to dry.

Papers. Rinse prints for 1 minute to remove excess hypo. Treat single-weight papers for 2 minutes, with agitation, in Kodak hypo clearing agent solution and then wash them for at least 10 minutes. Observe the normal recommendations concerning water flow. The prints must, of course, be agitated and separated throughout the washing time.

Rinse double-weight papers for 1 minute in clean water, then immerse them in Kodak hypo clearing agent solution for 3 minutes. Wash the prints for a minimum of 20 minutes with normal water flow and constant agitation.

Prints can be transferred to the hypo clearing agent solution directly from the fixer without an intermediate rinse. This practice, however, considerably reduces the capacity of the hypo clearing agent solution. For capacity of solution with and without intermediate rinsing, see the accompanying table.

Processing Prints for Maximum Stability

It is difficult, if not impossible, to remove the last traces of processing chemicals from photographic papers by ordinary means. For the maximum possible stability, therefore, you should use a hypo eliminator after washing.

Even when the last traces of hypo have been removed from a print by chemical means, the silver image is liable to be attacked by various substances in the atmosphere. Treatment with Kodak gold protective solution GP-1 makes the image less susceptible to such deterioration.

Alternatively, a selenium protective coating can be obtained by adding Kodak rapid selenium toner to the Kodak hypo clearing agent treatment—or other washing aid—at a rate of 90 millilitres of toner per litre (3 ounces per quart) of clearing agent solution. For details of the hypo eliminator and gold protective coating treatments, see ARCHIVAL PROCESSING.

• *See also:* DRYING FILMS AND PRINTS; FIXERS AND FIXING.

Washoff Emulsion

Washoff emulsions are usually silver bromide emulsions of relatively slow speed. They are prepared with unhardened gelatin, which is normally soluble in warm water. When processed in a tanning developer, the gelatin is hardened in proportion to the silver image developed. When washed in warm water after processing, only the unexposed or non-image portions wash away.

An early washoff emulsion was made for the washoff relief process. Its modern counterpart is the dye transfer process. This emulsion is of low to normal printing contrast and contains absorbing dyes in the emulsion so that exposures of low intensity are restricted to a limited depth, and exposures of greater intensity will penetrate to greater depths. When the film is processed in a tanning developer, a continuous-tone image composed of varying thicknesses of gelatin is produced. The film has to be exposed through the base so that it will remain attached to the substrate. If the film were to be exposed from the emulsion side, the image would be lying on top of a layer of soluble gelatin and would wash away completely when processed.

Another type of washoff film is currently being manufactured. It consists of a high-contrast emulsion on a plastic base and is used in drafting rooms for duplication of drawings. It requires only exposure, development in a tanning developer, and washoff in warm water to produce a transparent drawing that can be used to make blueprints and other types of paper copy. One advantage of this process is the ease of making corrections; all that is needed is a wet eraser.

 **Water Conservation**

Water conservation has become important because of increasing demands on water supplies and growing disposal problems. In many areas of the United States, the cost of water for photographic processing is increasing. Three additional factors may become important in using water commercially:

1. Increasing overall demands by commercial users could outstrip the supply.
2. With the increase in use, sewer and treatment systems have to be expanded, adding significantly to the cost of water usage.
3. In many locations in the world, including some parts of the United States, the availability of usable water is already limited.

The photographic processing industry now attempts to use water as efficiently as possible. The principal use of water in this industry is in washing the photographic material. It is in this area that significant reductions in water use might be found.

This article explains some of the things that affect the efficiency of the washing action and suggests some ways of using less water for washing photographic films and papers. Large users of water will benefit most from the suggestions. Nevertheless, individuals and small labs are encouraged to adopt as many water-conservation techniques as practical because waste at any level is inefficient and costly.

Conservation

Water conservation in photographic processing can be divided into three areas:

1. General housekeeping.
2. Washing.
3. Reuse.

Although this article is concerned primarily with the use of wash water in photographic processing, there are ways of conserving water that have no bearing on the washing function.

Some of the ways of saving water are:

1. Hot water used for heating processing solutions can be recirculated in a steam-heated hot-water loop. Likewise, compressors that are cooled by running water that goes to the sewer can be cooled with the recirculating loop and a cooling heat exchanger. These heating and cooling systems, if they are running day and night all week, can be controlled with a standby system that reduces flow during hours when the processing machines are not in operation.
2. Total wash-water consumption can be greatly reduced if the water is shut off when no film is being processed.

Simple waste awareness is also a means of conserving water. Examples of this are fixing leaking faucets, shutting off needlessly running hoses, washing and rinsing equipment no more than necessary to remove contamination, and not exceeding recommended wash-water rates.

Washing. Between 64 and 95 percent of the water used in photographic processing is used to wash the film or paper in some way. Therefore, anything that can be done to reduce the amount of water needed to remove adequately the chemicals from the emulsion will be a substantial saving.

In a carefully designed film process, surprisingly little water is required to satisfy the chemical requirements. Wash-water flow rates have, in the past, been set to satisfy other requirements. Some of these are controlling dirt accumulation and reducing the effects of biological growths in the wash systems.

Some of the factors that have been pointed out as important to washing efficiency can be manipulated to reduce the amount of wash water consumed.

Agitation. Agitation has two requirements:

1. Sufficient movement in the vicinity of the film or paper surface.
2. Rapid replacement of exhausted solution with fresh water.

A flat fan spray has been found to be the most effective way of providing both adequate movement and rapid replacement of exhausted solution. Agitation effects have been tested by using submerged wiper bars, submerged squeegees, and submerged spray nozzles.

Squeegees. Of all the ways of reducing wash-water consumption, the one that combines the greatest ease with the best results is the installation of squeegees between processing solutions and water washes. Carry-over of processing solutions into the wash water tends to reduce the effectiveness of the wash. That means either more time or a higher flow rate is required in this situation. In some processes, the use of squeegees allows the reduction of 50 percent in wash-water rates.

Squeegees consisting of polyurethane blades in contact with both sides of the film or paper are probably the easiest and least expensive to use. There are other types of squeegees, for example:

Air knives, which are highly effective but require the use of a compressed air system.

Rotary buffers, which are useful for wide films or papers but which must be carefully cleaned to prevent scratching. Power is also required to operate these buffers.

Belt turnarounds with soft-core rollers, which can be used on slow-speed transport of wide films; but these, too, require external power and are less effective at high machine speeds than at low ones.

Dissolved Salts. Adding salts to wash water in order to increase washing efficiency should be done with caution. Simulated seawater has been used as a substitute for tap water in washing several color products, but adverse effects might result from this practice.

In those processes where seawater gives an unwanted effect, it would be expected that many brackish waters would give significantly smaller effects, depending upon the composition of the brackish water. Brackish waters of low salt concentration probably would be all right to use, but solutions of high salt concentration or with dissolved natural salts, minerals, or organic matter may be wholly unsatisfactory for processing. A better solution is to precede a wash with a clearing bath such as Kodak hypo clearing agent.* It has been found that for many films a 1- to 2-minute bath in this clearing agent permitted a wash time of 5 minutes or less.

Countercurrent Washing. Countercurrent washing cannot be used in all locations in a process because of time considerations. In general, countercurrent washing takes longer to remove chemicals from emulsions because the film goes through the tank having the poorer washing power first, and the reactions occurring have a longer time to continue than in parallel or deep-tank washing. Nevertheless, considerably lower water flow is used in the countercurrent method.

High Temperature. Operating at higher wash temperatures, although an effective way of decreasing water consumption, may require more energy than is practical.

Reuse. Several methods are under study for making wash water reusable. The two most promising ones are ion exchange and reverse osmosis.

---

*Kodak hypo clearing agent is a preparation of inorganic salts that have been selected because they are harmless to the silver image. (*See:* WASHING.)

The advantage of these two methods of purification is that they can interface with most photographic processing systems using a simple input-output hookup to the processing equipment. This results in a closed loop and a reduction in water usage up to 99 percent. Two major drawbacks to these methods are:

1. The capital expense of the equipment needed.
2. The lack of a simple means of monitoring the condition of the water so as to determine accurately when it is pure enough for use.

Reverse Osmosis. This method uses a semipermeable membrane and pressure to separate chemicals from the wash water, thus purifying the wash water for reuse. This method depends upon very high pressure on the wash water to force most of the water molecules through a semipermeable membrane, whereas most of the salts remain in a concentrated brine solution, thus producing quite pure water and a smaller amount of concentrated salts. Some objectionable materials do pass through the membrane, a fact that limits its use in such things as mixing processing solutions. Energy is required to produce the pressure needed in this method, so the relative advantages of energy conservation and water conservation must be weighed. There are some ways of reusing the energy, since it ends up in the form of hot water.

Ion Exchange. This method replaces more objectionable substances with less objectionable ones, from a photographic standpoint, making the wash water reusable. Home water softeners utilize one form of ion exchange.

Image Quality

Most of the conservation methods mentioned have been shown to cause no reduction in photographic quality. Nevertheless, as has been often observed, there are no simple changes in the photographic process. Changes in time, temperature, and agitation in the washing steps can—and usually do—affect photographic quality.

It has also been pointed out that processing problems can occur as the result of adding squeegees and changing the location of squeegees in a process, if this is not done with care and with careful testing.

Environmental Impact

One of the consequences of lowering wash rates is an increase in the concentration of materials in the effluent. Local sewer codes regulate some constituents of photographic processing in effluent, and an increase in the concentration of these may cause a process operator to be in violation of the code. The most commonly regulated substances are silver and cyanide. Using silver recovery techniques and regenerating bleaches that contain ferrocyanide can substantially reduce the concentration of these substances in the effluent. Biological Oxygen Demand (BOD) and Chemical Oxygen Demand (COD) also are frequently regulated. These measure the extent to which chemicals deplete the oxygen supply of water into which they are dumped. Most photographic chemicals, like domestic sewage, fall into the oxygen-demanding category, are amenable to biological treatment, and are best handled by a municipal treatment plant that has secondary treatment stages.

• *See also:* ARCHIVAL PROCESSING; PROCESS CONTROL; SILVER RECOVERY; WASHING.

Waterhouse Stops

Waterhouse stops were a system of lens diaphragms in which each aperture was made as a carefully machined hole in a thin, brass plate. These plates, or diaphragms, were inserted into the lens barrel through a slot cut in the side, at a point that placed the diaphragm at the calculated position between the lens elements.

Note that the term "Waterhouse stops" refers only to stops that are made in individual pieces to be inserted one at a time as needed. Similar diaphragms include long plates of metal with a series of apertures in them, intended to be slid through the lens barrel, and circular metal plates with a circle of apertures in them, brought into place by revolving the disc. These latter are not, strictly speaking, Waterhouse stops, though they resemble them and work in much the same way. However, the term Waterhouse has come to have a generic use for all types of fixed apertures used in photography.

Waterhouse stops were used until quite recently in photoengraving because the apertures were fixed and unchangeable, which is very important in half-tone screen photography; a small error in setting an iris type of diaphragm can have considerable effect on the tone rendition of the image when a glass screen is used. In addition, certain special effects could be obtained by using stops with apertures of various shapes other than circular. Most diaphragms used today are adjustable stops made of thin, metal blades.

• *See also:* DIAPHRAGM; *f*-STOP.

Watt-Second

A watt-second is a measure of power equal to the power of 1 watt operating for 1 second (1 ampere $\times$ 1 volt $\times$ 1 second). The correct name for this unit is Joule (rhymes with *pool*).

Electronic flash units were formerly rated in joules or watt-seconds, based on the formula:

$$J = \frac{CE^2}{2}$$

where: C was the capacitance of the unit in microfarads, and E the applied voltage in kilovolts. This system of rating, however, did not take into account the efficiency of the flashtube nor the reflector in which it is used. For this reason, there was no exact relation between the light output and the watt-second rating of a self-contained unit. Consequently, the system has been largely abandoned, and flash units are currently rated in beam or effective candle-power-seconds (BCPS, ECPS) based on measurements of light output within the area actually illuminated for picture-taking.

• *See also:* ECPS; ELECTRONIC FLASH.

Wavelength

The length of a wave, in the case of repetitive wave forms, is the distance from a point on one wave to the identical point on the next wave. It is usually measured from peak to peak. It can also be measured on the time baseline, but you must be careful, in this case, to include both a negative and a positive peak, for the wave crosses the baseline once in be-

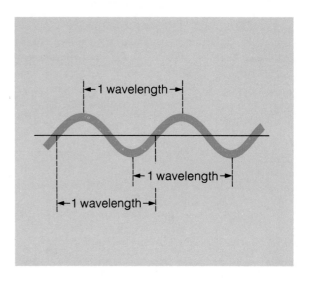

Wavelengths are conventionally measured from peak to peak in either a positive phase or a negative trough. They can also be measured along the time base (straight line) by including a positive peak and a negative trough.

tween, and if you measure from one crossing to the next, you are actually measuring only a half wave.

Wavelengths are given in standard length units, as are any other lengths. They vary enormously in size, however, so that different units are used. Thus, radio waves are measured in metres, and microwaves in centimetres. Light waves are far shorter; the currently used unit is the *nanometre* (nm), which is one billionth of a metre. (A former name for the nanometre was millimicron.)

Visible light has wavelengths varying from 400 (violet) to 700 nm (deep red). Ultraviolet radiation has wavelengths shorter than visible light (from 200 to 400 nm), and infrared radiation has longer wavelengths (upwards of 700 nm). An old measure, formerly used for measuring wavelength, was the Angstrom unit; 1 Å = 0.1 nm. It is now generally obsolete.

It is the custom to classify longer wavelengths, such as radio waves, by their frequency—that is, the number of waves passing a given point in one second. The unit is the hertz (Hz) and is equal to one wavelength per second; large frequencies are measured in kilohertz (1 kHz = 1000 Hz) and in megahertz (1 mHz = 1,000,000 Hz). Since the velocity of electromagnetic radiation is nearly 300,000,000 metres per second, a radio wave of 10 metres in length will have a frequency of 30,000,000 Hz or 30 mHz. Frequency measurements are not often used with light radiation because the wavelengths are so short that the corresponding Hertz values are astronomical. In the case of sound waves, the same type of frequency measurements are used, but the velocity of sound is much less; it is about 335 metres per second.

• *See also:* COLOR THEORY; LIGHT.

Wedding Photography

Weddings are very important occasions in the lives of people. The wedding photographer, therefore, has a special responsibility to produce a pictorial record that captures as much of the excitement, joy, and glamor of the event as possible. This task taxes the creative ability as well as the technical skill of a photographer. Moreover, reliability is of great importance, because a wedding cannot be photographed over again.

How to Become a Wedding Photographer

It can be said that any competent photographer can take photographs at a wedding, but to produce a first-class wedding album requires something more than just technical competence. The wedding photographer must be an opportunist. Some scenes last only for seconds and they must be recorded with certainty. Generally, the time taken to pose and shoot the picture is minimal. Also, a knowledge of wedding etiquette is necessary, as is the ability to handle and direct people diplomatically. All this requires both training by knowledgeable people and a good deal of practice.

The Freelance Wedding Photographer

If a photographer has gained enough experience and has the necessary equipment, he or she can work as a freelance wedding photographer. There are some disadvantages to this method. There will not be a studio, and some brides insist on having some studio shots. However, the majority of modern weddings are taken in casual surroundings.

The Preliminaries

After being approached by a couple to take their wedding photographs, the photographer should sit down with them and discuss such matters as price and the type of photography they prefer—formal, natural, or candid. Also, mention should be made of motion-picture coverage, because this may appeal to some people who had not given the matter previous thought.

Price. Later in this article is a sequential list of the pictures usually taken at a wedding. The price should be quoted for this kind of coverage. Be sure that each couple knows what they will get for the money. Some people may not want so many shots or they may not be able to afford the cost. Then, a compromise can be made on price, but be sure everyone gets the same good-quality photography.

Type of Coverage. The words formal, natural, or candid do not mean the same things to everyone. To make sure that customers know what these terms mean, display representative samples that show the difference clearly. It is probable that a photographer will be asked for a mixture of the three styles. In that case, the formal shots should not be made too formal nor the candids too candid. The result will be a nice blend of different styles.

Wedding Movies. A movie of the day's events makes an excellent supplement to the wedding album. People who already own a super-8 projector are good sales prospects. Remember that an assistant may be needed to help shoot a movie as well as stills. See the later section on this topic.

Advice on Makeup and Colors. The bride should be advised to use makeup sparingly, because it tends to be exaggerated in a color photograph. Black eyeliner and glossy or highly colored lipsticks should be avoided. Blush should spread beyond the edge of the cheekbone, and hair should not cover an eye, or eyes. If the bridegroom is cleanshaven, he should be asked to shave as late on the wedding day as possible, particularly if he has a dark beard.

It is helpful to remind the bride that colors do not always photograph exactly as they are seen by the human eye. This depends on the particular colors and on the color quality of the light at the time the photograph is taken.

Taking Pictures in the Church. Nowadays, few clergymen object to photographs being taken during the wedding ceremony. On occasion, one will object to flash pictures, but this is not a problem in most churches now, because ASA 400 film yields adequate exposure even in comparatively dim light. In any case, permission should be gotten from the officiating clergyman before taking the pictures.

Equipment for Wedding Photography

Cameras. Cameras that take 120, 220, or 70 mm film are preferred by most experienced wedding photographers. Many good-quality cameras that yield negatives of the so-called ideal format (2¼″ × 2¾″) are available. The former is preferable, because it enables enlarging to 8″ × 10″ without much cropping of the negative. The 2¼″ × 2¼″ negative must be cropped to get an 8″ × 10″ enlargement, and so a greater degree of enlargement is required. A 35 mm single-lens reflex camera is the most versatile instrument, and if purely candid wedding pictures are required, this size should be considered. A large variety of different lenses is not usually required at a wedding, but a telephoto lens with a moderate focal length is useful for reducing the distortion caused by using a short-focal-length lens for close-ups.

Some medium-format cameras can use interchangeable backs or inserts—a very useful feature when quick reloading of film is necessary. In addition, Polaroid backs can be used to test exposures under uncertain lighting conditions.

Leaf shutters are preferred over the focal-plane type, because focal-plane shutters are limited to a shutter speed of up to 1/60 sec. with electronic flash. A tripod makes slow shutter speeds usable, but consider other forms of support, such as a wall, a pillar, or a chair. The small, pocket-type tripods are easy to carry and they can be very useful on some occasions.

Electronic Flash Units. These units, sometimes called strobes, are available in wide variety. Wedding photography requires three units with a guide number of 110 or higher, with ASA 100 film. A recycling time of less than 5 seconds is essential. Otherwise, picture opportunities in a quickly changing scene will be missed.

PC cords of various lengths and slave units make off-camera lighting possible. Units that have variable output features make complicated lighting relatively easy. Attach the flash unit to the camera with a suitable bracket so that the light is not close

to the lens, otherwise a phenomenon known as red eye may result. (*See:* RED EYE.)

Exposure Meters. Some photographers rely on exposure meters, while others are adept at assessing exposures by observation. The method to use is a personal choice, but if *properly used,* a meter should result in more accurate exposure. Incident-light metering is used in shade, while reflected-light readings are more useful where high-contrast lighting exists. Spot meters, which have an angle of acceptance of as little as 1 degree, can be useful in measuring the light falling on a small area or object.

Films for Wedding Photography

Today, the wedding photographer has at hand an array of color films that were previously unavailable. Color film with an ASA speed of 100, such as Kodak Vericolor II professional film, is excellent for general purposes. Its characteristics of moderate contrast and good exposure latitude make this film a first choice for the difficult subject matter so often encountered in wedding photography.

When a faster film is needed, Kodacolor 400 film, with an ASA speed of 400, can be used. Many wedding shots that once required the use of flash or other additional lighting can be made in available light with this film. Thus, the cost of batteries, renewal of flash supplies, and other items is saved. Moreover, by saving the time necessary to set up lights, to check synchronization of flash and shutter, and to wait for electronic units to recycle, time can be devoted to making pictures.

Preparation and Checking Equipment

To guard against equipment failure, anything that might malfunction should be checked either on the day of the wedding or the night before. Since anything mechanical or electrical can fail, a complete set of backup equipment is necessary. This includes cameras, lenses, and strobe units, as well as articles such as PC cords, batteries, and the like. Also, take along a set of jeweler's screwdrivers, a pair of pliers, a roll of black adhesive tape, and — the most useful of photographic accessories — a changing bag.

Picture-Taking Locations

At some weddings, all of the photographs are taken in one place; at others, several locations may be used at the request of the couple. These locations include the bride's home, the church, a studio, a park, and the reception hall.

Pictures in the Bride's Home. Conditions are normally difficult on the wedding morning at this location, but helpfulness and diplomacy on the part of the photographer will usually achieve results. From a technical standpoint, be careful about backgrounds. Avoid drapes with distracting patterns and highly reflective surfaces. Remember that when you photograph someone in a mirror, focus on the mirror image and not on the edge of the mirror; otherwise, the picture will be out of focus.

At the Church. People like and want pictures of the wedding ceremony, but they do not want the taking of photographs to be obtrusive. Avoid cameras with noisy shutters, and take available-light photos if possible. See the suggested list for wedding photographs later in this article.

In the Studio or Park. Formal pictures of the bride, groom, and the bridal party can be taken in the studio or in a park. The latter location is usually preferred if suitable settings can be found. However, some couples ask for formal pictures to be taken at the altar or outside the church. This is a matter for prior arrangement with the people concerned.

At the Reception Hall. Once the reception begins, most of the important photographs will have been taken, except such photos as the bride throwing the bouquet, the cutting of the cake, and so on. There are a number of possibilities for unusual photographs to be obtained at a wedding reception. Be on the lookout for them. Remember also that many salable photographs of the guests can be taken here.

(Left) A semi-formal portrait of the bride and groom is almost mandatory among the poses desired for a wedding album. A park or garden makes an ideal setting for such a shot; backlighting behind the bride's veil is always effective. (Right) A romantic long shot, especially when the setting is particularly beautiful, will also be successful. Here again, backlighting is used to fine advantage.

Suggested List of Possible Wedding Photographs

The following checklist is representative of the photographs usually taken at an American wedding. Customs in other countries are sometimes different, so that a list of photographs might not be the same.

The checklist need not be followed to the letter; it should be modified as the occasion demands. Always duplicate important photographs as an insurance against failure because of movement of the subject, damage to the negative, or some other unforeseen happening.

Bride's Home
Bride in mirror
Bride and her mother
Bride and her father
Bride's parents
Bride and her brothers and sisters
Bride and her complete family
Bride and her maid of honor
Bride and bridesmaids
Full-length shot of bride
Family leaving bride's home
Bride's father helping her into car

At the Church
Bridegroom and best man waiting
Bride kisses father as they enter the church
Available-light shot of church interior
Bride and groom from front
Bride's family in pew
Bridegroom's family in pew
Close-up shot of ring exchange
Close-up shot of wine drinking
Bride and groom kiss
Bride and groom leaving
Receiving line
Rice or confetti throwing
Bridal party on church steps, or in other location
Bride entering car
Bride and groom in car

Formal Pictures at Studio or Other Location
Bride (various)
Bridegroom (various)
Full bridal party
Bride and groom (various)
Bride and all bridesmaids
Groom and ushers
Groom and best man
Bride, groom, maid of honor, and best man
Bridegroom and his parents
Bridegroom's parents
Bride and her parents
Bride and groom with parents (various)
Bride and both mothers
Bridegroom and both fathers
Bride's parents
The four parents together

At the Reception Hall
Bride and groom entering reception hall
Best man (or others) toasting the couple
Bride and groom toasting
Party at head table
Shot of wedding cake
Ceremony of cutting the cake
Bride and her father dancing
Bridegroom and his mother dancing
Overview of the dancing
Various people dancing with bride and bridegroom
Bride's parents at their table
Bridegroom's parents at their table
Throwing the bride's bouquet
Various couples dancing
Any other pictures that are appropriate
Close-up of couple's hands showing rings and flowers against a background of the bride's gown
Bride and groom waving goodbye.

The above list does not include all of the picture-taking opportunities that might occur at a wedding, nor is it necessary to photograph everything suggested on the list. In many cases, circumstances dictate what pictures will be taken and the number that will be required.

Posing People at a Wedding

Today, most people prefer "natural" poses to those of a more formal kind. This does not mean that a photographer can dispense with posing people at a wedding, but it does suggest that as little formal posing be done as possible. In any case, there is not

A photo of the "getaway car," if there is one, should not be missed. It will provide considerable entertainment for the reminiscing couple.

much time for it, because events at a wedding must move quickly.

To make people feel at ease is the most important task of a photographer. If a person feels at ease, then he or she will look that way in the photograph. Then a few simple directions are all that is needed to complete the pose. Here are a few hints on simple posing of people.

Stance. Ask the subject to point one of his or her feet toward the photographer and drop the weight onto the other hip. Thus, the body is turned slightly. Men can stand with hands in pockets, or lean against a wall with arms folded. Women can stand with clasped hands. Usually, three-quarter-length shots of individuals are preferable to full-length shots.

Couples. A man and woman together should stand facing each other in a partially turned position. The couple can hold hands, but this might depend on their relationship. If there is a large height differential between the two, the taller person can sit while the shorter one stands.

Groups. Photographing groups is a skill, and the wedding photographer should cultivate it. First, the appropriate people must be assembled, and then be persuaded to stand (or sit) in suitable attitudes. Attention must be paid to backgrounds because undesirable objects in a background are distracting.

Each person should be asked to look toward an imaginary center. In a wedding group, the center would probably be where the bride and groom are standing. To avoid distortion of figures at the ends of the group, use a lens with focal length a little longer than that considered normal for the format.

In making the exposure, watch out for people with careless postures, with their heads turned away, or their eyes closed.

The Bride and Groom. If any wedding pictures can be said to be more important than others, the photographs of the bride and groom together are these. A number of pictures of the couple are usually made. Full-length formal photographs of the bride alone and the bride and groom together show the bride's gown to the best advantage. Other poses include the bride and groom looking at each other, kissing, and laughing. Special effects can be created either in the camera or in the lab. Camera effects include selective focus, misty pictures of the bride, and vignettes made with filters partially coated with petroleum jelly or clear lacquer. A matte box is also

(Right) Photographs of the bridal party show off the bride's gown and the ensembles of her attendants. For a formal picture such as this, a graceful effect will also be achieved by posing the subjects slightly turned from the camera rather than facing it directly.

(Left) An informal grouping of the groom and his party is another "must" for any set of wedding pictures.

Wedding Photography

used to create interesting effects, such as placing the image of the bride and groom inside hearts or other shapes. Cross star (diffraction) filters make highlights shimmer, and they can be used to soften wrinkles in an older person's skin.

Professional photofinishers who cater to wedding photographers' needs provide a range of special effects that have been popular for a long time. These effects include soft-focus or diffused images, double-exposures, and multiple-printing techniques.

Lighting for Wedding Photography

Where lighting is concerned, photographing people at a wedding is very much the same as photographing people anywhere. One difference, however, is that time and sometimes space are limited, so there is little time at a wedding for fancy lighting or complicated setups. Versatility in lighting is the keynote. Daylight, electronic flash, or available light may be used indoors in rapid succession.

Daylight. Daylight can be almost constant for hours, or it may vary momentarily. Cloudy-bright conditions are ideal. In bright sunshine, place the people in a position so that the sun provides an oblique backlighting. Otherwise, try to find a suitable place in the shade. If there are rapidly moving clouds in an otherwise clear sky, watch out for variations in the light and alter exposure accordingly. If the sun is very high in the sky, fill-in flash helps to reduce unavoidable shadows. A simple way to use fill-in flash is to expose for the daylight and position the unit to provide one stop less exposure than the highlighted areas of the subject. Variable-output flash units are the most suitable for this purpose.

Single Flash. The easiest and most often used form of artificial light at a wedding is a single flash unit on the camera. This type of lighting gives a somewhat uninteresting effect and tends to create objectionable shadows. Bouncing the light off a ceiling helps to soften the light and provide better modeling in faces. (*See:* BOUNCE LIGHT.) Umbrellas and other reflectors can also be used to provide softer

Another important photograph will show the bride and groom's champagne toast to each other. Be sure to catch playful moments as well as romantic ones.

lighting with a single flash. (*See:* UMBRELLA LIGHTING.)

Use of Multiple Flash. Better lighting effects can be obtained by using more than one flash. The most simple of such arrangements is to use a movable lightstand to hold the main light in a fairly high position. A slave unit is plugged into the main light and is triggered by a fill light on the camera. Exposure is calculated on the distance between the main light and the subject.

Note that when other people are taking flash pictures, their flashes may set off a photographer's slave units if the units are light-activated. The problem can be avoided by using radio-activated slaves, but these units are expensive and sometimes cumbersome to carry.

Available Light. With fast lenses and the very fast color films manufactured today, many pictures that once needed the use of flash can be made with available light. The advantages of dispensing with flash equipment are obvious, and available-light pictures are often more pleasing to the customer than

films are adequate, but for available-light shots, high-speed films are necessary.

Shooting Technique. First, prepare a storyboard, rather than shooting at random. Encourage animation, but try to get people to talk and act naturally. Keep scenes brief and vary the distance. Use the zoom lens. In church, use existing light and keep well back from the action, so that camera noise is not obtrusive.

Sound Movies. Today a movie film that includes sound can be made with relatively simple equipment. In years to come, such a sound film would become of incalculable value to the people concerned. At the planning session, this aspect of wedding photography should be pointed out to the prospective bride and groom.

• *See also:* AVAILABLE-LIGHT PHOTOGRAPHY; BOUNCE LIGHT; ELECTRONIC FLASH; FLASH PHOTOGRAPHY; LIGHTING; PORTRAITURE; RED EYE; UMBRELLA LIGHTING.

Further Reading: Arin, M.K. *Successful Wedding Photography.* Garden City, NY: Amphoto, 1967; Feltner, Don and Castle, Paul. *Fifty-four Thousand Dollars a Year in Spare-Time Wedding Photography.* Upper Darby, PA: Studio Press, 1977; Szasz, Suzanne. *Modern Wedding Photography,* rev. ed. Garden City, NY: Amphoto, 1978; Tydings, Kenneth S. *Candid Wedding Photography Guide.* Garden City, NY: Amphoto, 1959.

are flash shots. In churches, particularly, the possibilities for tasteful available-light shots of the wedding ceremony are numerous.

Wedding Movies

As mentioned before, a motion picture of a wedding is a very desirable supplement to the wedding album. In no other way can the movement, excitement, and varying expressions be recorded except in a movie.

Motion-Picture Equipment. Movie cameras require such features as a lens fast enough for available-light pictures and the capability to use 100- or 200-foot cartridges of silent or sound film. A zoom lens is a great advantage. A substantial and steady tripod is essential. Incident-light exposure meters are generally used, and two large 3400 K lights on stands provide the lighting indoors. On occasion, extension cords as much as 100 feet long will be needed.

Films for Wedding Movies. Super-8 films, either silent or sound, are widely used for wedding movies. For outdoor work, slow- to medium-speed

Wedge Spectrogram

A *spectrogram* is a calibrated photographic record of part of the electromagnetic spectrum produced by a particular source of exposing energy. When the source produces a standard known spectrum, the spectrogram of a particular emulsion shows the range of wavelengths the emulsion can record. When a continuously graduated neutral density filter—a density wedge—is used to vary the intensity of the entire spectrum during exposure, the resulting *wedge spectrogram* shows the relative sensitivity of the emulsion to each wavelength.

Because they can be made quickly and easily, wedge spectrograms are an especially useful means for photographic scientists to investigate the color sensitivity characteristics of films and papers.

The Wedge Spectrograph

Spectrograms are exposed in a spectrograph, an instrument which produces a standard spectrum and incorporates various exposure controls. For photographic investigations in the visible and near-ultraviolet range, the light source of a spectrograph provides either standard tungsten (usually 3200 K) illumination or—by means of a suitable lamp and filter combination—a simulation of daylight.

A very narrow slit passes a thin beam of light from the source to a diffraction grating which spreads the light by diffraction into an evenly spaced spectrum; the spectrum is projected onto the emulsion being investigated. Various lenses—not shown in the accompanying diagram—concentrate the light on the slit and focus the spectrum onto the emulsion. A simple shutter between the source and the slit controls exposure.

(A prism can be used instead of a diffraction grating, but it does not produce an evenly spaced spectrum in the visible wavelength range. Prisms of various optical materials other than glass are used to provide spectra of energy outside the visible range, for example, infrared and x-ray wavelengths.)

The illuminating source is operated at a standard intensity to produce a consistent output. Its strength is varied by a density wedge located at the slit so that the light is uniformly attenuated before it is dispersed into a spectrum. The density wedge and the diffraction grating are oriented so that wavelength increases (blue to red) from left to right in a spectrogram, and exposure decreases from bottom to top. A wavelength reference scale is usually incorporated in the spectrograph so that it calibrates the spectrograms across the lower edge of the exposed area.

The Spectrogram

The wedge spectrogram produced by a test exposure graphically shows the relative wavelength sensitivity by the height of the exposed area at each point. Since the illumination was progressively weaker in the upward direction, greater height cor-

This schematic simplifies a wedge spectrograph to its basic elements. Light is reduced to a very narrow beam by the slit (A). Its intensity is modulated by the density wedge (B) across the slit. A diffraction grating (C) disperses the beam into an evenly spaced spectrum. The scale (D) provides wavelength and sensitivity references. Condenser lenses, the shutter used between the light source and the slit, and focusing lenses are omitted from the drawing for simplicity.

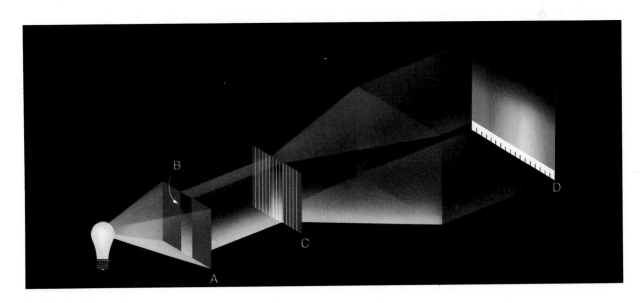

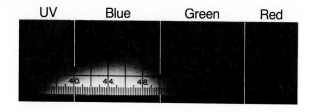

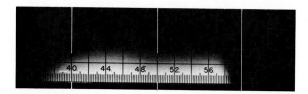

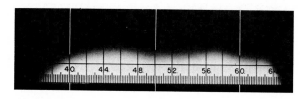

A wedge spectrogram is a graph of the effective sensitivity/wavelength relationship throughout the spectrum for a particular photographic material and light source. Shown (from top) are wedge spectrograms for blue-sensitive, orthochromatic, and panchromatic emulsions. Spectrogram figures times 10 equal wavelengths in nanometres.

responds to greater sensitivity. In evaluating a wedge spectrogram, it must be remembered that the *logarithm* of sensitivity is shown in the vertical direction; therefore, each major vertical scale division represents a $10\times$ increase in sensitivity.

Wedge spectrograms are especially valuable for the comparative evaluation of the spectral sensitivity of different emulsions. The accompanying spectrograms show the response of blue-sensitive (unsensitized), orthochromatic, and panchromatic film emulsions to a daylight spectrum.

See also: EMULSION; GRAY SCALES; NEUTRAL DENSITY; SENSITOMETRY; SPECTROGRAPHY.

Wedgwood, Thomas

(1771–1805)
English amateur scientist, son of Josiah Wedgwood, famous English pottery manufacturer

At the very beginning of the nineteenth century, Thomas Wedgwood worked with Humphrey Davy in investigating the production of images by the action of light upon silver nitrate; they did not succeed in fixing their images, however, and the process remained a curiosity. The two published a scientific paper on the subject and were undoubtedly the first to produce images on paper and leather by photographic means.

Wedgwood's work may have had an influence on Fox Talbot, who was successful in making permanent paper negatives and positive prints from the negatives some 30 years later.

Weights and Measures

The United States is in the process of converting to the International System (Systeme Internationale, SI) of weights and measures, commonly known as the *metric system*. Throughout this encyclopedia preference is given to SI, or metric units, except where U.S. customary units identify an established standard—for example, $4'' \times 5''$ film, and $8'' \times 10''$ prints.

The accompanying tables will assist in computing equivalents within either system, and especially in making conversions from one system to the other.

Measurement units for light, temperature, and some other factors are included in other articles; see the list of cross-references at the end of this article.

U.S. CUSTOMARY (AVOIRDUPOIS) WEIGHT		
1 dram	=	27.343 grains
16 drams	=	1 ounce
16 ounces	=	1 pound

OUNCES AND EQUIVALENTS IN GRAINS

Ounces	Grains	Ounces	Grains	Ounces	Grains	Ounces	Grains
⅛	54.7	1	437.5	2 ¾	1203	4 ½	1969
¼	109.0	1 ¼	546.0	3	1312	4 ¾	2078
⅜	164.0	1 ½	656.0	3 ¼	1421	5 ¼	2296
½	219.0	1 ¾	765.0	3 ½	1531	5 ½	2406
⅝	273.5	2	875.0	3 ¾	1640	6	2625
¾	328.0	2 ¼	984.0	4	1750	6 ¼	2734
⅞	382.9	2 ½	1094.0	4 ¼	1859	6 ½	2844

APOTHECARIES WEIGHT*

20 grains	=	1 scruple	
3 scruples	=	1 dram	
8 drams	=	1 ounce	
12 ounces	=	1 pound	

½ scruple	=	10 grains	1 dram	=	60 grains
1 scruple	=	20 grains	2 drams	=	120 grains
2 scruples	=	40 grains	3 drams	=	180 grains

*Old formulas were often given in this system as the scruple and dram weights were very convenient as substitutes for small amounts in grains in an avoirdupois formula. The grains are the same in both systems.

U.S. FLUID MEASURE*

60 minims	=	1 dram
8 drams	=	1 ounce=480 minims
4 ounces	=	1 gill
16 ounces	=	1 pint
32 ounces	=	1 quart
128 ounces	=	1 gallon

*Note that the above are U.S. measures. The British or Imperial pint contains 20 ounces, an Imperial quart 40 ounces, and an Imperial gallon 160 ounces. Due allowance must always be made when handling these quantities in English formulas if the terms pint, quart, and gallon are used instead of the quantity being expressed in ounces.

The Metric System: SI Units and Symbols

The designation SI is the official abbreviation for a system of measurement known as the International System of Units. It is a modernized metric system adopted by the International Standards Organization (ISO), numerous other standards organizations, and by national governments worldwide.

SI consists of seven base units, two supplementary units, a series of derived units consistent with the base and supplementary units, and a series of prefixes for forming multiples and submultiples of the various units. The SI system is designed to be "coherent." That is, when a derived unit is expressed algebraically in terms of base units, each having a value of one, the derived unit itself has the value one.

SI BASE UNITS

Quantity	Unit	Symbol
Length	Metre	m
Mass	Kilogram	kg
Time	Second	s
Electric current	Ampere	A
Thermodynamic temperature	Kelvin	K
Amount of substance	Mole	mol
Luminous intensity	Candela	cd

SUPPLEMENTARY UNITS

Quantity	Unit	Symbol
Plane angle	Radian	rad
Solid angle	Steradian	sr

USEFUL EQUIVALENTS

Linear

millimetres ÷ 10	= centimetres	1 millimetre	= 0.03937 inch
millimetres ÷ 1000	= metres	millimetres ÷ 25.4	= inches
centimetres ÷ 100	= metres	1 centimetre	= 0.3937 inch
centimetres × 10	= millimetres	1 metre	= 39.3704 inches
metres × 100	= centimetres	1 metre	= 3.2808 feet
metres × 1000	= millimetres	1 metre	= 1.0936 yards
1 inch	= 25.4 millimetres	1 kilometre	= 0.6213 mile
1 foot	= 0.3048 metre	kilometres ÷ 1.6093	= miles
1 yard	= 0.9144 metre	1 kilometre	= 3280.833 feet
1 mile	= 1.6093 kilometres		

Volume

millilitres ÷ 1000	= litres	1 cubic yard	= 0.765 cubic metre
litres × 1000	= millilitres	1 litre	= 1.0567 quarts (U.S.)
1 minim (water)	= 0.06161 millilitre	1 litre	= 0.26418 gallon (U.S.)
1 fluid dram	= 3.6966 millilitres	1 litre	= 33.8147 fluid ounces
1 fluid ounce	= 29.5729 millilitres	1 cubic centimetre	= 0.061 cubic inch
1 ounce apothecary (water)	= 31.1035 millilitres	cubic centimetres ÷ 16.387	= cubic inches
1 pint (16 ounces U.S.)	= 0.4732 litre	millilitres ÷ 3.6966	= fluid drams
1 quart (32 ounces U.S.)	= 0.9464 litre	millilitres ÷ 29.5729	= fluid ounces
1 gallon (128 ounces U.S.)	= 3.7853 litres	1 cubic metre	= 35.3357 cubic feet
1 millilitre	= 16.23 minims (water)	1 cubic metre	= 1.3079 cubic yards
1 millilitre	= 0.2705 fluid dram	1 cubic metre	= 264.15 gallons (U.S.)
1 millilitre	= 0.0338 fluid ounce	1 litre	= 61.0232 cubic inches
1 cubic inch	= 16.3871 cubic centimetres	litres ÷ 3.7853	= gallons (U.S.) (231 cubic inches)
1 cubic foot	= 0.0283 cubic metre	litres ÷ 28.3170	= cubic feet

Weight

1 grain	= 64.7989 milligrams	1 milligram	= 0.01543 grain
1 ounce avoirdupois	= 28.3495 grams	1 gram	= 15.4323 grains
1 ounce troy	= 31.1035 grams	1 kilogram	= 2.2046 pounds avoirdupois
1 pound avoirdupois	= 0.4536 kilogram	1 kilogram	= 2.6792 pounds troy
1 pound troy	= 0.3732 kilogram	1 kilogram	= 35.2739 ounces avoirdupois
1 pound avoirdupois	= 453.5924 grams	1 kilogram	= 35.1507 ounces troy

Miscellaneous

1 gallon (U.S.)	= 231 cubic inches	1 ounce avoirdupois (water)	= 0.9623 fluid ounce
1 gallon (U.S.)	= 8.313 pounds avoirdupois	1 cubic inch (water)	= 252.892 grains
1 gallon (U.S.)	= 58418.144 grains	1 litre (water)	= 1 kilogram
1 pound avoirdupois (water)	= 0.1203 gallon	1 litre of water × specific gravity of liquid	= weight in grams of liquid
1 fluid ounce (water)	= 456.392 grains	1 U.S. gallon	= 0.83267 Imperial gallon
1 fluid ounce (water)	= 1.0391 ounces avoirdupois	1 Imperial gallon	= 1.201 U.S. gallons

Conversion Factors

Grains per 32 fluid oz. × 0.06847	= grams per litre	Grams per litre × 0.03338	= ounces per 32 fluid oz.
Ounces per 32 fluid oz. × 29.96	= grams per litre	Grams per litre × 0.002086	= pounds per 32 fluid oz.
Pounds per 32 fluid oz. × 479.3	= grams per litre	Ounces (fluid) per 32 oz. × 31.25	= cubic centimetres per litre
Grams per litre × 14.60	= grains per 32 fluid oz.	Millilitres per litre × 0.032	= ounces (fluid) per 32 oz.

Prefixes

The prefixes used in metric notation are:

tera- T = 1,000,000,000,000 times; trillion; 10^{12}

giga- G = 1,000,000,000 times; billion; 10^9

mega- M = 1,000,000; million; 10^6

kilo- k = 1,000; thousand; 10^3

hecto- h = 100; hundred; 10^2

deka- da = 10 times; ten; 10^1 (or simply 10)

---

deci- d = 0.1; tenth; 10^{-1}

centi- c = 0.01; hundredth; 10^{-2}

milli- m = 0.001; thousandth; 10^{-3}

micro- μ = 0.000,001; millionth; 10^{-6}

nano- n = 0.000,000,001; billionth; 10^{-9}

pico- p = 0.000,000,000,001; trillionth; 10^{-12}

NOTE: Compound prefixes such as millimicro- are not used.

The unit of length is the metre, and the unit of mass is the kilogram. A decimetre is one-tenth metre, a decigram is one-tenth gram. A centimetre is one-hundredth metre, and a centigram is one-hundredth of a gram. A dekagram is 10 grams, a hectogram is 100 grams, and a kilogram is 1000 grams.

Some nonstandard units or designations encountered in photographic literature are:

Angstrom, Å = 0.1 nanometre;

thus, nm × 10 = A

micron μ = micrometre μm = 10^{-6} metre

millimicron mμ = nanometre = 10^{-9} metre

In photography, only a few of these prefixes are ever used, the general practice being to write the multiples in full and the subdivisions decimally, as: 50.0 grams, 2.5 grams, and so on. Plate and film sizes are often expressed in centimetres or millimetres, and the focal length of lenses may be stated either in centimetres or millimetres. Because the litre is not exactly a cubic decimetre (or 1000 cubic centimetres), the use of the term *cubic centimetre (cc)* is not exactly correct and in scientific work has been abandoned in favor of the term *millilitre (ml)*. The difference is so trifling in all but very large quantities that photographers may safely ignore it.

Temperature

The SI unit of thermodynamic temperature is the Kelvin. However, wide use is made of the degree Celsius for expressing temperature levels and temperature intervals. The Celsius scale (formerly called the centigrade scale) is related directly to thermodynamic temperature (Kelvin) as follows:

The temperature interval 1 degree Celsius equals one Kelvin exactly.

Celsius temperature (t) is related to thermodynamic temperature (T) by the equation:

$$t = T - 273.15$$

Comparison tables of Celsius and Fahrenheit temperatures are included in the article TEMPERATURE SCALES. Conversion formulas are:

$$C = \frac{(F - 32) \times 5}{9}$$

$$F = \frac{C \times 9}{5} + 32$$

Temperature affects the volume of liquids. The practice of buying certain liquids by weight instead of volume is a logical one. Acids are sold in this way, by weight, and a heavy acid, like sulfuric acid, which has a specific gravity of 1.8, takes up less space than a lighter one. While most photographic formulas do not need to be compounded with extreme accuracy, it is just as well to work with the solutions at an average room temperature of about 20 C (68 F).

• *See also:* COLOR TEMPERATURE; LIGHT; LIGHT: UNITS OF MEASUREMENT; MIXING PHOTOGRAPHIC SOLUTIONS; SPECTRUM; TEMPERATURE SCALES; WAVELENGTH.

Wet Collodion Process

The wet collodion, or "wet plate," process was the first truly practical method of making negatives on glass. Introduced by Frederick Scott Archer in 1851, it dominated photography until the introduction of gelatin-emulsion dry plates in the mid-1870's. It was called a "wet" process because the plate had to be coated and sensitized immediately before use, and then exposed and processed while the collodion remained tacky—a working time of about 20 minutes was available on the average.

Collodion

The key element in the process was collodion, a solution of gun-cotton (pyroxylin, nitrocellulose) in alcohol and ether. This solution could be painted, or more often flowed, onto any surface, where it would adhere with great permanency when dry. It formed a tough, waterproof, transparent, and flexible film, much like modern plastic sheeting. When collodion prepared for photographic use was flowed onto a glass plate, it would begin to set as the alcohol and ether evaporated. While in a tacky state, it could be sensitized, exposed, and processed; the "pores" of the collodion were open enough to let processing solutions reach halide crystals, but the collodion itself was unaffected because it was not soluble in water. If the plate was allowed to dry after sensitizing, it could be exposed, but no image could be developed or fixed because the dry collodion was perfectly waterproof.

When Archer began his experiments, collodion was used in hospitals to cover wounds, and to suture incisions and similar areas to protect them from infection and to permit washing of adjacent areas of the body. It was far superior to cloth bandages because of its impermeability, adhesion, and flexibility. It was also used in the theater to adhere false hair, beards, and other makeup elements; known as "spirit gum," its use persisted into the 1950's, when it was supplanted by liquid latex and similar more modern materials.

The strength of collodion and its adhesiveness made it far superior to albumen, which had been used as binder for glass-plate emulsions. It would not yellow, crack, and flake as albumen tended to do with only slight aging. Once dry, the collodion could be slit at the edges and the plate immersed in a chemical bath, which would allow the image-bearing film to be stripped off for transfer to another support or to be used as a flexible negative for printing. Archer had envisioned this as a special advantage for field photographers, who would have to carry a few pieces of glass that could be reused during extended trips. In fact, few photographers worked that way; it was cumbersome and time-consuming, and sometimes damaged the negative.

However, the stripping procedure was adopted in graphic arts photography, where the collodion process was used, in order to take advantage of the flatness of glass plates and the absence of dimensional changes in the image until the introduction of modern plastic film bases. The process of removing elements from plates taken at various magnifications and combining them into a composite master negative for platemaking is still called "stripping."

The nearly perfect adhesive qualities of collodion made it easy to produce novelty photographs on objects of wood, porcelain, stone, glass, metal, leather, or almost any other material. And it led to two major alternatives to paper prints—the ambrotype and the ferrotype (tintype), described in separate articles.

The Wet Collodion Process

Archer's original instructions, published in *The Chemist* (London, March 1851), explained how to make collodion as a starting point. Cotton-wool (absorbent cotton) was immersed in a mixture of equal parts of nitric and sulfuric acids for 15 seconds and

This engraving from Gaston Tissandier's History and Handbook of Photography *(1877) shows two photographers in the field with their dark-tent used for making wet collodion negatives. Photo courtesy International Museum of Photography, Rochester, N.Y.*

then washed thoroughly in water. It was then dissolved in a mixture of ethyl alcohol and ether to form collodion. For photographic use, sodium or potassium iodide and a small amount of potassium bromide were added. So long as evaporation was prevented, the prepared collodion would keep indefinitely. However, the preparation required care and was more than a little dangerous. Gun-cotton can be explosive, but of more concern was its high flammability, and that of the alcohol and ether, in an era of kerosene lamps and gas fixtures. Most photographers preferred to buy iodized collodion ready-mixed from a chemist or photographic supplier.

With the necessary materials and chemicals at hand, the process was as follows:

1. A glass plate was polished with pumice or jeweler's rouge to remove all surface dirt and grease (which would prevent adhesion of the collodion), rinsed clean with alcohol, and quickly dried over a small flame.

2. Iodized collodion was flowed into the center of the plate, which was then tilted back and forth to let the collodion run out to the edges to form an even coating. Getting the knack of this was the first big step in mastering the wet-plate process. After a few minutes, the collodion would begin to set, and any excess could be poured back into the container. In cold weather, the bottle of collodion had to be warmed, and the chill removed from the plate, before coating. In hot conditions, the collodion might not set sufficiently to stay on the plate.

3. The plate was sensitized by immersing it in a solution of silver nitrate (65 grams per litre of water) for about 1 minute. A reaction took place between the silver salt and the compounds in the collodion, forming light-sensitive silver iodobromide crystals in the coating. This was often done in a closed box to exclude light.

4. Under safelight conditions, the sensitized plate was placed in a holder with a dark slide, taken to the camera, and exposed. Exposures ranged from 1 to 15 seconds, on the average, although late in the period shorter exposures were possible.

5. The plate was taken back to the darkroom (or portable field tent made of light-safe orange or red canvas) and developed with constant agitation in an open tray. Often the developer was poured or washed over the surface of the plate repeatedly. The developer was either pyrogallol or iron sulfate in a solution of acetic acid and water.

6. The developed image was fixed in hypo, washed, and the plate placed in a stand to dry.

The developed collodion image was a whitish gray; if backed with black, it looked positive, which was the technique used to produce an ambrotype. For negatives, photographers often intensified the image, toning it dark brown or black.

• *See also:* AMBROTYPE; ARCHER, FREDERICK SCOTT; COLLODION; FERROTYPE; HISTORY OF PHOTOGRAPHY.

Wet Negatives, Printing

In certain cases, it is essential to have a print from a negative in the shortest possible time. A good deal of time can be saved by eliminating the washing and drying steps after developing the negative. The method is simply to develop and fix the film, then rinse it quickly in water to remove a substantial portion of the fixer. The film is then lightly squeegeed in order to remove water droplets and placed in a glassless negative carrier in the enlarger. Then prints are made as usual. It is essential that the enlarger be fitted with heat-absorbing glasses to avoid damaging the wet gelatin of the negative.

After printing, the negative may be completely washed and dried in the normal way. If this is to be done, it is well to return it first to the fixing bath for complete fixing and additional hardening. Washing is then done as usual. If the negative is no longer needed after printing, it can be discarded.

At one time, passport studios offered finished pictures from a negative in 5 minutes; this was done in an even shorter version of the process described above. Since the prints were to be made by contact, the negative could not be fixed, because the hypo in them would ruin the printing paper. Therefore, the negative was merely developed and rinsed in water and printed in contact with a sheet of wet contact-printing paper. The residual silver halides in the negative merely made a longer printing exposure necessary, but had no other effect on the final image.

The prints were developed, fixed, and washed briefly. They were delivered to the customer still damp, or in some cases, they were dried with a hot-air blower. The negative was not fixed or washed at all; it was discarded once the prints had been delivered.

Other methods of printing wet negatives included such methods as squeegeeing the wet emulsion to a sheet of cellulose acetate plastic, which could be wiped dry and printed in contact. Since the plastic protected the negative emulsion from that of contact-printing paper, the negative could be fully fixed before printing. This method was used where it was intended that the negative be kept for future use. It was peeled from the plastic sheet, refixed shortly, and washed and dried as usual.

Modern film processors, stabilization papers, fast-drying resin-coated papers, and other processing aids now shorten processing time to the point where wet-negative printing is seldom necessary.

• *See also:* RAPID PROCESSING.

Wetting Agent

A wetting agent is a substance that, when added to water or certain other chemical solutions and solvents, reduces the surface tension of the liquid. This causes liquid to wet the surface evenly without air bells and to run off without leaving droplets.

A variety of products have been used as wetting agents for photographic applications. These include a group of derivatives of sodium sulfosuccinate generally available under the trade names Aerosol® or Alphasol®. Other wetting agents used especially as additives in developers are alcohols (ethyl, butyl, hexyl) and triethanolamine.

Wetting agents are used in a wide variety of commercial products. Since the effects of wetting agents on photographic materials may be unpredictable, it is best to use a solution recommended specifically for photographic use. One such product is Kodak Photo-Flo solution. It is a powerful wetting agent that is safe for photographic use. Its recommended uses include the following:

1. A final process bath for the prevention of watermarks before film drying.
2. A prebath before intensification or reduction.
3. A means of facilitating the application of watercolors, opaques, and retouching dyes.

Photo-Flo solution is formulated to minimize the formation of sludge or precipitates when mixed with hard water or when contaminated with traces of fixer introduced by incompletely washed films.
• *See also:* DRYING.

Wide-Angle Photography

Wide-angle lenses are generally considered to include all lenses that have angles of coverage ranging from about 60 degrees to about 180 degrees. Lenses with narrower angles of coverage are either telephoto lenses or normal lenses; lenses with extremely wide angles of coverage are fisheye lenses. (*See:* FISHEYE LENS; TELEPHOTOGRAPHY.)

Wide-Angle Design
Traditionally, wide-angle lenses had symmetrical designs and relatively small apertures due to difficulties in correcting optical aberrations. One disadvantage of these lenses, which rendered them particularly unsuitable for color work, was the unevenness of illumination they delivered to the film—bright toward the center of the image but dark at the edges and corners. The reversed-telephoto design, originally developed by Angenieux of France, overcame these difficulties by providing even illumination and wider lens apertures, as well as making the back focus longer so that they could be used with single-lens reflex cameras. Today most wide-angle lenses for 35 mm cameras are of reversed-telephoto design; this is also known as inverted-telephoto de-

Wide-angle lenses will encompass more of a scene than would be covered with a normal lens. They may also be used creatively to increase apparent picture depth or to produce apparent distortions. Photo at left was taken with a 50 mm (normal) lens, photo at center with a 20 mm lens, and photo at right with a 16 mm lens. Camera-to-subject distance was the same for all three pictures. Photos courtesy Minolta Corp.

sign. Wide-angle lenses for view cameras are nearly always of the symmetrical design.

A reversed-telephoto lens can be likened to a positive lens that has a negative lens attached to its front.

"Distortions"

Wide-angle lenses are rectilinear, which means that they will image parallel lines as parallel lines provided the lens axis is at 90 degrees to the lines. What is generally referred to as "distortion" in photographs taken with wide-angle lenses is actually exaggerated perspective, which results from taking the picture close to the subject.

Perspective. Many photographers believe that wide-angle lenses change perspective. This simply is not true, as the accompanying photographs illustrate. Perspective is quite the same in photographs of the same scene taken at the same distance with wide-angle and with normal lenses, but it appears different because of the relationship of the camera position when the picture was taken and the viewing distance of the two-dimensional final image. See the article PERSPECTIVE for a full explanation of this effect. The photographer can use this apparent distortion to his or her advantage in certain kinds of pictures.

Using Wide-Angle Lenses

Wide-angle lenses are often used simply to encompass more of a scene than would be covered with a normal lens; they are also used creatively to increase apparent picture depth or to produce apparent distortions. The photographer who is aware of how to control perspective can use wide-angle lenses to advantage when particular subjects call for it. However, photographers should be aware of the following points when using wide-angle lenses.

Focusing and Depth of Field. Exact focusing in dim light with wide-angle lenses may constitute a problem because of the great depth of field inherent in wide-angle lenses. When working under adverse lighting conditions, larger-aperture lenses should be used. Magnifying eyepiece attachments may be useful for critical focusing. Use of the focusing and depth-of-field scales on the lens is often the best way to provide good definition in the pictures.

Portraiture. When using a wide-angle lens, if you get too close to a subject in order to fill the picture frame, a direct frontal view will depict facial features in an unappealing way. Photographing downward and close to a face will exaggerate the size of the forehead. Shooting a head close-up from a low angle will exaggerate the size of the chin. If there is no other choice but to use a wide-angle lens, it is best to take the picture from a distance that will provide a three-quarter view, and to have the camera at eye level.

Exposure. Because there may be great variations in light levels within the wide scene area of a wide-angle lens, it is important that exposure determinations be based on the most significant areas of coverage. While this is true of all picture-taking, it constitutes a particular problem in wide-angle photography, especially when behind-the-lens exposure meters are used. One technique is to measure the scene with a normal lens on the camera, and to take the actual photograph with the wide-angle lens.

Flash Photography. In flash photography, bounce- and multiple-flash techniques should be used with lenses wider than 35 mm. If a single flash is used with straight frontal lighting in conjunction with a wide-angle lens, the light may not extend to the edges of the scene. Rather, a circular or rectangular area of brightness—depending on the reflector shape—will be seen in the center of the picture. However, some flash units have special lenses that widen the light angle of the unit.

• *See also:* FISHEYE LENS; LENSES; OPTICS; PANORAMIC PHOTOGRAPHY; PERSPECTIVE; TELEPHOTOGRAPHY; ZOOM LENS.

Winterizing Equipment

Winterizing photo equipment is a highly specialized operation, best entrusted to the manufacturer or a competent, independent camera service representative. Essentially, the procedure calls for dismantling the camera and removing the original lubricants. The shutter, lens diaphragm, film transport mechanism, and other moving parts are then relubricated with materials that will not thicken when the camera is exposed to extreme cold. Powdered graphite has been, and in some cases still is, used for the purpose. However, newer, so-called "broad-range" lubricants (Teflon and silicone) have become increasingly popular, not only because of their effectiveness at low temperatures but also because they can be left in the camera permanently. In fact, such lubricants now are being used in manufacture. A camera that has been lubricated with a broad-range lubricant, either in manufacture or as part of a winterizing operation, need not be dewinterized and relubricated when it is returned to use under normal conditions.

When cameras are stripped down for winterizing, weakened or damaged parts may be discovered and can be replaced, to avoid possible failure under the extra stress of severe arctic temperatures.

There is often difficulty in operating small levers and knobs on cameras when the photographer is wearing thick gloves. To make camera operation easier, extensions can sometimes be added to levers, and knobs can be replaced with larger ones.

Exposure Meters

Photoelectric exposure meters do not require special winterizing and are usually reliable, even in very low temperatures. However, it is good practice to carry replacement batteries for CdS meters and to have a selenium-cell meter (which does not require batteries) in reserve for making comparison readings or as a substitute should the CdS meter fail.

Tripods

Tripods ordinarily do not require professional winterizing, although the photographer may want to remove any existing lubricants by rinsing the legs and pan-tilt head in kerosene. Wooden tripods are preferred by some workers, but either metal or wooden tripods should be satisfactory. Tripod heads for motion-picture equipment should be winterized if they include gyros, motors, or other revolving parts.

Flash

Extremely low temperatures have a detrimental effect on electronic flash units. The capacitor loses efficiency, with the result that the exposure guide number is lowered. Nickel cadmium (Ni-cad) batteries, when subjected to temperatures of −20 C

(−4 F), operate at only about 60 percent capacity and give fewer flashes per charge. Ni-cad batteries should not be recharged at temperatures below 10 C (50 F), since this is likely to cause them to vent and become permanently damaged. Contributing to the uncertainty is the fact that the exact effect of cold weather on the light output of an electronic flash unit cannot be predicted accurately. Efficiency will vary from one unit to another, due to differences in batteries and capacitors.

If electronic flash is necessary, a possible compromise is to use an arrangement in which power is delivered directly to the capacitor of the flash unit from a separate heavy-duty (510-volt) dry battery kept warm under the photographer's clothing.

Conventional flashbulbs are bulky and take up valuable storage space. Also, the battery power supply is unreliable due to the loss of efficiency in the extreme cold.

• *See also:* WINTER PHOTOGRAPHY.

Winter Photography

Photography under severe winter or arctic conditions is likely to impose unusual stresses on cameras, equipment, film, and indeed, on the photographer, too. The basic cause of most of the problems is, of course, the extreme cold. Normally, in the temperate zones winter temperatures do not fall much below −23 to −29 C (−10 to −20 F) for extended periods of time. In arctic regions, however, winter temperatures of −34 to −40 C (−30 to −40 F) are fairly common, and readings of −51 C (−60 F) or even lower are not unusual.

Problems

Problems that may be encountered in the field include the following:

Camera shutters tend to become sluggish and unreliable, or even fail completely.
Lens diaphragms often bind.
Film transport mechanisms stiffen up, making it difficult to advance the film from one exposure to the next.
Dry batteries lose efficiency, often delivering only a small portion of their energy

(the efficiency of battery-operated flash units and motion-picture camera drives may be seriously impaired).
Films may become brittle and break in the camera.
The photographer is apt to be less alert, and even the simplest and most familiar physical actions will be difficult to perform.
There is an increased hazard of static marks.

While the problems can be severe, they are by no means insurmountable. Careful advance preparation will pay rich dividends in the form of easier and more reliable equipment operation and better pictorial results. Obviously, the first step in preparation is to select the most suitable equipment, with due regard for the work to be done and the results desired,

Selecting Equipment

Each kind of camera has its adherents, and no one type seems to be outstandingly superior to the others. However, considering the working conditions, good judgment dictates that the camera or cameras selected should be compact, lightweight, easy to use, dependable, adaptable to various needs, and readily portable.

35 mm Cameras. Many 35 mm cameras fulfill the basic requirements of arctic photography and offer users the advantages of lens interchangeability and the widest choice of film emulsions. The availability of 20- and 36-exposure magazines minimizes the need for changing films under adverse conditions. Both rangefinder and single-lens reflex types are widely used; the choice is dictated largely by personal preference, although it may be noted that rangefinder cameras tend to be somewhat smaller and lighter and to have fewer mechanical movements. Rangefinder cameras are also easier to focus, particularly in dim light, and the shutter action is smooth and quiet. Single-lens reflex cameras offer advantages in using interchangeable lenses and in close-up work, since the subject is viewed through the camera lens.

Some of the rangefinder cameras and most single-lens reflex cameras have built-in exposure meters coupled to automatic lens diaphragms. These fea-

Snow and ice are visual elements which offer the creative photographer new opportunities for experimentation. In this photograph, the star-like image of the sun offsets the vertical lines of icicles backlighted by the sun.

tures are definitely advantageous, since they simplify the photographer's work and allow him or her more freedom to concentrate on getting good pictures.

Some thought should be given to the camera shutter. In cold weather, leaf-type between-the-lens shutters are more reliable than focal-plane shutters, but few 35 mm cameras have them. Of the focal-plane shutters, those made of metal are considered more likely to give even exposure over the full film frame under extremely cold conditions than shutters made of treated cloth.

Roll-Film Cameras. Some single- and twin-lens reflex cameras using 120- or 220-size roll film have much of the convenience of 35 mm models, with the added advantage of a larger picture size. The more versatile single-lens reflex cameras have interchangeable magazine backs that hold 12- or 24-exposure rolls. This feature is attractive because with only one camera and a few extra backs the photographer can easily switch from one film type to another whenever he or she wishes. Since the backs are small and light, they can easily be carried under the photographer's parka where the film will be kept warm and ready for use when wanted.

Sheet-Film Cameras. If still larger negatives or transparencies are required, 4″ × 5″ sheet films can be used in a press- or commercial-type hand camera. The extra size and weight of these cameras can be a serious disadvantage, and this is compounded by the problem of storing and carrying sheet-film holders. Also, a camera bellows can become stiff at low temperatures and break or come apart instead of expanding and contracting as a bellows should. Film packs are not suited to picture-taking in the extreme cold because of the danger that the film, made less flexible by the cold, will break when the paper tab is pulled to move the film to the back of the pack after exposure.

Sheet-film cameras are heavy and too large to be carried under the photographer's clothing when not in use. Everything considered, they should be avoided for arctic photography unless, of course, the benefits of having larger size negatives and transparencies outweigh the disadvantages of the sheet-film equipment.

Motion-Picture Cameras. Electrically powered motion-picture cameras are generally preferred over spring-driven models, if a generator or other reliable source of electricity is available. Batteries are not a dependable power source when exposed to extreme cold for extended periods of time. Film in rolls is less likely to break in the camera than film in magazines.

Magazine and cartridge motion-picture cameras allow quicker and easier loading than roll-film models, and this is an advantage for reloading in the field. Whereas motion-picture cameras can be winterized, there is no practical way to winterize magazines or cartridges to keep them operative in the extreme cold. If they *are* used, each day's working reserve carried into the field should be kept as warm as possible under the photographer's parka. Another possibility is to carry the film supply in an insulated thermal bag, along with one or two small hand warmers. Cameras in use can be similarly protected to some extent by keeping them in an insulated "blimp" covering with hand warmers. The blimp

Street scenes photographed during a snowstorm can provide good exercises in expression of mood.

will help to retain the heat given off by the warmers in the same way that thermal clothing retains body heat and keeps the wearer warm. A blimp covering alone, without an integral source of heat, is of no practical value except, possibly, to protect the camera against windblown snow.

Winterizing Equipment

All cameras, still or motion-picture, whether newly purchased or long used, should be properly prepared before being taken into the field. (*See:* WINTERIZING EQUIPMENT.)

Films

Films retain their flexibility and other physical characteristics as long as they remain at normal temperatures unopened in their original packaging. After being loaded into the camera and subjected to extreme cold, a film loses some of its humidity and may become brittle and break in the camera. However, this danger is minimized in a camera that has been winterized properly. Film should be advanced from one exposure to the next with a slow, steady motion of the transport lever or crank, since this lessens the strain on the film and thus reduces the likelihood of breakage, and static marks, as well.

With motion-picture films, rapid loss of moisture at low temperatures may cause curling in the gate and brittleness. Such problems are minimized by using films on Estar base, which maintains flexibility and strength better than acetate base.

Color films may lose speed and change in color balance, and exposure meters may lose accuracy. The extent of these changes cannot be predicted in advance. The wisest course is to use film freely, bracketing exposures by several half-stops over and under the meter reading on important subjects.

Keeping Warm

The ideal working outfit will provide adequate warmth without unnecessary bulk and will allow maximum mobility. An expedition outfitter or dealer in cold-weather clothing can make specific recommendations appropriate to the temperatures and conditions likely to be encountered.

Hand covering presents a special problem, because it must not only provide warmth, but also allow free use of the fingers for manipulating the camera controls. One practical solution is to wear thin silk, cotton, or woolen gloves under heavy lined mittens. One or both mittens can be removed when pictures are actually being taken. The inner gloves will give adequate protection for the few seconds needed to focus the camera and trip the shutter, and the hands will quickly recover their normal warmth after the mittens are put back on. Silk gloves are favored over wool or cotton. If the mittens are on a string attached to the parka's cuffs, they will always be handy and will not get lost.

One handy item of apparel is a photographer's vest. This garment, consisting mainly of pockets, is worn under the parka and provides safe, convenient spaces for carrying films, spare batteries, filters, extra lenses, exposure meters, and other miscellaneous items. Being located next to the photographer, these items are kept warm by body heat. A skier's belt serves a similar purpose. When worn with the pockets at the front, the belt not only provides extra space but also a kind of shelf or rest that comes in handy for reloading cameras and changing magazine backs or batteries.

Procedures and Precautions

Since most of the problems of arctic photography are caused by the extreme cold, it follows that they may be alleviated by keeping materials and equipment as warm as conditions and ingenuity will permit.

Carrying Film and Accessories. Whenever possible, films, cameras, extra lenses, and other accessories actually needed in the field should be carried under the photographer's clothing, where they will

A gray-white sky and snow-covered ground provide an almost unbroken background for this lone, bare tree; the feeling of winter's desolation is unmistakable.

Winter Photography

benefit from the body heat and be protected from the wind except for the few seconds or minutes when they are actually in use. Do not allow equipment to remain out in the cold any longer than necessary, because there will then be risk of condensation if it is returned to higher temperature and humidity under the clothing.

To conserve valuable space, films should be removed from their cartons, but not from their vapor-tight packaging; however, each film should be identified as to its type. Dry batteries for flash units or exposure meters will maintain their efficiency longer if carried in a shirt pocket, as close to the body as possible. The working camera is best carried on a neck strap at about chest height; it can then be removed from the protection of the parka for use and returned to cover immediately thereafter. A spare camera body and one or (at most) two extra lenses can readily be distributed in other pockets of the photographer's vest or compartments of the skier's belt around the waist. Several small hand warmers, using lighter fluid as fuel, will supplement body heat and help to keep the spare camera and extra lenses in good operating condition. Some photographers also tape a warmer to the back of the working camera, since this gets the most exposure to cold.

Changing Film. Roll and 35 mm cameras can be reloaded in the field if they can be protected against blowing snow. With a little practice, a photographer can learn to change film under his or her parka. A large towel or blanket can also be used to protect the open camera from flying snow.

Frostbite. An important thing to keep in mind is the ever-present danger of frostbite, a particular threat when hands or face come in direct contact with the metal of the camera body. Cameras that are used at eye level and must be brought close to the face for proper viewing and accurate focusing should have their exposed metal areas covered with heavy electrical tape, plastic foam, or some other insulating material. Under no circumstances should the photographer touch the camera with wet hands, because the skin will freeze fast to the cold metal almost instantly.

Condensation. Condensation forms when warm, moist air comes in contact with a cold surface, such as occurs when cameras, lenses, and other pieces of equipment that have been carried in the field are brought into a warm room. Condensation disappears when a cold camera is allowed to warm up to room temperature. Therefore, the camera can be left to dry off naturally, or it can be placed in a covered container with activated silica gel.

If the cold camera is in a tight-fitting case, or wrapped in an airtight plastic bag, the condensation will form on the outside of the container. The camera will be dry when it is removed from its container after reaching room temperature. Condensation does not form when a warm camera is exposed to cold air.

Dropped Camera. If the camera is dropped into the snow, pick it up and shake it hard. Do not try to blow the snow off because your warm, moist breath will freeze almost instantly, leaving the camera with a deposit of frost that is not easily removed.

Pictorial Effects

For best pictorial results in either black-and-white or color, snow pictures should be taken with back- or sidelighting. This captures the sparkle of sunlight striking individual snow granules and gives a feeling of depth impossible to get from a flatly lighted scene or one taken on a dull, overcast day.

Filters. The pictorial beauty of snow subjects taken on black-and-white films will be enhanced by using a medium-yellow filter over the camera lens. This filter darkens sky tones and increases overall contrast by absorbing some of the blue skylight illuminating shadow areas. Still more tone control can be obtained by substituting a red filter over the lens. This exaggerates contrast still more, creating the very dramatic effect of sparkling white snow with its many intermediate gray shadow tones against an almost black sky.

Color films can capture the scenes in the most natural way. All Kodak color films intended for use outdoors are balanced to give pleasing results in sunlight. Pictures taken during the period between 1 hour after sunrise and 1 hour before sunset will give good color rendering. Warmer tones—yellow, orange, and red—predominate in pictures taken earlier or later in the day, including sunrise and sunset.

Filters are seldom necessary with color films unless special color effects are desired. However, a skylight filter can be used to good effect in reducing excess bluishness. This filter can be used at all times to protect the camera lens, if desired.

Backlighting from a low winter sun offers excellent pictorial results. Diffracted light gives a striking center of interest to what might otherwise be a rather ordinary shot of a stand of evergreens on a snowy slope.

Polarizing filters are invaluable for creating special effects because they give the photographer wide control, allowing him or her to darken the tone of blue skies in color pictures without affecting the color rendition of other subjects in the scene. The darkening effect is greatest under clear sky conditions and when the sun is at right angles to the lens axis. The sun position is thus one that gives side-lighting.

Lens Hood. A lens hood should always be used to avoid flare from the sun or from the snow.

Exposure

There is no substitute for accurate focusing and correct exposure. However, this need not mean that the process must be repeated for every picture. For scenic pictures, for example, the camera will most likely be focused on the hyperfocal distance, for the greatest possible depth of field. As long as the lighting conditions and subject matter do not change appreciably, the exposure should remain fairly constant.

Snow is such a good reflector of light that side- and backlighted subjects are well lighted on the shadow side. This effect reduces the need for change in exposure with lighting direction. The accompanying table gives suggested adjustments to the basic exposure for a normal subject.

In the higher latitudes, the altitude of the sun is an important consideration. Normal exposure tables are based on a sun altitude of at least 30 degrees; if the sun is lower in the sky, an extra ½ to 1 stop more exposure should be given.

If you use an exposure meter to measure light reflected from sunlit snow, it will read high, perhaps off the scale entirely. It will indicate only half, or even a quarter, of the exposure actually required. Meters are fooled by snow because they are cali-

(Above) Daylight-balanced films give good, natural color rendition to pictures taken during the middle of the day. (Left) Photos taken near sunrise or sunset will have predominantly warmer tones; however, this is not likely to affect the generally wintery feeling of such pictures, and may actually enhance that feeling.

EXPOSURE CORRECTIONS FOR BRIGHT SUN ON SNOW (Adjustments from Normal Bright-Sun Exposure)			
	Frontlighted	**Sidelighted**	**Backlighted**
Scenics	1 stop less	1 stop less	1 stop less
Medium distance, people	1 stop less	1 stop less	None
Close-ups of people	None	½ stop more	1 stop more

brated for the usual proportion and darkness of shadows, neither of which occur in snow scenes. The best procedure is to take the meter reading from the gray side of a Kodak neutral test card. Use a lens opening 1 stop larger than the meter indicates as the basic setting for a frontlighted scene; then apply the adjustments given in the table. Under overcast conditions, the meter reading from the test card can be used to calculate the exposure directly for subjects of average reflectance, without any adjustments.

If the camera shutter slows down because of the cold, over exposure will result even though the settings are made for correct exposure. The photographer can often hear that the shutter speed is slowing down from cold. When this happens, use higher-than-called-for shutter-speed settings and bracket the exposures.

• *See also:* BAD-WEATHER PHOTOGRAPHY; WINTERIZING EQUIPMENT.

Wolcott, Alexander S.

(1804–1844)
American daguerreotypist and photographic inventor

On October 7, 1839, in New York City, Alexander Wolcott took what is believed to be the first practical (exposure less than 30 seconds) photographic portrait. It was a profile view of his associate, John Johnson, about 9 mm (⅜ inch) high on a daguerreotype plate.

In March of 1840, Wolcott and Johnson opened the world's first professional photographic portrait studio, in New York. Sitters were illuminated by sunlight reflected by a large double-mirror arrangement through a rectangular tank of a blue-colored solution. (Daguerreotype plates were not sensitive to

red or green wavelengths; the "liquid filter" also reduced the heat somewhat.) Photographs were made with a unique camera of Wolcott's invention, for which he received the first patent in the United States relating to photography, in May 1840.

In order to gather enough light for the short exposures required in portraiture, the camera had a concave mirror mounted at the rear interior, instead of a lens. The mirror was 7 inches in diameter and had a focal length of 12 inches. It concentrated light onto a small (about 2-inch-square) daguerreotype plate that was mounted facing the mirror on a pedestal that could be moved to focus objects at various distances. The mirror principle had been known since before 1672, when Isaac Newton built the first reflecting telescope. It is possible that its photographic application was suggested by Henry Fitz, a telescope- and lens-maker, who actually designed and built Wolcott's camera. The idea came full circle with the invention of the Schmidt photographic telescope in 1930, which is essentially a precision-made

The Wolcott mirror camera measured 38.1 X 21.6 X 20.3 cm (15" X 8½" X 8"). The photographer focused by peering through the door at the top while moving the small pedestal either toward or away from the mirror. A focusing plate in the pedestal was replaced by a sensitized daguerreotype plate for the exposure, which was controlled by a cover (not shown) over the open end of the camera.

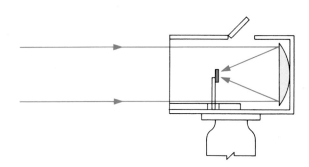

Wolcott camera with a corrector lens to eliminate mirror-induced aberrations.

To overcome the disadvantage of the small image size, Wolcott invented an enlarging copy camera, patented in 1843. The daguerreotype to be copied was placed in the camera at one end, where it was illuminated by sunlight directed through an opening in the top. A series of achromatic lenses enlarged and focused the image onto a daguerreotype plate or calotype (paper negative) material at the other end. The apparatus could be adjusted to provide various degrees of enlargement.

• *See also:* CAMERAS; HISTORY OF PHOTOGRAPHY.

Wollaston, William Hyde

(1766–1828)
English scientist

Trained as a physician, Wollaston gave up medicine for research in astronomy, optics, and metallurgy, in all of which he made significant contributions.

Investigating solar energy, Wollaston was the first to note the dark lines of the solar spectrum (named Faunhofer lines, after the scientist who investigated and classified them, inventing the science of spectroscopy). He then observed that paper sensitized with a silver chloride solution and exposed to a solar spectrum would begin darkening in response to invisible energy in the region beyond the visible violet. He attributed the action to what he called "chemical rays" to distinguish them from light rays; they are of course the ultraviolet. In this work, he duplicated and extended experiments that were fundamental to the invention of photography, first published by the Swedish chemist Carl Wilhelm Scheele in 1777.

Research into the optical properties of crystals led Wollaston to invent the goniometer to measure the angles of crystals. In 1807 he patented a prismatic drawing instrument called the camera lucida, because it formed images in full light rather than the dark enclosure of a camera obscura. In order to obtain improved images in the camera obscura, Wollaston invented the meniscus lens—which produced a flatter field than the simple double-convex lenses then in use—and incorporated it

in a periscopic camera obscura in 1812. (The meniscus was used for the first "eyes open" daguerreotype portraits of 1 to 2½ minutes' exposure by Susse, in France in 1839. At the same time, Alexander Wolcott was achieving 30-second portraits with a lensless camera in New York.)

Although he died eleven years before the daguerreotype was perfected, Wollaston knew of early progress toward the invention of photography. He was a vice-president and past secretary of the Royal Society, and met with Nicéphore Niépce in 1827. In the course of a trip to England, Niépce proposed to exhibit and discuss his "heliographic drawings" made with and without the camera obscura; the latter were contact prints from engravings. The offer was declined because full disclosure was one of the rules of the society's proceedings, but Niépce would not agree to reveal the details of his method for fear of losing a potential commercial advantage.

Wollaston's work in metallurgy laid the foundation for modern technology with such metals as tantalum, niobium, molybdenum, and tungsten. He made a fortune by devising a method of powdering platina and using heat, compression, and hammering to produce sheets of platinum in commercial quantities. He discovered the related metals rhodium and palladium, and the mineral Wollastonite is named in his honor.

• *See also:* CAMERAS; HISTORY OF PHOTOGRAPHY; NIÉPCE; NICÉPHORE; WOLCOTT, ALEXANDER S.

Woodbury, Walter Bentley

(1834–1885)
English professional photographer and inventor

Walter Woodbury is best known for the invention of a reproduction process, the Woodburytype, patented in 1864. Essentially a mass-production, mechanized method of making carbon prints, the Woodburytype produced exquisite true continuous-tone images completely free of grain, and without the halftone dot or line pattern required in other photomechanical reproduction processes. It was widely used from the 1860's until the turn of the century for the finest quality book illustrations, reproductions of art, and similar applications.

To make a Woodburytype, a gelatin-bichromate emulsion was exposed to a negative and then developed in warm water. The highlight and middletone areas that received less exposure washed away, leaving the relief thickest in the areas corresponding to the dark tone of the subject, where light passing through the negative had hardened the gelatin. The hardened relief was mounted on a firm backing and pressed into a sheet of very soft lead alloy (type metal) in a hydraulic press. The result was a mold in the metal. Five or six molds could be made from one gelatin relief, and more than 12,000 prints could be made from each mold.

Prints were made by filling the mold with a gelatin and pigment mixture—usually black or brown, but any color could be used—and pressing it in contact with the sheet being printed. The gelatin adhered to the sheet (the final support could also be glass, porcelain, or other materials), forming a positive image, because the mold—being deepest in the dark-tone areas—held more pigment in dark areas than in light areas.

As a professional photographer, Woodbury wanted his process to be used by individuals as well as for mass production, but the need for hydraulic presses made that impossible. He solved this problem by inventing a variation, the Stannotype, in 1879, for which he later received the Progress Medal of the Royal Society. In this process, the relief was made from a positive image, and a reverse mold formed by running it through a set of rubber rollers with a sheet of tinfoil. The mold could be strengthened by electroplating it with copper if several prints were desired, or new molds could be made quickly and easily.

Woodbury obtained more than 20 patents for a great variety of inventions. His apparatus for inexpensive aerial photography consisted of a camera with a continuous roll of sensitized paper, a clockwork mechanism to advance it, and a rotary shutter. These were actuated by an electromagnet, powered through a single wire running to a battery on the ground when the camera was hoisted by a small unmanned balloon.

Woodbury also made a number of improvements in projecting lanterns, kaleidoscopes, stereoscopes, exposure devices, cameras, barometers and hygrometers, and even railway signal systems.

• *See also:* CARBON AND CARBRO PRINTING.

Writing on Films and Papers

It is often necessary to mark numbers, names, titles, etc., on negatives or on prints, and there are several ways of doing so, depending upon whether a temporary or a permanent marking is required.

For permanent markings, it will be found that many ball-point pens will write on the emulsion side of negatives, and on all but the glossy surfaces of print papers. Some felt-tip pens and markers will mark on glossy surfaces, others will not, and it is usually necessary to try the marker in question to find out whether or not it will work. It is the inks that are solvent-based (rather than water-based) that mark on the glossy surfaces. These are usually labeled "permanent" or "waterproof."

For temporary markings on films and on the emulsion side of papers, you may use the well-known "china marker" type of crayon pencil; these come in a variety of colors, and their marks usually rub off quite easily. Kodak negative pencils are wax-based markers made specifically for photographic use. If any difficulty is encountered removing the mark of a china marker, a bit of lighter fluid will usually remove a mark quickly and cleanly.

One fault in the usual china marker is that its "lead" is quite thick; it makes broad marks that are, in some cases, unsightly. Further, if prints are stacked under pressure, the wax marks are likely to transfer. For marking in the margins of negatives, where very small writing may need to be done, there is a special type of pencil that appears to be a simple lead pencil but has the property of marking on smooth surfaces that would not accept the graphite of an ordinary pencil. Sold under various trademarks, the best known is the All-Stabilo made by Schwan in Germany. The most useful is the soft black No. 8008, which is obtainable in most art supply stores. Pencils of this type are also available in colors.

Fine, felt-tip solvent-type markers also write well on negatives. They work well on the emulsion side of all negatives, and on the base side of roll and sheet film negatives that have a gelatin back-coating. They may not work on the base side of 35 mm films.

Some "washable" felt-tip markers work quite well on the gelatin surfaces of prints and negatives.

Xenon Arc Lamp

In high-pressure lamps, xenon displays an essentially continuous spectrum throughout the ultraviolet, visible, and near-infrared. The color quality of xenon lamps is similar to that of daylight with a color temperature of 5000 to 6000 K. Typical continuous-burning short-arc lamps containing xenon gas have fused quartz bulbs with tungsten electrodes. Such lamps are usually run with a special power supply that may provide for dimming or fractional power settings. Since spectral output is not strongly dependent on operating pressure, lower power operation does not seriously affect the color temperature.

Pulsed Xenon Arc Lamps

The first approach to the use of xenon arc lamps for continuous-burning applications was a compromise. It was already known that flashtubes could be fired repetitively for short periods without excessive overheating. Thus, a new light source was developed for photomechanical use. This consisted simply of a bank of xenon-filled tubes operating through a special power supply that caused them to flash repeatedly at high rates so the light output appeared continuous. They are now used to illuminate copyboards of large process cameras. Other models are available for illuminating contact-printing frames.

The circuitry used with these lamps is somewhat different from that of electronic flash units. It is essentially a peaking circuit operating from the 60 Hz power line; it thus produces 120 flashes per second (one flash on each half of the ac cycle). The individual flashes are only about 1/1000 sec. in duration, so that the lamp has a duty cycle of about 1:8; this helps prevent overheating.

Typical examples of these lamps include the General Electric PXA lamps, which are made in both long straight models for copyboard illumination, and coiled types for contact-printing and platemaking. Others include the Ascorlux, and Xenolume lamp systems that differ mainly in their power-supply circuits.

Xenon Arcs for Projection

Small xenon arcs, such as the GE Marc-300 and the Sylvania Colorarc, are supplied for use in 16 mm projectors intended for auditorium projection. Their light output is comparable with a small high-intensity carbon arc, and it is adequate for pictures of 3 × 4 m (9' × 12') in size or larger, depending upon the type of screen used. These lamps have also been used in a few 8 mm projectors, and also in projectors for 50 × 50 mm (2" × 2") slides. They consume only 300 watts and have a life of about 25 hours, although they will still operate past that point. (Lamp life is rated as the time required to reach the point where output is 50 percent that of a new lamp.)

Unlike incandescent lamps, the xenon arc increases in luminance with wattage; thus, larger lamps are capable of producing brighter screen images. The xenon arc has replaced the high-intensity carbon arc lamp in many theaters. It is available in sizes from about 450 watts to as large as 4000 watts. For theatrical purposes, the lamp is designed for longer life at a somewhat higher initial cost. The 450-watt lamp is suited for small indoor theaters of up to 500 seats. The 4000-watt unit has sometimes been used in large drive-in theaters.

It is important to emphasize that xenon arc lamps cannot be used interchangeably in ordinary projectors. They must be operated through their specially designed power supplies, and the power supply must be matched exactly to the lamp in use.

• *See also:* ELECTRONIC FLASH; LIGHTING; PHOTOMECHANICAL REPRODUCTION METHODS; PROJECTORS.

Xerography

Xerography is an electrophotographic method of producing images. Exposure forms an image pattern of electrostatic charges that is equivalent to the latent image of conventional photography. This charge pattern attracts particles of pigment to develop the image to a visible state. In fixation, the pigment is permanently fused to a base material by radiant energy or by the action of a solvent.

In its fundamental form, xerography is a completely dry process (Greek *xeros* = "dry"), although some variations of the process may develop or fix the image with liquids. It is primarily employed for copying documents, drawings, diagrams, and halftone reproductions in offices, animation studios, reprographic concerns, and similar locations. Advanced equipment can also make reproductions from transparencies, in full-color if desired, or use a laser beam to create images from digital inputs as generated by a computer. In the latter case, the xerographic image is not a copy, but an original in the fullest sense.

Depending upon the equipment and the particular process used, current xerographic machines can produce black-and-white copies at a rate of more than 3000 an hour; color copies can be produced at between 100 and 200 copies an hour. Xerographic machines are self-contained and require no special training to operate. No stencil or duplicating master is required, and the copies are completely dry as they emerge from the machine.

Electrostatic Sensitizing

Xerography depends on the formation of an electrostatic charge on either the photoconductive selenium coating of a metal plate, paper with a zinc oxide coating, or a transparent film-base material.

The electrostatic surface charge is produced by a corona discharge of energy created when a high voltage is applied to a single fine wire or a screen of wires close to the photoconductive surface. Generally, a positive charge is created on a selenium plate and film-base materials, a negative charge on zinc oxide papers. Metal plates are commonly mounted on a drum that revolves past the discharge source.

The electrostatic charge sensitizes the coating so that it can be affected by exposure; it will remain at a useful strength from about 20 seconds to an hour or more, depending on the material, the coating, and atmospheric conditions. Sensitizing does not change the chemical or physical composition of the coating, so the charge can be renewed as required.

The subsequent steps in xerography are exposure, development, image transfer, and fixing. All the steps except fixing depend upon electrical charges and photoconductivity.

Exposure

The sensitized surface can be exposed in a camera system or by contact. Most xerographic copying machines are essentially self-processing camera systems in which a lens and mirror system focuses an image of the subject onto the electrostatically sensitized surface. This offers the possibility of making enlarged or reduced images by changing lens elements or object-image distances in the optical system. Conventional cameras are not suitable for exposure, primarily because of the difficulty of insulating the sensitized material so that its charge cannot be neutralized. Systems in which the exposure is made directly onto the final print material, rather than onto a transfer plate, often employ contact exposure.

The exposing energy may be light, x-rays, or other radiation. The fundamental sensitivity to light in a black-and-white copier is in the blue-violet region. Electrophotographic coatings with extended-range sensitivity have a response that is essentially panchromatic. Such materials are exposed through color separation filters in order to produce color copies.

Exposure makes the sensitized coating conductive so that the surface charge is reduced or erased in each exposed area. When exposure is made to a positive image, what remains on the plate, film, or oxide paper is a pattern of charged areas that correspond to the dark portions of the subject—an electrostatic latent image.

Development

The image is made visible by treatment with a colored pigment powder; for the moment, only the single powder used for black-and-white copies will be considered. The powder, or *toner,* has an electrical charge that causes it to be attracted to either the charged or the uncharged areas of the latent image. For positive-to-positive reproduction, the toner has a charge opposite that of the latent image. Therefore, it is attracted to the charged portions and develops the dark subject areas.

Electrostatic sensitizing in xerography: (A) As the dielectric coating passes a corona discharge unit, an electrostatic charge is created on the surface. Either the corona unit or the coated unit may move, depending only on design decisions. (B) The sensitizing charge is uniform over the entire coated surface, and it may be negative or positive. Exposure in xerography: (C) Light causes the sensitized coating to become conductive, so that the charge is neutralized in the exposed areas. (D) The remaining charge-pattern is a latent image that corresponds to the dark portions of the exposing subject or image. Development of the xerographic image: (E) In positive-to-positive reproduction, a toner with an opposite charge is attracted to the latent image charges. (F) In negative-to-positive reproduction, the toner has a like charge; it is repelled by the charged areas and is deposited in the uncharged areas. (G) Either method results in the development of the dark areas of the image. There will be a distinct dot pattern composed of unfused particles of toner. Continuous-tone development: (H) The latent-image charge is strong at the borders of areas, causing strong development of lines and edges. Weaker charges across unexposed areas result in insufficient deposits of toner. (I) A development electrode can equalize the charges across large areas; therefore they attract equal amounts of toner for full development. Image transfer: (J) As the print material and the developed image pass under a corona discharge, toner is attracted to the print sheet. (The distance between them is greatly exaggerated for clarity. (K) In single-image reproduction, all the toner is transferred; multiple reproduction takes only part of the toner for each copy. Fixing the xerographic image: (L) The image is fused to the print material by heat, radiant energy, or solvent vapor. (M) The final image is a positive reproduction of the exposing image.

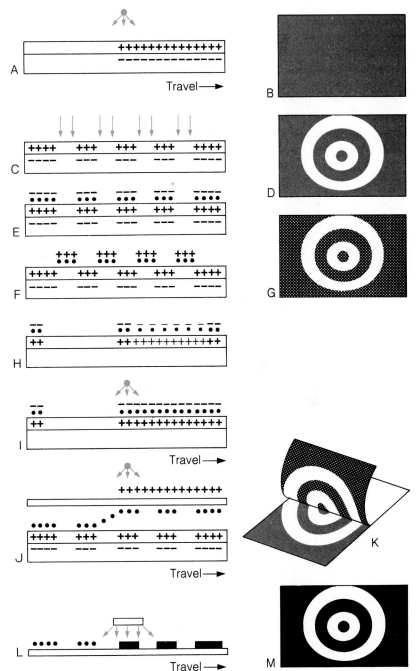

In negative-positive reproduction, exposure to a negative causes the charged portions of the latent image to correspond to the subject highlights. To develop a positive image, the toner has the same charge so that it is repelled by the charged portions and is attracted to the uncharged portions of the latent image. Again, the toner brings out the dark areas of the subject.

There are several methods of applying the toner to develop the image. In *cascade development,* the developer consists of large carrier particles that have a weak charge capable of attracting a coating of toner particles. As the developer is sifted or cascaded over the latent image, the stronger image charges attract the toner from the carriers. Carrier particles that have lost some toner are capable of picking up any that has floated free; as a result, this kind of development produces images with good contrast and clean backgrounds.

In *magnetic-brush* development, the toner particles cling to larger ferromagnetic particles that are attracted to the pole of a magnet. As the coated magnet brushes over the image surface, toner is attracted and held according to the negative-positive charge relationship. *Powder cloud* development uses many closely spaced air jets to blow appropriately charged toner across the latent image. *Liquid development* is achieved by mist-spraying, floating, or immersing the charged surface in a liquid such as a hydrocarbon that holds the toner particles in colloidal suspension. Electrophoresis causes toner to precipitate out of the liquid onto the appropriately charged image areas.

The charged areas of the latent image have fringe fields that hold the toner particles in place. These are strongest at the edges of charged areas and so provide good development of lines and edges. However, the electrostatic charge is considerably weaker across the center of a large area, with the result that weak and uneven deposits of toner may be formed. This can be counteracted by the use of a development electrode to create a charge of equal strength throughout such areas as the toner is being applied.

If development has taken place on the surface of the final image-bearing material, the last step is fixing. In selenium-plate xerographic systems, the developed image must be transferred from the image plate to the final base material before fixing.

Transfer

A sheet of paper or suitable transparency material is brought very close to or in contact with the developed image surface as it passes beneath a corona discharge electrode. A charge is induced in the receiving material that is stronger than the charge on the selenium plate, and the toner pigment is attracted from the plate to the image sheet. When several copies are to be made from one exposure, the transfer charge can be adjusted so that only part of the toner is transferred each time. The density and covering power of the toner after fixation is sufficient to assure that there is little difference between the quality of a single copy and of multiple copies.

Fixing

The image is made permanent by fusing it to the surface of the print material. This can be done by heat or radiant energy above about 120 C (248 F), which melts the toner, or by the vapor of a solvent that causes the toner to become tacky and adhere to the print material.

Color Xerography

The principles of color separation photography and subtractive color image formation can be used to provide full-color reproductions from full-color opaque or transparency originals. In equipment with this capability, it is also possible to obtain single-color separations from a full-color original, or a single-color copy of a black-and-white original. Three separate subtractive color toners are used—cyan, magenta, and yellow. From these toners, seven colors can be created: red, blue, green, cyan, magenta, yellow, and black.

A full-color copy requires three exposure-development cycles before the final image is fixed:

1. The xerographic drum or plate is exposed to the original through a green filter; the resulting image is developed with a magenta toner and transferred to the copy paper.
2. An image is exposed through a blue filter, developed with a yellow toner, and transferred in exact registration over the magenta toner.
3. The final exposure is through a red filter; the image is developed with a cyan toner and transferred in exact registration over the magenta and yellow toners.

To achieve this image, the photographer made a picture of her own face by placing it in direct contact with the scanning glass of a color photocopier. The print was then put through the machine several more times to accumulate the desired number of overlays. As few as three and as many as twelve overlays may be added to any one image. Photo by Susan Kaprov.

Then the composite image is fused to the copy paper. (The principles by which red, green, and blue filters analyze a full-color image and the principles of subtractive color synthesis are covered in the articles COLOR SEPARATION PHOTOGRAPHY and COLOR THEORY.) Individual colors can be printed by adjusting the copier controls for just one or two exposure-development cycles with selected toners.

• *See also:* COLOR SEPARATION PHOTOGRAPHY; COLOR THEORY; ELECTROPHOTOGRAPHY.

X-Ray

X-rays are a form of electromagnetic radiation discovered by Roentgen in 1895. In wavelength, they occupy a space in the electromagnetic spectrum just below the ultraviolet, and they range from "hard" x-rays (about 0.5 nm) to "soft" or Grenz rays (about 10 nm). The hard rays are so-called because of their greater penetrating power.

Film

X-rays affect photographic films in much the same way as light. Since, however, a film is affected only by radiation which it absorbs, and since x-rays pass freely through many substances, including photographic emulsion, special films are usually provided for use in radiography. Most of these films have a relatively thick layer of emulsion on each side of the base, so as to absorb as many of the rays as possible and thus secure denser images. This is especially important in medical and dental work, where it is desired to keep the exposure of the patient to these potentially damaging rays to the absolute minimum. Most medical x-ray films are used with intensifying screens, which increase the light energy to the film, further reducing patient exposure.

Airport Security

In recent years, a system of x-ray baggage checking has been in use at airports. In this system, a very short exposure is given, and the image is amplified by a photomultiplier system, similar to a television system. It is generally claimed that the exposure is short enough so as not to do any damage to photographic films carried in luggage. There is some question as to whether this is actually the case, especially in many foreign airports. In any case, if the journey requires several changes of planes at different airports, a film may receive a total exposure which, being cumulative, can cause definite fogging. For this reason, it is well to carry films in a separate bag, and to insist on hand inspection of this bag at the airport inspection station.

Some supposedly protective bags, made of paper and lined with lead foil, are offered for sale to travelers; it is claimed that enclosing films in these bags will protect them from x-rays. It is dubious whether the relatively thin lead foil used in these bags has any great effectiveness in protecting films from cumulative radiation exposure, and it is probably better to insist upon hand inspection.

• *See also:* RADIOGRAPHY; SPECTRUM.

Yearbook Photography

Every year, numerous photographs are reproduced in school yearbooks. Although most of the photography is done by large firms who specialize in school photography, many yearbook pictures are taken by students who have a more intimate knowledge of the school, its faculty, and its students. However, there is nothing to prevent a photographer or a group of photographers from bidding for the yearbook photography at a certain school. Requests for the opportunity to bid should be made to the school principal or to the editor of the school's yearbook.

Professional yearbook photography should not be undertaken without giving some consideration to the nature of the work. The number of students, student groups, and individuals to be photographed may seem overwhelming to the uninitiated. In addition, it is a seasonal business, and the yearbook's publication deadline must be met regardless of how much photography is involved. Photographers interested in entering the field can obtain information from School Photographers Association, Professional Photographers of America, 1090 Executive Way, DesPlaines, Illinois 60616.

Equipment

The majority of professional yearbook photography is done on 70 mm bulk film in 100-foot rolls. Two cameras in this field are the Nord and the Beattie-Coleman Portronic. The latter can accommodate 35 mm film stock and expose 70 mm as either 70 mm, or 70 mm split-frame. Some yearbook photography uses 46 mm film for greater economy.

Student Participation in Yearbook Photography

Different schools have different policies in regard to what is published in the yearbook, but the yearbook staff will usually decide the ratio of student photography to outside professional work. However, the availability of good-quality student pictures of the right kind might easily determine what this ratio will be. A student photographer with a good camera and some imagination can make a valuable photographic contribution to the yearbook. He or she is on the spot to photograph impromptu scenes, is aware of events that are taking place, and is able to mix freely with other students at any time. Thus, the student photographer has a great advantage over the professional in this respect.

What to Photograph

Yearbook editors are much like any other editors in that they prefer photographs that are unusual, that seem to live, or that have a touch of humor. Humor in photography, whether by a professional or a student, is difficult to achieve; be careful not to make anyone seem ridiculous.

Sporting events yield many good yearbook pictures, but try to photograph the unusual or the spectacular, rather than the hackneyed. Do not neglect practice sessions. Sometimes pictures of these situations can tell more about a team or an individual player than a regular game picture can. Be sure to ask the coach's permission, however.

A classroom setting offers many picture-taking opportunities, but again, be sure to ask the teacher's permission. Many classes will be carrying out special projects or activities that should be recorded. Keep in contact with the teachers; know what they are

(Left) Imaginative student photographers may have the advantage over professionals by their on-the-spot availability to photograph impromptu scenes. This eye-stopper was made by a high school student who chose a high camera angle to take advantage of the streamers converging on her center of interest. Photo by Carol Weisman.

A

B

C

D

Classroom photographs should be included in the yearbook. Keep track of special projects or activities, and always be sure to have the teacher's permission.

doing. Classroom pictures can be serious studies of teacher and students hard at work.

Groups and clubs often meet after school and are usually pleased to have pictures taken of their activities. Again, it is wise to ask the club adviser's permission before proceeding. Many groups meet after school when outside light gets dim, so be prepared to take flash pictures or existing-light pictures. Parties also provide picture-taking opportunities,

particularly if the photographer is able to move around and take unposed pictures of guests.

Keep informed about special events such as appearances of guest speakers, dedications, and ground-breaking ceremonies. Be particularly alert to the many opportunities for good, informal pictures that exist around every school. It is rarely possible to set up informal pictures without making them look artificial, so look for unusual and interesting

(Facing page) Sports events are an important part of most yearbooks, but care must be taken to avoid the obvious. (A) A pre-game scene photographed by existing light in the locker room is much more interesting than the usual "lineup" shown in most team photographs. (B) A record-setting broad jump is best recorded by the selection of a good camera angle; the sports photographer must learn to anticipate action such as this. (C) Mud and bad weather often plague sporting events; this should not discourage the photographer. (D) Pep talks and winning moments are not the only side of athletic events. Here, an alert photographer caught the coach in one of his less cheerful moods.

(Below) Graduation is obviously the most important event of the school year. While it is popular to depict the new graduates as "solemn" or "hopeful," many of them look just like this one.

(Below left) Certain subjects really lend themselves to photographic illustration. Move in close to show detail. *(Below right)* Pictures of spectators add variety to photo coverage of sports events and other entertainment. Keep such crowd shots close enough so that the subjects remain individualized.

(Facing page) Good informal portraits reveal the many faces of a campus. Use existing light with an uncluttered background, and move in close. Then concentrate on getting a natural expression.

pictures in the midst of the ordinary—in the halls, on the school grounds, or in the cafeteria.

Tips for Better Pictures

Here are a few simple hints for making good yearbook pictures.

1. Avoid cluttered foregrounds and include only a few things in each picture. Do not forget to look behind the subject to make sure that the background is not distracting.
2. Get pictures of people—people are interesting and make news—but do not shoot large groups, especially "line-ups."
3. Get close. People like to see things up close.
4. Do not leave large gaps between the subjects.
5. Capture action. Have people doing something, but do not forget the spectators. They may be newsworthy, too.

Reproducing Pictures for the Yearbook

No printing process can reproduce the full range of tones found in a good photo. The printer must try to hold detail in the important light and dark parts of the picture. It is true that a skilled printer can make some high-contrast and low-contrast pictures look acceptable, but this can be costly and time-consuming, and results will be inferior to those obtained from a print with normal contrast.

A print does not have to be glossy for best results. Any smooth photographic paper will do—a white-base paper is preferable. Some printers prefer prints on glossy paper that has been dried without the glossy finish.

The best print for yearbook reproduction should have the following characteristics:

1. A sharp image on smooth, white paper, with highlights that are clean-looking, not gray.
2. A full range of tones, from clean whites through many intermediate grays, to a good, deep black.
3. Detail in all important areas of the picture. This is especially true of the highlight areas, the lighter tones of the picture. Usually the tonal range of the print should include a deep black.

Such prints are achieved by good, basic photography—correct exposure, correct processing of the negative, and correct printing. If you make your own prints, you will have no problem; if someone else makes them, accept for reproduction only those prints that fit the above description.

• *See also:* AVAILABLE-LIGHT PHOTOGRAPHY; CANDID PICTURES; CAREERS IN PHOTOGRAPHY; COMMENCEMENT-DAY PICTURES; EXISTING-LIGHT PHOTOGRAPHY; FLASH PHOTOGRAPHY; NEWS PHOTOGRAPHY; SPORTS PHOTOGRAPHY.

Young, Thomas

(1773–1829)
English scientist and physician

Young made numerous investigations into the nature of light, and laid the foundations for the wave theory of light by his explanations of a number of interference phenomena, which until that time were not completely understood. In 1802, Young propounded a theory of color, which stated that color is a sensation, not a substance, and that as far as the viewer is concerned, the sensation produced by any color can be matched by a proper mixture of three fundamental colors called "primaries." Artists had been mixing colors for years without any systematic knowledge of why it could be done. Young postulated the existence of three color receptors in the human eye, one sensitive to each primary color. Based on Young's observations, Helmholtz later organized a comprehensive theory of color, known today as the "Young-Helmholtz Color Theory." The success of color photography, which is based on Young's three primary colors theory, attests to the fundamental correctness of his ideas.

Zeiss, Carl

(1816–1888)
Head of the famous Carl Zeiss Jena Works, German
manufacturers of lenses, cameras, binoculars, microscopes,
and many other types of optical instruments

Zeiss formed the Zeiss foundation to support scientific research and publishing. In much the same way that George Eastman gathered scientists together to do research on photography, Zeiss gathered optical scientists together to further the knowledge of optics. Chief among these scientists were Professor Ernst Abbe and Dr. Paul Rudolph.

Zeiss had Abbe collaborate with the Otto Schott Glass Works (also in Jena) in the development of the new barium optical glasses that revolutionized lens design. Abbe and Rudolph designed many camera lenses that became famous.

Zeiss made Abbe a partner, and when Zeiss died, Abbe became the sole proprietor of the Carl Zeiss Works. He in turn set up the business so that the employees eventually became the owners.

After World War II, the Western powers moved much of the Zeiss factory to West Germany. The East Germans later reactivated the Jena factory, however, so that today there are two Zeiss factories.

Zirconium Arc Lamp

The zirconium arc lamp is also known as a "concentrated arc" lamp. It consists of a glass envelope that contains a tubular cathode filled with zirconium oxide. The cathode is surrounded by a metal ring-shaped anode. The arc forms between the two and emits a well-defined circular spot of light.

At the temperature of the arc, the molten zirconium-cathode surface provides a high-luminance output. Color temperature is about 3000 to 3200 K. The cathode diameter varies from about 0.08 mm (0.003 inch) for the 2-watt lamp, to about 1.5 mm (0.06 inch) for the 100-watt lamp. The small size and high brightness of the source make the zirconium arc useful for microscope illumination.

It has been found that the light of the zirconium lamp can be modulated with an audio-frequency signal, and these lamps have been used in "light-beam sound transmission" systems.

Zoetrope

This early toy, which created the illusion of a moving picture, was popular before the introduction of cinematography. Essentially, the zoetrope consisted of a light metal cylinder, about 12 inches or larger in diameter, mounted on a shaft so it could be spun by hand. The top half of the cylinder contained a series of equally spaced slits. Around the inside of the lower half was a strip of paper containing a series of drawings like an animated cartoon. There were as many pictures around the paper strip as there were slots in the upper part of the drum.

When the drum was set in motion, by looking through the slits, one could see the successive pictures, each visible for only an instant. The effect was that of a continuously moving picture, repeating at each revolution of the cylinder.

A similar toy, working in the same manner but differently made, was the praxinoscope.
• *See also:* PRAXINOSCOPE; ZOOPRAXISCOPE.

Zone Focusing

For fast-breaking news stories, sports events, and similar action subjects, there is often no time to focus for each individual picture. In this case, a system known as "zone focusing" is used: The photographer estimates where the action is likely to take place and sets the camera focus and aperture so that the depth of field will take care of any likely movement of the subject.

Some inexpensive cameras utilize a variation of this system. Instead of a focusing scale marked in metres or feet, it has two or three lens settings, marked for "portraits," "full-length figures," and "landscapes." In some cases, the camera scale is not marked in words but merely has small pictures or symbols representing the three types of subjects. Generally, these cameras have lenses of small aperture and great depth of field, and the zone focusing system is quite adequate for all ordinary purposes.
• *See also:* DEPTH OF FIELD; FOCUSING SYSTEMS; HYPERFOCAL DISTANCE; VIEWING AND FOCUSING.

Zone System

The zone system is a practical, methodical approach to contrast and tone control in black-and-white photography. It is intended to permit the photographer to "previsualize" the expressive tonal range of a final print of a subject, and then to select an exposure and development combination that will produce a negative that will yield the desired image on a normal-contrast-grade paper with straightforward, un-manipulated printing techniques.

The zone system is, in fact, a refinement of the principle "expose for the shadows and develop for the highlights," adapted to modern panchromatic films, which cannot be developed by inspection. It expands this basic approach to allow a decision as to which shadows or dark areas to expose for and what dark print tone will represent them, and to control which key highlight value will be represented by a particular light tone in the print.

Ansel Adams and Fred Archer first formulated the zone system about 1939 for use as a teaching and learning method for their students at the Art Center School in Los Angeles. It was not an invention, but a codifying of what had been learned about the behavior of photographic materials since the invention of sensitometry by Hurter and Driffield in the 1870's and 80's. It attempted to provide a workable system for photographers who had no knowledge of sensitometry, but who wanted pragmatic methods of control to solve practical problems of photographic expression.

The zone system was first fully explained in print in Book 2, *The Negative,* and Book 3, *The Print,* of Adams' *Basic Photo Series.* (Current editions are published by Amphoto, Garden City, NY.) The system has been adapted, expanded upon, and interpreted by many others, leading to a number of "tone control" methods that for the most part are only slight modifications of the basic zone system. Of all the material produced, two works are especially valuable supplements to the Adams books in studying the zone system. These are *The New Zone System Manual,* by White, Zakia, and Lorenz (1975), and *Zone Systemizer,* by Dowdell and Zakia (1973); both are published by Morgan and Morgan, Dobbs Ferry, NY.

Zones and Gray Scales

The concept of a "zone" is related to the way black-and-white photography reproduces subject brightnesses—as a continuous range of tones from black to white.

Since basic photographic controls are related to doubling or halving exposure—one-stop changes—it is convenient to mark off corresponding intervals across the continuous gray scale. If the space between these intervals is equally divided, each one-stop interval marks the midpoint of a small local range, or *zone,* of gray tones. The tonal range in any one zone is what would be produced by up to a half-stop less and a half-stop more exposure than that of the midpoint.

There is a small range of subject brightnesses that will produce the exposures represented in any one zone; they will be recorded as a corresponding

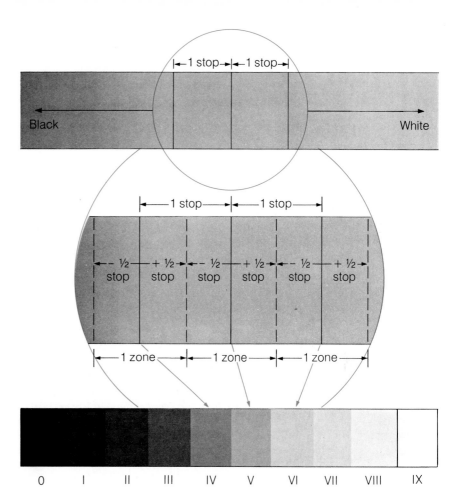

Formation of a stepped, or zoned, gray scale. (A) A continuous-tone photographic scale can be divided into intervals equivalent to one-stop exposure differences. (B) Each interval can be considered the midpoint of half-stop variations in exposure; the local tones on each side of such a midpoint comprise one zone. (C) The midpoint gray tones are used to represent all others in each step of a zoned gray scale. The print equivalents of the tones in each zone are described in the text.

range of densities in the negative, and they will be reproduced as a corresponding range of tones in a print. Thus the concept of the zone as an exposure range links subject, negative, and print.

Originally, "zone" was used to identify the steps in all of these interrelated ranges. However, it is clearer to refer to subject brightness (or luminance) values, negative density values, and print tone values. The term *zone* is used to refer to the exposure scale of the negative, not the recorded densities. It is a conceptual term that is especially useful for relating negative exposures to a stepped or zoned gray scale.

It is neither practical nor convenient to make reference to a continuous-tone gray scale, because there are no established reference points. It is easier to let the midpoint gray tone in each zone stand for all the other, closely related grays in that zone. This divides the gray scale into a series of steps, producing a zoned gray scale or a "zone ruler." The zoned scale is divided into 10 steps from black to white, because the average outdoor, sun-illuminated subject as measured with a meter typically has about a 9-stop range (from zone 0 to zone IX is 9 stops) from subject areas to be recorded as total black in the print, to areas to be recorded as white with no detail.

Normal film can record and normal-grade paper can print many more than 10 shades of gray, of course, but they are intermediate shades produced by small negative exposure differences. A film developing time is found by trial and error that will produce a negative density range that will print this normal subject range on normal-contrast-grade paper with a given enlarger. Normal-contrast paper is considered to be No. 2 grade in the United States, but may be No. 3 grade in Europe. This paper, with

The average outdoor subject, illuminated by sunlight, typically has a range of about 9 stops between areas that record as total black and those that record as white with no detail. Photo by George Zucconi.

its 10 zones as printed, becomes the standard in the zone system. While the average subject has 10 zones, there are subjects that have very bright values that produce zone X, XI, XII, and higher exposures, and negatives can produce correspondingly higher densities. The standard paper, however, cannot print that many full-stop steps. The practical photographic problem that the zone system is designed to solve is how to reproduce the brightness range of the subject, whatever it is, within the given value range of the print.

Zone Numbers

The steps of a zoned gray scale are numbered in terms of their corresponding negative exposure steps, or zones. Roman numerals are used to prevent confusion with the figures used for shutter speeds, *f*-numbers, and the like, and to serve as a reminder that "zone" is a concept, not a physical entity. The zone numbers and corresponding print values are:

0 Complete black, without texture or detail; the maximum black the paper can produce.

I Almost black; the first distinguishable tone lighter than maximum black; first sign of shadow-area detail, but without texture.

II Deep gray-black; first tone in which some texture may be recorded in shadow details, depending upon the subject.

III Gray-black; the first step to record full texture in shadow details; usually the key zone in determining the actual exposure.

IV Dark gray; the tone that usually represents major shadow values.

V Middle gray; the pivotal zone of the scale; a tone equivalent to the gray of an 18-percent reflectance neutral test card. Most exposure meters are calibrated to indicate exposures that will reproduce the metered brightness as a zone V gray. Represents dark skin.

VI Gray; commonly represents average sunlighted Caucasian skin tones and equivalent brightness values.

VII Light gray; textured highlights; lightest tone in which full texture can be recorded.

VIII Very-light gray, off-white; the last trace of untextured detail.

IX Complete white; the maximum white the paper can produce; no evidence of response to exposure.

Zoned steps from 0 to IX are indicated on this photograph. Some of the tonal values apparent in the original print may be lost in the screen process used to print this volume. See the text for print values corresponding to the zone numbers. Photo by George Zucconi.

In the zone system, the actual exposure for a picture is chosen to place a key value in a selected zone. For example, assume that the meter-indicated exposure of the wall at the left was Zone IV (dark gray), but that the photographer wished to bring out more detail. He therefore would have exposed it for Zone VI. In so doing, the wall at the right, which might originally have exposed as Zone VII, is now moved up the scale to Zone IX. Ordinarily, this would result in complete loss of detail. Appropriate development, however, brought the lighter values back down the scale to Zone VII, the point where texture could once again be recorded. Photo by George Zucconi.

Zones and Exposure

Two principles are fundamental to understanding how the zone approach to exposure is used.

1. Each zone represents the effect of an exposure that is one stop different from the exposures that produce the tones in each of the adjacent zones.
2. Any single subject value can be exposed so that it will register in any selected zone.

Averaging exposure meters calculate zone V exposures. If you take a reading of a black shirt, the meter-indicated exposure will cause it to print as a middle gray. But because of principle number 1 above, if you give one stop less exposure—that is, expose it in zone IV—it will print as the next darker gray; if you give two stops less exposure, it will print two steps darker. Similarly, a subject value can be moved up the gray scale by giving one stop more exposure than the meter indicates for each step of change that is desired.

This technique is called *placing* exposure. In the zone system, the actual exposure for a picture is chosen to place a key value—usually a dark area—in a selected zone.

However, when exposure is changed for one value, all other values are similarly affected. When a black shirt is given two stops less than meter-indicated exposure, a light-gray rock, a piece of white paper, and all other elements in the picture will also be shifted two zones down the scale. But, the lighter values can be shifted back up the scale by appropriate development.

Thus, exposure determines how dark values are recorded, and development controls how middle and light values are recorded.

True Film Speed

Although zones represent the effect of full-stop differences in exposure, they are not represented by equal differences in negative density values. Smaller density differences result in the darkest tones because they are recorded on the toe of the characteristic curve of a film's response, where equal exposure increases produce smaller density increases than on the straight-line portion of the curve (where middle and highlight values are recorded). This has the advantage of producing negatives with normal middle tone and highlight densities so that graininess is not increased, but it demands precise exposure—there is no latitude for underexposure.

Precise exposure depends on knowing the true speed of a film for *your working conditions*. The assigned ASA speed is an accurate indication of a film's sensitivity under standard test conditions. But your lens apertures, lens and camera flare, meter response, developer formula, and developing procedures may not add up to standard test conditions; it is likely you will obtain optimum results by using an adjusted film-speed rating, or personal exposure index (EI).

In practical terms, true film speed is indicated by the exposure required to produce enough negative density to print the first visible tone lighter than maximum black. In terms of zones, maximum black results from zone 0 exposure, which is no exposure at all; the only density in the negative is that of the film base plus the inevitable trace of chemical fog produced by development (gross fog). The first printable tone is produced by the density that results from a zone I exposure. This represents the minimum amount of exposure to which the film can respond. The following test will identify a zone I exposure; then determine the true film speed.

Film-Speed Test

1. Set up an even-toned light-gray surface large enough to fill the camera's field of view. Keep the lens focused at infinity so that *f*-stop settings will have maximum accuracy; focus is not important, only exposure for tone. Light the surface evenly; check this carefully with a meter.

2. Take a reflected-light meter reading from the test surface, with the meter set at the manufacturer's ASA rating for the film. The meter will indicate equivalent zone V exposures.

3. You want to test for zone I exposures, four stops less than zone V, so calculate downward from the meter indications to arrive at an exposure that is four stops less. For example, if the meter indicates 1/30 at *f*/4, you might calculate 1/125 at *f*/8—two shutter speeds faster and two *f*-stops smaller total, the equivalent of a four-stop reduction in exposure. This is the "calculated zone I exposure."

4. Make the following exposure series of the test surface. Vary the *f*-stop setting, not the shutter speed, for the greatest accuracy.

(a) Calculated zone I exposure.
(b) One stop more exposure than (a).
(c) Two stops more exposure than (a).
(d) One stop less exposure than (a).
(e) Two stops less exposure than (a).
(f) A blank exposure, with the lens cap on. This will provide a blank piece of film for a zone 0 reference.

5. Process the film. Use your usual developer and normal developing time. However, the developer formula is important. If you decide to use a different developer at a later time, you should repeat this film-speed test. A true film speed is valid only for a particular emulsion and developer combination, and a single developing time at a given temperature and a consistent agitation.

6. Evaluate the negatives to identify the zone I exposure, either with a densitometer, or by a practical printing test. In any event, the printing test should be used to confirm densitometer results on the basis of actual printing conditions.

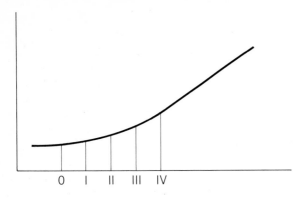

True film speed can be determined from the minimum exposure required to produce the first tone distinguishable from maximum black in a print. This is the zone I exposure. Zone 0 represents no exposure effect at all; the negative density is merely that of the film base plus fog.

(a) Densitometer method. Read the density of the blank exposure to determine zone 0 (film-base-plus-fog, or fb-f) density. Read the density of each of the other exposures. Identify the exposure that is approximately 0.1 greater than fb-f density. In practice, the density of this exposure may range from 0.075 to 0.15 more than fb-f. This is the zone I exposure. Check your results with the printing test. Lower values (0.075 to 0.10) are better for negatives to be printed on condenser enlargers, while 0.10 to 0.15 values are better for negatives to be printed on diffusion enlargers.

(b) Printing test. Expose a piece of printing paper for a short time to raw white light, and process it to obtain a maximum-black reference patch. Insert the blank exposure negative in the enlarger, and raise the enlarger to cover the area of your usual prints. Make a stepped test strip through the blank film to determine the *minimum* time required to produce a maximum black. (*See:* TEST STRIPS.) Compare the test-strip steps with the maximum-black reference patch to do this. This is your standard printing time. Use the standard printing time to print each of the other test exposures. Do not change *f*-stops. Compare them with the reference patch to determine which one shows a tone just lighter than maximum black. This is the zone I exposure.

7. Refer back to the actual exposures you made to the test surface to determine the film speed:

If zone I exposure resulted from	True film speed is
Calculated zone I exposure	ASA speed
+1 stop	ASA ÷ 2
+2 stops	ASA ÷ 4
−1 stop	ASA × 2
−2 stops	ASA × 4

Use the true film speed to make all zone system light readings and exposure calculations. It, not the manufacturer's ASA rating, is your personal exposure index for that film-developer combination.

Basic Zone System Procedure

The zone system deals with subject luminance values, commonly called reflected-light brightnesses. Therefore, readings must be made with a reflected-light, not an incident-light, exposure meter. Two readings are required: one for a dark area, to *place* the shadow values and calculate actual exposure; the other for a light area, to see where the highlights *fall* and to determine the amount of development. The meter must be set to the true film speed of the emulsion in use.

Because it determines exposure, the dark value chosen for metering is of great importance. Usually it should be the darkest area in which you wish to see full texture and detail in the final print. In that case, it will be placed in zone III. Sometimes—especially in low-key photography—a major element is to be rendered as a distinct dark shape without local texture. A reading from that kind of area should be placed in zone II.

Placing Shadow Values. To place a value on zone III, simply take a meter reading (which will indicate zone V exposure) and calculate two stops *less* exposure. For example, if the meter reading of the shadowed side of a tree trunk is *f*/2.8 at 1/30, an exposure of *f*/5.6 at 1/30 will place it in zone III. (Another stop less exposure would place it in zone II.) You must be sure that the meter reading takes in only the textured dark area.

The calculated "placing" exposure—or an equivalent speed-aperture combination—is the actual exposure you must give to the film. In the above example, the camera controls should be set to *f*/5.6 at 1/30 (or equivalent) to take the picture.

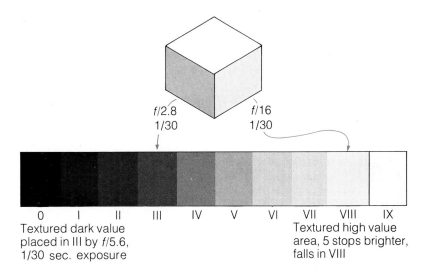

The basic zone system procedure utilizes meter readings made from the most important textured dark and light areas of the subject. Since the meter calculates a zone V exposure, reducing exposure two stops places the dark value in zone III. The highlight value is five stops brighter, so it falls five zones higher, in VIII. This is a normal range and indicates normal development. A "fall" in VII or lower would indicate the need for N+ development. Conversely, a reading of IX or higher would indicate N− development, as explained in text.

f/2.8
1/30

f/16
1/30

0   I   II   III   IV   V   VI   VII   VIII   IX

Textured dark value placed in III by f/5.6, 1/30 sec. exposure

Textured high value area, 5 stops brighter, falls in VIII

Highlight "Fall." Before exposing the film, determine where the highlights "fall," or will be registered, on the zone scale. Take a meter reading of the brightest textured subject area; often this is a white shirt in direct light, or a similar picture element. Do not read specular highlights such as reflections of light sources on water, glass, or polished surfaces.

Compare the dark-area meter reading (*not* the calculated "placing" exposure) with the highlight reading, and count the number of stops between them at a common shutter speed. For example, if the two readings are *f*/2.8 at 1/30 and *f*/16 at 1/30, there is a five-stop range (4, 5.6, 8, 11, 16). Thus the highlights will fall five zones higher than the zone in which the shadow values are exposed. In the example, the shadows are placed in zone III, so the highlights will fall in zone VIII.

A normal-range subject has this five-stop or five-zone spread, from III to VIII, between textured shadows and textured highlights. A longer or shorter range usually requires altered development. Note that many discussions identify an average or normal subject as one having a seven-stop brightness range. This simply indicates that measurements are made from areas that will not be rendered with full texture in the print—that is, values that will be exposed in zones I and VIII.

Zone System Development

Normal development is that which causes a subject luminance value to appear in its own zone of the final-print gray scale. For example, with a dark value placed in zone III and other important values falling in zones V, VII, and VIII as a result, normal development will produce negative densities that will give these areas corresponding step III, V, VII, and VIII grays in the print.

If a subject has a greater-than-normal brightness range, the textured highlight value will fall beyond zone VIII when the textured shadow value is placed in zone III. In that case, reduced or "normal-minus" (N−) development is required. Reduced development holds down negative densities; the degree of reduction is described in terms of the number of zones a particular value is shifted. For example, if a subject value that falls in zone IX is developed to just enough density to print as a normal zone VIII value, it has been shifted one zone down the scale. This is "normal-minus-one-zone," or N−1 development. N−2 development would cause an exposure value falling in zone X to print in zone VIII, and so on. "Minus" development compacts or compresses the subject-value range into the print-value range.

A "flat," or low-contrast, subject has a shorter-than-normal brightness range. To avoid a flat print, the negative can be given additional, "normal-plus" (N+) development. Normal-plus-one-zone (N+1) development expands the subject values within the print range by moving a zone VII value, for example, to an VIII print value.

Other values also move when plus and minus developments are used. The high values (VII–IX

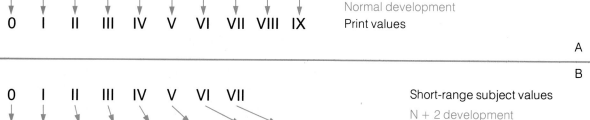

Zone system development. (A) Normal development produces negative densities that maintain the relative separation of subject values in a print. (B) Plus and minus developments shift the lightness in a print, but cannot change the sequence of the subject values. N+2 development expands a subject two zones; N−2 development compacts the subject the same amount. The degree of shift increases as the subject value becomes higher. Low values are established by exposure rather than development; therefore they shift only slightly. Changing the EI for N− and N+ development keeps a constant negative density in the I zone.

and up) are affected most; the middle values (IV–VI) shift less; and the low values (I–III) are affected hardly at all. Again: Negative exposure determines shadow values, and development controls highlights in the final print.

Normal and various plus and minus developments must be established by methodical tests with a given film-developer combination. Such tests are called zone system calibrations; they are beyond the scope of this article. The most comprehensive method of making calibrations with current materials is described in *The New Zone System Manual,* by White, Lorenz, and Zakia. A good set of calibration tests is also described in the *Zone VI Workshop,* by Fred Picker.

Changing developing times to change negative density ranges changes film speed. The speed is lowered at N− development, and it increases at N+ development. After the developing times have been found for each of the N− and N+ developments, a new test at each developing time must be run to find the exposure index. Although the amount of change differs with different film and developers, the following speed-change values can be used as starting figures for tests.

Development	Speed Loss
N−3	−1 stop
N−2	−⅔ stop
N−1	⅓ stop
N	none
N+1	+⅓ stop
N+2	+⅔ stop
N+3	+1 stop

For example, if your subject is very contrasty and you find that it needs an N−3 development, give one stop more exposure because the film loses approximately one stop with N−3 development.

Zone System Applications

The zone system achieves its greatest flexibility when used with sheet films, for they can be sorted into batches for various development treatments. Roll and 35 mm films often are exposed to subjects with a wide variety of brightness ranges. In such cases, the zone system method of determining exposure will insure that shadow values are properly recorded. Development is then determined by the most important images on the film, or by a tested normal standard; negatives that have other-than-normal contrast can be printed on compensating grades of paper.

Zone system concepts can also be applied to problems of color film exposure. The *Zone Systemizer,* by Dowdell and Zakia, has a useful discussion of this application.

An alternative method of finding developing times that give consistent negative density ranges and that compensate for the contrast controlling factors in the photographic process can be found in the article CONTRAST. This method utilizes nomographs and contrast-index curves to find developing times, and minimizes the amount of testing that has to be done.

• *See also:* BLACK-AND-WHITE PRINTING; CONTRAST; CONTRAST INDEX; DEVELOPERS AND DEVELOPING; EXPOSURE; EXPOSURE METERS AND CALCULATORS; EXPOSURE TECHNIQUES; GRAY CARD; GRAY SCALES; TEST STRIPS; TONE REPRODUCTION.

Further Reading: Adams, Ansel. *Basic Photo Series, Book 1: The Negative.* Boston, MA: New York Graphic Society, 1948; _____. *Basic Photo Series, Book 2: The Print.* Boston, MA: New York Graphic Society, 1950; Dowdell, John and Richard Zakia. *Zone Systemizer.* Dobbs Ferry, NY: Morgan & Morgan, 1973; Picker, Fred. *Zone VI Workshop.* Garden City, NY: Amphoto, 1974; Saltzer, Joseph. *A Zone System for All Formats.* Garden City, NY: Amphoto, 1978; Sanders, Norman. *Photographic Tone Control.* Dobbs Ferry, NY: Morgan & Morgan, 1977; White, Minor. *Zone System Manual.* Dobbs Ferry, NY: Morgan & Morgan, 1968; White, Minor, Peter Lorenz, and Richard Zakia. *The New Zone System Manual.* Dobbs Ferry, NY: Morgan & Morgan, 1976.

Zoom Lens

A zoom lens is a lens with a focal length that is continuously variable between certain limits. It permits the optical image to be varied in size without altering the focus. To zoom in on a subject means to enlarge it continuously and rapidly until it appears to be very close."

Development

Zoom lenses were developed originally for motion-picture photography, where smooth, uninterrupted changes in image size often enhance the visual impact of the scene being photographed. Still photographers were quick to appreciate the ability of the zoom lens to take the place of several fixed-focus lenses; today, zoom lenses with a wide variety of focal-length ranges are available.

Single-lens reflex cameras are especially well suited to the use of zoom lenses, because these cameras have the ideal viewing/focusing arrangement to utilize the zoom capability to great advantage.

Zoom Ratio. The relationship between the shortest and the longest zoom settings is called the zoom ratio. It is derived by dividing both extremes of the zoom range by the minimum focal length. A 50–100 mm zoom lens has a zoom ratio of 1:2; an 80–240 mm zoom lens has a zoom ratio of 1:3; a 50–300 mm zoom has a ratio of 1:6. You may also see the zoom ratio expressed as a magnification factor that indicates how many times larger the image formed at the maximum focal length is compared to the image formed at the minimum focal length. This style of designation would render a 1:2 ratio as $2\times$, 1:3 as $3\times$, 1:6 as $6\times$, and so on.

Although the zoom ratio or factor is a convenient means of describing the "zoom power" of a zoom lens, it is not necessarily a valid criterion for

With a zoom lens, the image may be varied in size without changing the focus. When used in still photography, a variety of interesting special effects can be obtained. Photo courtesy Minolta Corp.

comparing zoom lenses, because lenses that produce dissimilar image sizes, and thus apparently dissimilar perspectives, can have identical zoom ratios. For example, a 25–50 mm zoom lens has the same 1:2 zoom ratio as a 100–200 mm zoom. The former yields images ranging from pronounced wide-angle to normal, while the latter covers a range from short telephoto to medium-long telephoto.

Design. To limit cost, lens size, and weight, most zoom lenses are designed to cover moderate zoom ratios of 1:2 or 1:3. More extreme zoom ratios are available, particularly for movie cameras. Common zoom ranges are wide-angle to normal, medium wide-angle to short telephoto, normal to medium telephoto, and short or medium telephoto to long telephoto.

Zoom lenses are internally complex because of the special optical and mechanical provisions required to permit changing the focal length while maintaining image sharpness on film. (*See:* LENSES.) One of the distinguishing characteristics of a true zoom lens, in fact, is its ability to hold focus regardless of changes in focal length. (Lenses that permit changing focal length but do not hold focus are known as variable-focal-length lenses. They are less convenient to use than true zooms because they must be refocused each time the focal length is altered.)

In practice, the zoom control of a modern zoom lens not only changes the lens focal length by altering the relative spacing of the lens elements, but also makes other movements within the lens to maintain constant focus and light transmission.

Using Zoom Lenses

A more practical point of differentiation among zoom lenses is the method of controlling the zoom setting. Some zoom lenses have a single control for zooming and focusing, usually in the form of a large, textured collar or ring concentric with the lens barrel. Rotating the collar changes focus, while pushing it forward increases focal length and pulling it back toward the camera body decreases focal length. Lenses with independent zoom and focus controls generally provide two rotating collars on the lens barrel—one for focus and one for zoom adjustment. Other methods may also be encountered, such as a side-mounted focusing wheel with a centrally pivoted zoom lever.

Combined zoom/focus controls are fast-handling and are often preferred by photographers dealing with action subjects such as sports or news events. Other photographers who work more deliberately may favor separate zoom and focus controls because they feel there is less likelihood of inadvertently altering the focal length while focusing, or vice versa.

An extra feature built into some zoom lenses is a special close-focusing range, usually engaged via push button or by moving the zoom ring to a close-up detent. Close-focusing zoom lenses are frequently described by their manufacturers as "macro zooms," although the close-up setting seldom produces an image on film much larger than about one-third life size. This is a useful feature if you are interested in occasional close-up photography. For extensive close-up work, however, a macro lens specifically corrected for close-up photography and photomacrography will generally produce superior results.

Zoom Limitations

Zoom lenses, present some limitations that may or may not be significant, depending upon the type of photography you do and your personal preferences.

For example, although a zoom lens' focal-length range may effectively substitute for several fixed-focal-length lenses, the zoom lens approximates the size and weight of the longest lens it replaces. When using it at shorter focal-length settings, you still lift to your eye the mass of the longest focal length. Thus, using a zoom may reduce the total weight of equipment you carry, while it actually increases the energy you expend in making certain photographs.

As a rule, zoom lenses have moderate maximum apertures—about one to three *f*-stops slower than the fixed-focal-length lenses they replace. Therefore, zoom lenses are not well-suited to available-light photography when image criteria or subject characteristics preclude the use of high-speed films or relatively long exposures. Furthermore, the relatively great depth of field obtained at the modest maximum aperture may make precise focusing difficult at the shorter zoom settings. For this reason it is advisable to focus a zoom lens at the longest focal-length setting, where depth of field is minimized, and then zoom back to the shorter focal length.

Because it is easy to zoom to fairly long tele-photo settings with many zoom lenses, photographers sometimes forget that a shutter speed that is appropriate at a short-focal-length setting may be too slow for sharp hand-held photography at the telephoto extreme of the zoom range. The old rule of thumb that the shutter speed of a hand-held camera should be no slower than the fraction formed by placing one over the lens focal length expressed in millimetres is applicable to the use of zoom lenses, too.

Special Zoom Effects

Although the most obvious application of the zoom lens in still photography is to adjust image size conveniently, zoom lenses, in the hands of imaginative and skilled photographers, provide unique opportunities for creating striking images. As will be seen from the following examples, the common basis for several different zoom special effects is zooming the lens during a relatively long exposure.

Zoom Blur. The simplest special effect to produce with a zoom lens combines a single sharp image of the principal subject with an expanding or contracting zoom blur. This effect is generally produced by mounting the camera on a tripod and focusing on the main subject, with the zoom set to produce either the largest or smallest image that is critical to the composition. The choice of a large or small image as a starting point depends on whether you

A simple zoom effect combines a sharp central image of the main subject with expanding or contracting zoom blur. Overall exposure time must allow for two exposure segments: one for the basic sharp image, the other for the operation of the lens' zoom control. Photo by Brent Jones.

Zoom Lens

A series of sharp images linked by a zoom blur can be made by combining a series of flash or stroboscopic exposures with continuous light exposure; the camera shutter remains open during zooming.

want the zoom blur to contract inward from a sharp large subject rendition, or expand outward from a sharp small inner subject. The overall exposure time must be long enough to allow splitting the exposure into two segments. During one exposure segment, the basic sharp image of the subject is recorded. During the other exposure segment, the lens' zoom control is operated smoothly through the appropriate range. You might also choose to begin and end with sharp subject contours, with a zoom blur between them. Nearly endless variations can be devised with these basic techniques.

Multiple Images and Blur. Another interesting and dramatic use of the zoom lens is to create a series of sharp images of the subject of increasing or decreasing size, linked by a zoom blur to provide a sense of continuity and progression. This may be achieved by combining repetitive or stroboscopic flash exposures with continuous-light exposure, while zooming with the camera shutter open. The flash exposures record the series of ever-larger (or smaller) sharp images, while the continuous-light component traces the zoom blurs joining the sharp images. The effect can be varied by changing the zoom speed, the frequency of the flash exposures, and the relative intensities of the flash and continuous-light exposures. The camera is most often tripod-mounted for this technique, which is best achieved under controlled studio conditions. Black backgrounds are favored because of the multiple exposures involved.

Variations. The basic zoom techniques described above may be elaborated upon by introducing planned subject or camera movement, or both. Repetitive-flash zoom shots in color may be enhanced by using different-colored gels to change the color of each of the several flash renditions recorded on a single frame of film.

If you are tempted to make special-effects zoom shots, bear in mind that not every attempt will result in a technical or aesthetic triumph. Many variables are involved, and results are not entirely predictable. Probably the most helpful accessory you can use in meeting the challenges of experimental zoom photography is a small notebook. Take meticulous notes

of exactly how you set up and expose each shot. Eventually, your notebook will be your most reliable guide to repeating procedures that worked well and to avoid those that failed.

• *See also:* ACTION PHOTOGRAPHY; FOCAL LENGTH; LENSES; MULTIPLE EXPOSURE TECHNIQUES; MULTIPLE FLASH; SPORTS PHOTOGRAPHY; STROBOSCOPIC PHOTOGRAPHY; TELEPHOTOGRAPHY; WIDE-ANGLE PHOTOGRAPHY.

Zoo Photography

The artificial environments created by zoo authorities provide an opportunity to take extraordinary nature pictures without searching and stalking. Animals are confined and tolerant of the presence of humans. Many progressive zoos have built natural habitats that virtually duplicate the animals' original homes. Of course, a photographer may wish to use

The zoo's artificial environment provides the photographer with unusual opportunities. Since the animals are confined and generally accustomed to the presence of humans, they may be observed for long periods of time until the right photographic moment occurs. Photo by J. Mehaeko.

the zoo simply as an environment for pictures of children, people, animals, and the general happenings around the zoo. But in this article, methods are described of separating the animals from the surroundings and producing natural-appearing photographs.

The best time to visit a zoo for photography is on a rainy weekday morning when schools are in session. The relative peace and quiet will allow a photographer to set up and shoot at leisure. In addition, the animals will be rested, alert, and free from the distractions of crowds. However, if the zoo is outdoors, rainy weather can cause special problems with the camera. Be prepared for such an eventuality by being familiar with appropriate techniques.

See the article   BAD-WEATHER PHOTOGRAPHY.

Animal Behavior

Animal behavior varies widely from species to species. Animals of the same species vary in terms of activity, aggressiveness, and playfulness.

Most animals are territorial. They tend to occupy the same area day after day—particularly when resting or sleeping. The photographer can prefocus on that spot or territory and be sure the animal will rest there at some time during the visit.

Most animals have a fairly distinct pattern of exercise. They seem to prefer to play or to pace in the same area and in a predictable manner. By

Most animals are creatures of habit, and the photographer who studies their routine can catch them at the right time for his or her purposes. This polar bear is in a playful mood; the photographer's assistant catches his attention while the photographer concentrates on taking pictures.

It is a good time to photograph cubs when they are feeding, because there is less likelihood that mother or babies will move around too much within the enclosure. At the same time, this activity provides an excellent photographic subject. Photo by Louis Allen Schaefer.

studying the animal's routine, the observer can be prepared to wait and shoot. The key word in zoo photography is *patience*. Concentrate on one animal at a time and be prepared to do so for an hour or more to get that really good picture.

Some animals are relatively inactive by nature. Reptiles and amphibians fall into this category. Lizards, snakes, and alligators—because of their general sluggishness—are easy to keep in focus and easily illuminated by flash.

Most animals are usually alert and active just prior to feeding time. Most zoos post information about feeding times, or a zookeeper will know the schedule. Keepers are usually helpful in pointing out behavioral quirks of their charges.

Following their meal, most animals exhibit some cleaning or grooming activity and then return to their territorial area for sleep. The cleaning operations make for good photographic opportunities, as do the customary yawning and stretching that pre-

Zoo Photography

cede a nap or deep sleep. A patient viewer can photograph the reverse sequence of actions when the animal awakens.

Habitat Zoos

More and more zoos are attempting to do away with cages wherever possible. They design and maintain a habitat closely resembling the actual environment of the animals on display. Most habitat collections have a moat—and perhaps a low fence—to separate the spectators from the animals.

The photographer can pick a camera angle that will capture on film only the animal or animals and the natural-looking surroundings of their enclosures. A wide lens opening will decrease depth of field, which softens or blurs any unavoidable man-made elements in the frame.

The photographer who must deal with a fence should try to place the lens right at the fence with the wires outside the field of the lens. Again, use the widest lens opening available to reduce depth of field. Focus carefully on the most interesting aspect of the subject. When the animal to be photographed is close to the fence—or if the photographer is unable to get close to the fence — look for openings in the fence, or move around to get a more favorable angle.

The subject may be in an objectionable area of shadow. Consider lightening the scene with fill-in flash. If the sun is low in the sky—as in morning and

Choose a camera angle that shows as little man-made material as possible. However, it is unrealistic to sacrifice a good shot just because of some obstacle, such as the fence in this picture.

When dealing with fences or bars, use the widest lens opening possible to reduce depth of field and focus carefully on the animal itself. Photo by T. Wienand.

Zoo Photography

Do not overlook the humorous aspects of zoo photography. Photos such as these are not only amusing to the photographer; they may be salable as well. Photo by Bob White.

evening—it is possible to get interesting silhouette shots.

Zoo Interior Photography

Indoor zoos often display animals living in more or less natural surroundings, or with cage backgrounds of natural browns, greens, or blues.

Most zoos are illuminated indoors with skylights, and film that is balanced for daylight can be used. A roll or two of tungsten-balanced film, or an electronic flash unit, should suffice to cope with the exceptional lighting situation. Photographs through glass often present problems with reflections. Moving the camera in close to the glass or standing at an angle to the glass can reduce reflection problems. Cleaning the glass with lens tissue and the use of a polarizing filter can eliminate most reflections.

Flash in Zoo Photography

The photographer must combat flash reflections from protective glass in zoo photography. If the camera lens is directly against the glass of the cage, the flash can be in any position off the camera. When both flash and camera are at a distance from the glass, the flash can be held far enough from the camera to keep reflections out of the field of view. Sufficient separation of camera and flash may be a problem, but a long flash extension cord will help. An assistant who can hold the flash where it is needed is a great help. Straight cords are preferable to coiled cords, since the tension on the coiled cord can disconnect the unit at inconvenient moments.

• *See also:* ANIMAL AND PET PHOTOGRAPHY; BAD-WEATHER PHOTOGRAPHY; BINOCULARS, TAKING PICTURES THROUGH; FLASH PHOTOGRAPHY; GLARE AND REFLECTION CONTROL; INSECT PHOTOGRAPHY; NATURE PHOTOGRAPHY; POLARIZED-LIGHT PHOTOGRAPHY.

  Zoopraxiscope

Working from the principles of various devices such as the praxinoscope and the zoetrope, which created the illusion of movement from sequences of drawings, Eadweard Muybridge devised a method of adapting a magic lantern (slide projector) to produce the same effect, using separate photographic images.

He called the device the *zoopraxiscope* (from Greek roots meaning "life-action viewer"), and first demonstrated it at Palo Alto, California, in 1879, for Leland Stanford and his family. Stanford had hired Muybridge to make photographic analyses of the movements of racehorses; the result was the famous sequence that revealed that all four hooves of a trotting horse are at times off the ground simultaneously.

In the zoopraxiscope, individual glass slides were replaced by a large glass disk that had positive images from a movement-analysis sequence mounted around the circumference. A geared hand-crank caused the disc to revolve, bringing the images into projection position one after the other. To eliminate the blur of the images moving across the screen, a circular metal plate with a corresponding series of narrow slits was mounted next to the image disk. It revolved in the opposite direction so that as each image passed through the projection plane, a slit moved past in front of it. The action was much the same as that of a focal-plane shutter in stopping the movement of a subject. In later versions, the elongation of the subject in the projected image (a consequence of the slit movement—see SHUTTERS) was eliminated by copying each image with intentional compensating distortion when making up a disk.

Muybridge was a popular lecturer and used slides of his varied work. With the zoopraxiscope, his appearances became a sensation. Audiences were first startled and then wildly enthusiastic as the image of a horse or a running man on the screen would flicker, take on a ragged jumpiness, and finally flow into smooth, continuous motion as the necessary projection speed was reached. It did not seem to matter that the same 12 or 24 images would repeat the same movement over and over; the effect was visual magic, and audiences were enthralled.

Muybridge exhibited a variety of subjects with the zoopraxiscope in major American and European cities before beginning the major photographic work of his life—the study of human and animal locomotion—at the University of Pennsylvania. His success in bringing the projected photographic image seemingly to life has led some to consider him to be the man who invented motion pictures.

• *See also:* MAREY, ETIENNE JULES; MOTION STUDY; MUYBRIDGE, EADWEARD JAMES; PRAXINOSCOPE; SHUTTERS; ZOETROPE.

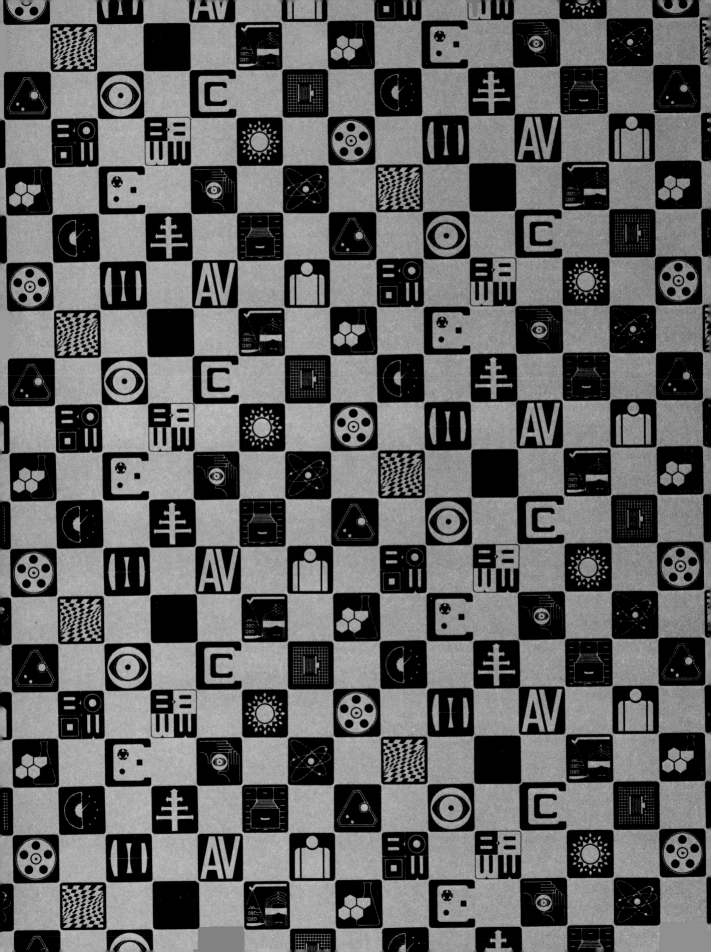

Guide for the Use of the Index

The proper use of this index will aid you in quickly locating the information you are seeking. Time spent reading this guide will mean time saved when you use this encyclopedia.

Entries in boldface type are for articles in the encyclopedia on that topic. Other entries are for subjects that are covered in certain articles but for which no separate article exists.

> Example: **Boric Acid**
> Boro-silicate crown glass
> Bounce flash
> **Bounce Light**

The system of alphabetizing in the index follows the same style used in the encyclopedia itself. Entries are alphabetized by letter sequence, with word breaks and hyphens not considered.

> Example: Architectural Photography
> Archival Processing
> Arc Lamps

Abbreviations are alphabetized according to the letters of the abbreviations, not by the words for which the letters stand.

> Example: Bromoil Process
> BSI Speeds
> Buffer

Once you locate the index item you want, you can use the notes at the bottom of the pages to help you select the volume you need.

In the index many subjects are organized in the form of detailed outlines. These outlines can be used to determine the overall coverage of a topic and to limit a search for specific information. The outlines can also be used as study guides to the various topics. Examples of such outlines are the listings for:

> Astrophotography
> Business Methods in Photography
> Copying

A

A and B Roll Editing, 1–4. *See also:* Animation; Editing movies; Splicing film
"checkerboard" technique (diagram), 1
dissolves, 3
effects, 3–4
equipment for, 2–3
fades and superimposures, 3–4
procedure, 2–3
Abbe, Ernst, 4, 1463, 1538, 1821, 2175, 2609
Abbe number, 4
Aberration, 4–7, 1535, 1537, 1538, 1826, 1923, 1964. *See also:* Achromatic; Anastigmat; Apochromatic; Barrel distortion
chromatic, 6, 1651, 1943
geometric, 4–6
lateral chromatic, 1824
longitudinal chromatic, 1824
spherical, 1652–1653, 1823, 1943
Abney, Sir William de Wiveleslie, 7, 1343
Abney effect. *See* Intermittency effect
Abridged Scientific Publications, 1638
Abstract photography, 1351–1354
Accelerator, 750–752, 771. *See also:* Activator
Acetate filters, 1059
Acetate to acetate splicing, 2296
Acetic Acid, 8, 120, 378, 380, 1087, 1160, 2342. *See also:* Fixers and fixing; Stop bath
Acetone, 8, 753
Achromatic, 8, 1560, 2543, 2544. *See also:* Aberration; Apochromatic; Lenses; Optics
Achromatic light, 1816
Achromatic magnifier, *Kodak,* 892
Achromatic reflection, 1561
Achromat lens, 1943, 2055
Acid, 8, 1661. *See also:* Alkali; Neutralization (chemistry); pH; Stop bath *and specific acids*
Acrol. *See* Amidol; Diaminophenol
Actinic, 9. *See also:* Black-and-white films; Light
Actinometer, 1389
Action Photography, 9–15. *See also:* Dance photography; Sports photography
animals and pets, 62, 68
animation, and 85
blur vs. sharpness, 10–12
focal-plane phenomena, 14–15
motion-stopping shutter speeds, 12–13
table of, 12
panning, 14
poise vs. pose, 14
speed and, 15
sporadic motion, 13
sports, 2303–2318
Activation process, 1859, 2111
Activator (chemistry), 378, 750–752, 1160, 1859. *See also:* Accelerator
Active surveillance photography, 2360, 2364–2366
camera positions for, 2364
equipment, 2364
films for, 2364–2366
Activol, 2175
Acutance, 15. *See also:* Mackie line; Resolving power
Adams, Ansel, 15–16, 1348, 1357, 2230, 2610. *See also:* Zone system
Adamson, Robert, 1342, 1356, 1358
Additive Color Synthesis, 17, 525–526, 1342, 1344, 2354. *See also:* Color theory; Subtractive color synthesis

Adjacency effect. *See* Edge effect
Adjustable cameras, 2391
Ad-type papers, 1290
Adurol, 17, 751, 769. *See also:* Chlorhydroquinone
Advertising, 310, 545, 1030–1032, 1144, 1365, 1405
Advertising Agencies, 17–18. *See also:* Advertising photography; Agencies, picture
art director in, 17–18
Advertising Photography, 18–29, 2531. *See also:* Advertising agencies; Business methods in photography; Fashion photography; Glamour photography; Model release; Photomechanical reproduction
catalogs, 27
content and message in, 20–23
establishing the mood in, 24
execution of the illustration in, 25–27
fashions, 1030–1032
function of, 18, 20
illustration, problems and solutions in, 27–28
logic and visual appeal in, 24
montage in, 1682
photographic quality in, 27
portfolio for, 1995–1996
posters, 28
television slides for, 2392–2393
Aerial cameras, 336
Aerial films, 573
Aerial Fog, 30. *See also:* Antifoggant; Development; Fogging
Aerial Perspective, 30, 1501. *See also:* Atmospheric haze; Filters; Infrared
brightness, 1877
color saturation, 1877–1878
contrast, 1877
filters to control (table), 1879
hue, 1878
sharpness, 1878–1879
Aerial Photography, 30–40, 227, 1199, 2415, 2595. *See also:* Infrared photography; Photogrammetry
aircraft for, 32–33
cameras, 35, 1907
during commercial flights, 30–31
in crime detection, 635
exposure, 38–39
films, 35–37
filters, 35, 36, 37
flights for photographic purposes, 32
infrared, 1425–1426
lenses, wide-angle, 37–38
montage in, 1682
photointerpretation in, 1904–1907
scale-determination in, 39–40
scale in oblique photographs (diagram), 40
shutter speed and lens aperture, 39
stereo, 2341–2342
types of photographs, 30
vertical scales (1000 ft altitude), table of, 39
weather for, 34–35
working with a pilot, 33–34
Afocal converters, 2382
Aftertreatment, 41. *See also:* Airbrush; Backgrounds, eliminating; Bleaching; Intensification; Reduction; Retouching; Spotting prints; Toning
Ag, 41, 117
test for, 119
Agencies, modeling, 1671, 1678
Agencies, Picture, 41–51, 1922. *See also:*

Advertising agencies; Legal aspects of photography; Model release; Selling pictures
contracts with, 49–50
cooperative, 50
feature, 46
historical, 47
information for, 48
news, 43–44
personal agent and, 50–51
rates and rights, 42
releases, 49
requirements of, 47–50
Agfacolor reversal film, 1345
Agfa Company, 60, 226
Agfa Rondinax tank, 2375
Agitation, 51–52, 748, 766, 810, 818, 821, 846, 928, 2375–2376, 2564. *See also:* Developers and developing; Gaseous-burst agitation; Mackie line
color film processing, 442–443
definition, 51
of long rolls, 2053
in tanks, 2375–2376
for toning, 2458
tray-tilt, 894–895
types of, 51–52
Airbrush, 52–54. *See also:* Aftertreatment; Backgrounds, eliminating; Retouching
masking, 53–54
operation of (diagram), 52
procedures, 54
retouching, 1938
color prints, 2162
uses of, 54
Airy, G.B., 790
Airy disc, 790, 792, 2112
Albada, Liewe Evert Willem van, 54
Albada Finder, 54
Albumen, 54–56, 222, 226. *See also:* Bayard, Hippolyte; Carte-de-visite
Albumen paper, 55
Albumen process, 957
Alcohol. *See* Glycerin
Alcohol, Denatured, 56
Alcohol, Ethyl, 56
Alcohol, Isopropyl, 56
Alcohol, Methyl, 56
Alkali, 57, 378, 1661. *See also:* Acid; Borax; Buffer
Alkaline Salts, 57
Allan, David, 2374
Alum, Chrome, 57, 1087
Alum, Potassium, 57–58
Aluminum, 1656
Aluminum-foil screens, 2081–2082
Aluminum nameplates, 1759–1760
Alum meal. *See* Alum, potassium
Ambrotype, 58, 1342. *See also:* Archer, Frederick Scott; Collodion
copying, 611
American Association for the Advancement of Science (AAAS), 623
American Association of School Photographers, Inc., 1901
American Bar Association, 1531
American National Standard Photographic Exposure Guide (ANSI PH2.7-1973), 1017
American National Standards Institute. *See* ANSI
American Racing Press Association, 1901
Americans, The (Frank), 838
American Society of Cinematographers, 1901
American Society of Magazine Photographers, 1901

American Society of Photogrammetry, 1901
American Society of Photographers, 1901
American Society of Picture Professionals, 1901
American Standards Association (ASA), 94, 244, 1695. *See also:* ANSI
Amidol, 58, 378, 751, 768. *See also:* Diaminophenol
Ammonia, 752, 787
Ammoniocitrate of iron. *See* Ferric ammonium citrate
Ammonium bichromate, 1297, 1299
Ammonium Chloride, 58–59
Ammonium hyposulfite. *See* Ammonium thiosulfate
Ammonium Persulfate, 59
Ammonium sulfocyanide. *See* Ammonium thiocyanate
Ammonium Thiocyanate, 59, 111. *See also:* Potassium thiocyanate
Ammonium Thiosulfate, 59, 377, 379. *See also:* Sodium thiosulfate
Ammonium thiosulfate reducer
  normal, 2124
  strong, 2124
Amphoto, 386
Anaglyph, 59, 2339, 2340. *See also:* Stereo photography
Analysis of information, photographic, 990
Analytical photography, 1754
Anamorphic Systems, 60, 385, 1345
Anastigmat, 60. *See also:* Aberration; Lenses; Optics
Anderson, Paul, 1977
Andresen, Momme, 60
Angier, Roswell, 838
Animal and Pet Photography, 60–72. *See also:* Action photography; Birds, photography of; Nature photography; Zoo photography
  cameras for, 62–63
  controlling the subject, 68–70
  domesticated animals, 60
  equipment for, 62–63, 71–72
  exposure, 65–66
  identification pictures, 62
  lighting
    indoor, 65
    outdoor, 63, 66
  photographing through glass, 68
  portraits, 61
  settings
    boxes vs. cages, 67–68
    diagrams of, 68, 69
    exterior, 66
    interior, 66–68
  show animals, 61–62, 68
  undomesticated and semitame animals, 61
  wild animals, 61, 71–72
Animal Locomotion and Human Locomotion (Muybridge), 1755
Animation, 73–94, 2442–2443. *See also:* A and B roll editing
  acceleration and deceleration, 77–78, 88
  animation stand, 80–82
    construction diagram, 81
  artistic expression, 78–79
  cameras for, 80
  cel, 74, 75–76, 82–85
  close-ups, 91
  cutaway and reaction shots, 91
  cutouts, 88, 93–94
  equipment, 80–82
  exposure sheet, 75–76
  graphs, charts, maps, et al., 88–89
  limited, 91

mouth movements, 89–91
movement cycles, 79–80
planning the film, 74–80
principles of, 73–74
progressive disclosure, 93
puppets, 77, 86–88
running time and film lengths for common projection speeds (table), 77
scratch-off, 91–93
special effects, 89–91
storyboard, 75
three-dimensional objects, 83, 85
timing, 76–77
  in titling, 2442
  on twos, 94
typical running time of (table), 76
Anschütz, Ottomar, 94
Ansco Printon, 1345
Ansel Adams: Images, 1953–1974, 15
ANSI (American National Standards Institute), **94,** 244, 1017, 1695, 1939, 2116. *See also:* ASA, ASAP speeds; BSI speeds; DIN speeds; GOST speeds; Sensitometry; Speed systems
  Standard Method for Determining Speed of Photographic Negative Materials (Monochrome, Continuous-Tone), PH2.5, 244
  Standard PH1.43-1971, 463
  Standard PH2.19-1959, 704
  Standard PH2.31-1969, 879
  Standard PH4.20-1958, 462–463
  Standard PH4.20-1958 (R 1970), 2486
  Standard PH22.164-1975, 1614
  Standard PH22.9-1976, 1710
Anthion. *See* Potassium persulfate
Antichlor. *See* Sodium thiosulfate
Anti-fog, *Kodak,* 1094, 1138, 1309
Antifoggant, 94–95, 378, 753, 768. *See also:* Aerial fog; Benzotriazole; Development; Fogging; 6-Nitrobenzimidazole nitrate
  use of (table), 95
Aperture, 95–96, 1136, 1190. *See also:* Diaphragm; *f*-Number; Focal length; *f*-Stop
  corrected settings (table), 1062
  lens diaphragm settings (table), 1194
  numerical, 1805, 1943
  relative, 1192–1194
  shutter speed and, 39
Aperture cards, 1645
Aperture diaphragm, 1944
"Aperture-preferred" exposure system, 165
Aplanat lens, 650
Apo-Artar lens, 2055
Apochromatic, 96. *See also:* Aberration; Achromatic; Lenses; Optics; Photomechanical reproduction
  color separation photography, 515, 605
  for photographing art, 124
Apochromat lens, 1943, 2055
Apo-*Ektar* lens, 2055
Apo-Tessor lens, 2055
Applied Optics and Optical Design (Kingslake), 1473
Applied Optics and Optical Engineering (Kingslake), 1473
Apron-type tanks, 2375
Aquarium, photographing an (diagram), 69
Arago, D.J.F., 647, 2112
Arbus, Diane, 1360
Archer, Frederick Scott, 58, **96,** 957, 1342, 2559, 2579, 2580, 2610. *See also:* Ambrotype
Architectural lighting, 426
Architectural Photographers Association, 1901

Architectural Photography, 97–111, 1783, 1788, 2530. *See also:* Camera movements; Model and miniature photography; View camera
camera positions, 103
  diagrams of, 102, 103
construction pictures, 97
consultation with client, 98–99
double printing, 108
equipment, 103–107
exposure
  double, 109
  time, 108–109
illustrative pictures, 97–98
lighting
  artificial, 109–110
  color temperature balance, 109
  exterior, 107
scale model, 111
spot meter, 104
technical approaches to
  exterior views, 100
  indoor views, 100–101
techniques of, 107–108
tripod, 104
understanding of, 99–100
Archival Processing (B&W Films and Papers), 111–120. *See also:* Black-and-white printing
deterioration, causes of, 111, 113
fixing, 113–114, 116
  negatives, 114
  prints, 114
hypo clearing agent, *Kodak* (table), 117, 118
  removal of, 118–119
protective coating procedure, 119–120
washing, 116–118
  negatives, 117
  prints, 117–118
  pure water vs. sea water, 116–117
  water temperature, 117
water-resistant paper base, 118
Arc Lamps, 120, 1580, 2494. *See also:* Artificial light; Lighting
Ardel Kinamatic, 1368
Argentum. *See* Ag
Argon-ion laser, 1522
Aristo Platino, 1981
Armat, Thomas, 120, 928
Arp, 1357
Arriflex camera, 1862
Art, Photography of, 121–137, 1356–1357, 2415. *See also:* Close-up photography; Color separation photography; Copying; Lighting; Photomacrography
cameras, 124–125
conservation and restoration in, 124
documentation in, 124
dramatization in, 123
equipment and materials, 124–130
exposure, 135–137
  color, determination of, 136–137
fidelity in, 121, 123
handling artworks, 130
  diagrams of, 130
infrared, 1429–1430
lighting, 126–127, 130, 132–135, 136
  diagrams, 132, 133, 135
  flat and relief artworks, 132
  three-dimensional artworks, 132–135
purpose and intent in, 121–124
techniques, 130–135
tripod, 124
Artificial Light, 138–139, 1568, 1569, 1570, 1572–1575. *See also:* Arc lamps; Electronic flash; Flash photogra-

2634

pp. 1–192 Vol. 1   pp. 193–376 Vol. 2   pp. 377–560 Vol. 3   pp. 561–744 Vol. 4
pp. 1481–1664 Vol. 9   pp. 1665–1848 Vol. 10   pp. 1849–2056 Vol. 11

pp. 745–936 Vol. 5   pp. 937–1112 Vol. 6   pp. 1113–1396 Vol. 7   pp. 1297–1480 Vol. 8
pp. 2057–2264 Vol. 12   pp. 2265–2472 Vol. 13   pp. 2473–2629 Vol. 14

2635

Bellows, 35, **224**, 334, 336, 339, 341, 391, 627. *See also:* Bellows extension; Cameras; View camera
double-rail, 407
Bellows Extension, 224–225, 1926, 1946, 1989. *See also:* Bellows; Close-up photography; View camera
close-up photography, 406–412
double, 407
duplicate slides and transparencies, 871
triple, 407
Bending power (of lenses), 1814
Benzene, 225–226
1,4-Benzenediamine. *See* Paraphenylenediamine
1,2-Benzenediol. *See* Pyrocatechin
1,2,3-Benzenetriol. *See* Pyrogallol
Benzol. *See* Benzene
Benzotriazole (*Kodak*** Anti-fog No. 1), 95, 226**, 753, 768. *See also:* Antifoggant; 6-Nitrobenzimidazole nitrate
Berthiot Orthor lens, 1539
Berthon, Rodolphe, 226. *See also:* Color films; Color theory
Bessy, Maurice, 1638
Between-the-lens shutter, 625, 2235
cathode-ray tube recording, 370
diagram, 340
Bichloride of mercury. *See* Mercuric chloride
Bichromate, 226, 433. *See also entries by individual processes*
Bichromate of potash. *See* Potassium bichromate
Biconvex lens, 1811
Bidirectional microphones, 1610
Bimat Process, 226–227. *See also:* Diffusion transfer process
Binoculars, Taking Pictures Through, 227–230, 2382–2383. *See also:* Telephotography; Telescopes, photographing through
cameras, 228–229
f-number, determination of, 230
focal length, determination of, 229–230
focusing, 229
specifications of binoculars, 229
Biograph Company, 789
Biographies
Abbe, Ernst, 4
Abney, Sir William de Wiveleslie, 7
Adams, Ansel, 15–16
Albada, Liewe Evert Willem van, 54
Andresen, Momme, 60
Anschütz, Ottomar, 94
Archer, Frederick Scott, 96
Armat, Thomas, 120
Baekeland, Leo Hendrik, 217
Barnack, Oskar, 217
Bayard, Hippolyte, 222
Becquerel, Edmond, 223
Berthon, Rodolphe, 226
Brewster, Sir David, 295
Chevalier, Charles Louis, 380
Chretien, Henri, 385
Clerc, Louis Philippe, 386
Crabtree, John I., 622–623
Daguerre, Louis Jacques Mandé, 647–648
Dallmeyer, John Henry, 650
Dallmeyer, Thomas Rudolph, 650
Deckel, Friedrich, 684
Demeny, Georges, 699
Dickson, William Kennedy Laurie, 789
Dollond, John, 845
Draper, John William, 845–846
Driffield, Vero Charles, 846
Ducos du Hauron, Louis, 864

Eastman, George, 911–914
Edgerton, Harold E., 928
Edison, Thomas Alva, 928
Evans, Ralph M., 989–990
Farmer, Ernest Howard, 1030
Fischer, Rudolf, 1084
Friese-Green, William, 1182
Gaumont, Léon, 1207
Gauss, Karl F., 1207
Godowsky, Leopold, 1242
Goerz, Carl Paul, 1242–1243
Herschel, Sir John F.W., 1313
Hoegh, Emil von, 1361
Hübl, Arthur von, 1388
Hunt, Robert, 1388–1389
Hurter, Ferdinand, 1389
Huygens, Christiaan, 1389
Ives, Frederick Eugene, 1461
Jenkins, C. Francis, 1463
Joly, John, 1464–1465
Jones, Henry Chapman, 1465
Jones, Lloyd A., 1465
Kingslake, Rudolf, 1473
Land, Edwin Herbert, 1489–1490
Lea, Matthew Carey, 1529
Lumière, Auguste, 1596–1597
Lumière, Louis, 1596–1597
Maddox, Richard Leach, 1601–1602
Manly, Thomas, 1622
Mannes, Leopold D., 1622
Marey, Etienne Jules, 1622–1623
Maxwell, James Clerk, 1629
Mees, Charles Edward Kenneth, 1636–1638
Méliès, Georges, 1638
Monckhoven, Desiré Charles Emanuel van, 1680
Morse, Samuel Finley Breese, 1687
Muybridge, Eadweard James, 1753–1755
Nadar (Gaspard Felix Tournachon), 1757–1758
Namias, Rodolfo, 1761
Niépce, Joseph Nicéphore, 1792–1793
Ostwald, Wilhelm, 1831
Pathé, Charles, 1862–1863
Paul, Robert W., 1863
Petzval, Josef M., 1853–1854
Rayleigh, Lord (John William Strutt), 2112
Rudolph, Paul, 2175
Talbot, William Henry Fox, 2373–2374
Taylor, Harold Dennis, 2376–2377
Vogel, Hermann Wilhelm, 2557
Voigtländer, Peter Wilhelm Friedrich, 2557
Warnerke, Leon, 2559
Wedgwood, Thomas, 2576
Wolcott, Alexander S., 2593–2594
Wollaston, William Hyde, 2594
Woodbury, Walter Bentley, 2594–2595
Young, Thomas, 2607
Zeiss, Carl, 2609
Biological Photographic Association, 1901
Biomedical Photography, 230–231, 1630. *See also:* Bright-field illumination; Cathode-ray tube recording; Clinical photography; Dark-field illumination; Dental photography; Electron micrography; Fiber optics; Medical photography; Motion-picture production; Photomacrography; Photomicrography; Radiography; Scientific photography; Stereo Photography; Thermal photography; Ultraviolet and fluorescence photography; X-ray
equipment, 1634–1635
disinfection of, 1635–1636

film, 1634
image size in, 1635
Birds, Photography of, 231–240. *See also:* Animal and pet photography; Nature photography; Telephotography; Zoo photography
cameras, 232–233
film, 233
lenses, 233
lighting, 239–240
preparation for, 231–232
techniques
in the field, 235–239
at home, 233–235
using a blind, 236–239
Birefringence, 1885, 1984
Birth of a Nation (Griffith), 1862
Bisson Frères, 1347
Bitzer, Billy, 1862
Black-and-White Films, 35, 241–252. *See also:* Actinic; Characteristic curve; Color films; Contrast index; Films and plates; Notch codes; Storage of sensitized materials and processing solutions
archival processing of, 111–120
art, photographing, 127
for available-light photography, 173
blue-sensitive, 242
characteristic curve, 241, 245, 246
graph, 245, 572, 588, 703
color sensitivity, 241–243
classification of, 242
contrast, 245–246, 571–574
contrast index curves for, 600–602
definition, character of, 243
degree of enlargement, 244, 251, 252
developers and developing, 745–770
emulsion
graininess, 243–244
resolving power, 243
exposure for, 1012
filters for, in infrared photography, 1417
fogging, 1137–1138
format availability and usage, 246–248
usage tables, 247, 248
gray-tone of colored objects, 241–242
for high-speed photography, 1336
image structure characteristics, 243–244
infrared, 35–36, 242, 1410, 1418–1419
Kodak films
extremely high-contrast, 248–249
high-contrast, 249–250
medium-contrast, 250–252
latensification of, 1524
long-roll films, 248
in low-temperature astrophotography, 157
mechanized processing of, 672–673
orthochromatic, 242
overexposure with, 1831
panchromatic, 242
for photographing art, 127
printing, 750–751
roll films, 248
sheet films, 246–247
speed, 244–245
wavelengths of light (diagram), 241
Black-and-white negatives, 1508–1509
duplicate, 866–868
retouching, 2150–2154
ring-around, 2171–2175
Black-and-white papers, 1854
Black-and-White Printing, 253–268, 672–673, 2505–2506. *See also:* Archival processing; Burning-in; Contact printing; Contrast; Contrast index; Darkroom, amateur; Densitometry;

2636

pp. 1–192 Vol. 1   pp. 193–376 Vol. 2   pp. 377–560 Vol. 3   pp. 561–744 Vol. 4
pp. 1481–1664 Vol. 9   pp. 1665–1848 Vol. 10   pp. 1849–2056 Vol. 11

pp. 745–936 Vol. 5   pp. 937–1112 Vol. 6   pp. 1113–1396 Vol. 7   pp. 1297–1480 Vol. 8
pp. 2057–2264 Vol. 12   pp. 2265–2472 Vol. 13   pp. 2473–2629 Vol. 14

2637

2638

pp. 1–192 Vol. 1   pp. 193–376 Vol. 2   pp. 377–560 Vol. 3   pp. 561–744 Vol. 4
pp. 1481–1664 Vol. 9   pp. 1665–1848 Vol. 10   pp. 1849–2056 Vol. 11

pp. 745–936 Vol. 5   pp. 937–1112 Vol. 6   pp. 1113–1396 Vol. 7   pp. 1297–1480 Vol. 8
pp. 2057–2264 Vol. 12   pp. 2265–2472 Vol. 13   pp. 2473–2629 Vol. 14

2639

pp. 745–936 Vol. 5   pp. 937–1112 Vol. 6   pp. 1113–1396 Vol. 7   pp. 1297–1480 Vol. 8
pp. 2057–2264 Vol. 12   pp. 2265–2472 Vol. 13   pp. 2473–2629 Vol. 14

2641

2642

pp. 1–192 Vol. 1 pp. 193–376 Vol. 2 pp. 377–560 Vol. 3 pp. 561–744 Vol. 4
pp. 1481–1664 Vol. 9 pp. 1665–1848 Vol. 10 pp. 1849–2056 Vol. 11

pp. 745–936 Vol. 5   pp. 937–1112 Vol. 6   pp. 1113–1396 Vol. 7   pp. 1297–1480 Vol. 8
pp. 2057–2264 Vol. 12   pp. 2265–2472 Vol. 13   pp. 2473–2629 Vol. 14

2643

Dermatitis, 1662
Desensitizing, 744. See also: Developers and developing
Desiccant, 2488–2489
Desiccation, 1195
Destruction of Lower Manhattan, The (Lyon), 837
Deutoiodide of mercury. *See* Mercuric iodide
Deutsche Gesellschaft für Photographie, 1902
Deutsche Industrie Norm. *See* DIN speeds
Developers and Developing, 157, 244, 245, 378, **745–770,** 964, 1160, 1656, 1789–1791, 2357. *See also:* Activator; Agitation; Alkali; Antifoggant; Black-and-white printing; Bromide; Chemistry of photography; Color film processing; Compensating developer; Contrast; Desensitizing; Development; Direct positive processing; Drum and tube processing; Drying films and prints; Fixers and fixing; Formulas for black-and-white processing; Mixing photographic solutions; Replenishment; Restrainer; Tanks *and specific developers*
agitation, 51
black-and-white prints, 265–266
cathode-ray tube recording, 372
chemical vs. physical, 770
cold-tone, 769
contamination of, 267
copy negatives, 610
developing times at several different temperatures (graph), 755
development times in *Kodak* developer *D-76* (tables), 759
development times in *Kodak Microdol-X* developer (table), 758
equipment for, 745–747, 750–751
errors in, 983–989
ferrous oxalate, 1529
fine-grain, 756–757
fogging, 1138–1139
formulation, 751
    accelerator, 750–752
    developing agents, 751–752
    dilution of, 754
    preservatives, 752–753
    proprietary and formula developers, 753
    restrainer, 753
graininess and, 1250–1251
high emulsion speed developer, 755–756
high-key photographs, 1323
jet-spray processing, 1463–1464
Kodachrome film, 1478
Kodak, formulas, 1163–1169, 1254
Kodak HC-110 developer capacity of working dilutions (table), 765
HC-110 developer storage life of unused solutions (table), 765
long roll films with *Polydol* developer (table), 767
long rolls, 2053–2054
low-contrast, 769–770
mixing and dissolving chemicals, 1160, 1163
murals, 1746–1747
paper developers, 768–770
platinum print process, 1978–1979
prints, procedures, 750–751
procedures and materials for, 745–751
roll and 135 films, 766
roll and 135 films with *Polydol* developer (table), 767

sensitized fabric, 1029
sheet films with *Polydol* developer (table), 767
stock solution, 754
tanks, 746
temperature coefficient of, 754
temperature of, 266–267
time of development (graph), 766
trays, 750
in the tropics, 2485–2486
warm-tone, 770
water supply for, 1656
working dilutions from *HC-110* stock solution (chart), 761
working-strength dilutions, uses of, 762
Developing agents, 751–752, 1160.
    characteristics of (table), 771
Developing solutions, 754, 771–772
Developing tanks. *See* Tanks, developing
Developing times, 763–765
Development, 378, **770–777,** 1160, 1199, 1205, 1243, 1244. *See also:* Activator; Acutance; Adjacency effect; Aerial fog; Antifoggant; Bimat process; Blocked highlights; Chemistry of photography; Color film processing; Densitometry; Developers and developing; Diffusion transfer process; Directional effects; Direct positive processing; Dye destruction color process; Edge effect; Emulsion; Fixers and fixing; Halide; Latent image; Reduction; Silver bromide; Silver halides; Stabilization process; Stop bath; Superadditivity; Tanning developer.
bracketing, 294
carbon and carbro printing, 354, 356–357
cathode-ray tube recording, 372
chemical vs. physical, 770
color, 776–777
contrast and, 573–574
coupler, 498
developing agents, 771
effects on sharpness, 2233–2234
fine-grain, 774–775
image effects created in, 1398–1399
infrared film, 1419
intensification in, 1453
of kallitypes, 1471–1472
latitude, 1529
nameplates, photographic, 1759–1760
photodevelopment, 1829–1830
process of, 772, 773
silver halide exposure and, 772–774
solutions for, 771–772
split, 775
stabilization process, 2319–2322
stain, 777
tanning, 777
time, methods for finding, 574–577
for toning, 2458
using gray scales, 1274–1275
variable-contrast paper, 2528–2530
water bath, 776
zone system, 2617–2618
Develop-out light beam oscillograph, 1827
Dial thermometers, 2432
Diaminophenol, 777
2, 4-Diaminophenol dihydrochloride. *See* Diaminophenol
2, 4-Diaminophenol hydrochloride. *See* Amidol
1: 3-Diamino-phenyldiazonium hydrochloride. *See* Pinakryptol
Diamol. *See* Amidol; Diaminophenol
Diaphragm, 777–783. *See also:* Aperture;

Depth of field; Diffraction; *f*-Number; *f*-Stop; Inverse-square law; Iris diaphragm; Lenses; Optics; Photomacrography
automatic, 779
brightness control and, 779
image brightness and, 780–781
image sharpness and, 781–783
iris, 778–779, 1460
markings, 1194
real and effective diameters of, 779–780
rotating and strip stops, 778
settings (table), 1194
slotted blades, 778
types (chart), 778
waterhouse stops, 778
Diapositive, 783, 1899
Diascopes, 2085
Diazo dyes, 1804
Diazo transparency, 1834
Diazotype, 784, 1029, 2035
Dibromo-o-cresol sulfonphthalein. *See* Bromcresol purple
Dichroic Filters, 483, 484, 488, 500, 504, **784–787,** 1311, 1561. *See also:* Beam splitter; Diffraction; Dichroic fog; Dispersion; Enlargers and enlarging; Filters; Light; Optics; Prisms; Refraction; Scientific photography
Dichroic Fog, 753, **787–788,** 1139
causes of, 787
prevention of, 788
removing, 788
Dickson, William Kennedy Laurie, 789
Diffraction, 789–793, 1342, 1562, 1824, 1923. *See also:* Beam splitter; Diaphragm; Dichroic filters; Dispersion; Light; Optics; Prisms; Refraction; Resolving power; Spectrography
image definition and, 790
wavelength analysis and, 792–793
Diffraction grating, 791, 824, 1562. *See also:* Beam splitter
Diffuse backlight, 1576–1577
Diffuse density, 699–700
specular vs., 704
Diffuse highlights, 705
Diffuse light, 1568
Diffuse reflection, 1560–1561
Diffusers, 794, 2332
Diffusion, 793–798, 2281. *See also:* Additive color synthesis; Bounce light; Callier effect; Densitometry; Diffusion transfer process; Enlargers and enlarging; Lighting; Reflectors; Tent lighting; Umbrella lighting
chemical, 793
controlled, 793
ground-glass, 967–968, 969
in image control, 797–798
integrated reflected, 968
in lighting, 793–797
opal glass, 968
Diffusion enlarger, 255, 261, 484, 575, 578, 590, 597, 599
Diffusion materials, 1516–1517
Diffusion sheeting, *Kodak,* 843
Diffusion Transfer Process, 798–810, 1345, 1346. *See also:* Additive color synthesis; *Bimat* process; Color films; Color theory; Development; Diffusion; Dufaycolor; Emulsion; Lenticular systems; Line-screen systems; Lumière color processes; Mosaic systems; Photomechanical reproduction; Subtractive color syn-

pp. 745–936 Vol. 5   pp. 937–1112 Vol. 6   pp. 1113–1396 Vol. 7   pp. 1297–1480 Vol. 8
pp. 2057–2264 Vol. 12   pp. 2265–2472 Vol. 13   pp. 2473–2629 Vol. 14

2645

pp. 745–936 Vol. 5   pp. 937–1112 Vol. 6   pp. 1113–1396 Vol. 7   pp. 1297–1480 Vol. 8
pp. 2057–2264 Vol. 12   pp. 2265–2472 Vol. 13   pp. 2473–2629 Vol. 14

2649

2650

pp. 1–192 Vol. 1   pp. 193–376 Vol. 2   pp. 377–560 Vol. 3   pp. 561–744 Vol. 4
pp. 1481–1664 Vol. 9   pp. 1665–1848 Vol. 10   pp. 1849–2056 Vol. 11

pp. 745–936 Vol. 5   pp. 937–1112 Vol. 6   pp. 1113–1396 Vol. 7   pp. 1297–1480 Vol. 8
pp. 2057–2264 Vol. 12   pp. 2265–2472 Vol. 13   pp. 2473–2629 Vol. 14

2651

pp. 745–936 Vol. 5   pp. 937–1112 Vol. 6   pp. 1113–1396 Vol. 7   pp. 1297–1480 Vol. 8
pp. 2057–2264 Vol. 12   pp. 2265–2472 Vol. 13   pp. 2473–2629 Vol. 14

2653

2654

pp. 1–192 Vol. 1   pp. 193–376 Vol. 2   pp. 377–560 Vol. 3   pp. 561–744 Vol. 4
pp. 1481–1664 Vol. 9   pp. 1665–1848 Vol. 10   pp. 1849–2056 Vol. 11

pp. 745–936 Vol. 5   pp. 937–1112 Vol. 6   pp. 1113–1396 Vol. 7   pp. 1297–1480 Vol. 8
pp. 2057–2264 Vol. 12   pp. 2265–2472 Vol. 13   pp. 2473–2629 Vol. 14

2655

2656

pp. 1–192 Vol. 1   pp. 193–376 Vol. 2   pp. 377–560 Vol. 3   pp. 561–744 Vol. 4
pp. 1481–1664 Vol. 9   pp. 1665–1848 Vol. 10   pp. 1849–2056 Vol. 11

pp. 745–936 Vol. 5   pp. 937–1112 Vol. 6   pp. 1113–1396 Vol. 7   pp. 1297–1480 Vol. 8
pp. 2057–2264 Vol. 12   pp. 2265–2472 Vol. 13   pp. 2473–2629 Vol. 14

2657

pp. 745–936 Vol. 5   pp. 937–1112 Vol. 6   pp. 1113–1396 Vol. 7   pp. 1297–1480 Vol. 8
pp. 2057–2264 Vol. 12   pp. 2265–2472 Vol. 13   pp. 2473–2629 Vol. 14

2659

Metallic lenticular screens, 2082
Metallography, 1948
Metal nameplates, 1758–1760
Metalphoto, 1758
Metal-vapor lasers, 1522
Meteors, photographing, 143
Meter cells, 1014
Methanecarboxylic acid. *See* Acetic acid
Methanol. *See* Alcohol, methyl
1-Methyl-2 (3-nitrostyryl) - 6 -ethoxyquino-
line methylsulfate. *See* Pinakryptol
Metol, 751, 754, 768, 775, 956, **1641,** 1681,
2357. *See also: Elon* developing
agent, *Kodak*
Metol-hydroquinone, 2357
Metric System, 1641, 1660, 2576. *See also:*
Mixing photographic solutions;
Temperature scales; Weights and
measures
Metrologic Instruments, Incorporated,
1368
Michals, Duane, 1351, 1354
Michigan Press Photographers Associa-
tion, 1902
Microcard, 1643
Microdensitometer, 1247–1248, 2228, 2229
Microdol-X developer, 753, 754, 756, 757,
1455, 2094
capacity, 757–758
replenishment, 758
Microfiche; Microfilm, 1642
Microfilm, 1643–1649
color, 1649
Microfilm cameras, 1644
Microform Data Systems, 1645
Microform reader-printers, 1648
Microform readers, 1647–1648
Micrographics, 1643–1649
color microfilm, 1649
data systems, 1648
materials, 1648–1649
microformats, 1644–1645
microforms, 1643–1645
micropublishing, 1649
production equipment, 1645–1647
reduction ratio, 1645
user equipment, 1647–1648
Microlex, 1643
Micro-opaques, 1643–1644
Microphones, 1608–1610
bidirectional, 1610
cardioid, 1610
general-purpose, 1610
omnidirectional, 1608–1610
ultradirectional, 1610
Microphotogrammetry, 1900
Microphotography, 1645, **1649–1650,**
1923. *See also:* Micrographics;
Photofabrication; Photomicrography; Photoresist
stereo, 2337
techniques of, 1650
uses of, 1649–1650
Microprint, 1643
Micropublishing, 1649
Micro-reciprocal degrees. *See* Mired
Microscopes, 1989
bright-field illuminated, 1941
compound, 1923, 1941–1944
electron, 952–954
illumination
in photomacrography, 1932–1937
in photomicrography, 1947–1951
light, 952
for photomacrography, 1923
for photomicrography, 1923
simple, 1923, 1925
Microstrip (microtape), 1643

Microtape. *See* Microstrip
Microtransparencies, vs. micro-opaques,
1643–1644
Microwaves, 1518
Middle ultraviolet, 2493–2494
Mili, Gjon, 2350
Milwaukee Press Photographers Associa-
tion, 1902
Miniature cameras, 336
Minimata (Smith), 837
Mired, 475, **1650–1651.** *See also:* Color
temperature; Color theory; Filters;
Light
color temperature, 520–522
nomograph for light source conversion,
521
values of color temperatures from 2000–
6900 K (table), 520
values of common light sources (table),
1651
Mirror dimension adjustments, 2074
Mirror Lenses, 1651–1653, 2381. *See also:*
Lenses; Mirrors; Optics
reflecting telephoto lens, 1653
secondary spectrum, 1652
Mirror reflex camera, 2386
Mirrors, 1654–1656, 1932. *See also:* Special
effects
choosing and positioning, 1655, 2075–
2076
coating, 1655–1656
dimension adjustments for, 2074
photographing mirror images, 1654–
1655
in projection systems, 2072
and projector alignment, 2077–2078
as reflectors, 2063
using, 1655
Mitchell BNCR camera, 1862
**Mixing Photographic Solutions, 1656–
1664.** *See also:* Chemistry of photography; Darkroom, professional;
Developers and developing; Disposal of photographic solutions;
Formulas for black-and-white processing; Storage of sensitized materials and processing solutions;
Weights and measures
cleanliness, 1657
decontaminating rubber gloves, 1664
filtration, 1657–1658
funnel, 1658
in-line, 1657–1658
handling precautions, 1661–1664
making measurements, 1659–1660
mixing large quantities, 1664
mixing solutions, 1658–1659
percentage solutions, 1660–1661
storing solutions, 1661
types of containers for, 1656–1657
water supply, 1656
Mobiles, 697–698
**Model and Miniature Photography, 1665–
1669.** *See also:* Architectural photography; Perspective; Tabletop
photography; Tent lighting
Modeling agency, 1671, 1678
Modeling school, 1671–1672, 1678
Model portfolios, 1671, 1679
Model Release, 49, 311, 1608, **1669–1670,**
1678, 1690. *See also:* Advertising
photography; Agencies, picture;
Business methods in photography;
Legal aspects of photography; Mod-
els and modeling; Selling pictures
medical photography, 1630–1631
Models and Modeling, 1670–1679. *See also:*
Business methods in photography;

Fashion photography; Glamour
photography; Model release; Theatrical photography
equipment for, 1674–1676
fashion, 1037–1038
fees for, 1678
in glamour photography, 1209, 1219–
1221
nude, 1678
posing, 1676–1677
Modern front-meniscus lens, 1538
Modulation transfer factors, 2232–2233
Modulation transfer function (MTF), 459,
2231–2233
Moholy-Nagy, Laszlo, 1353, 1681
Moiré Pattern, 433, 1680. *See also:*
Graphic arts photography; Halftone; Special effects
**Monckhoven, Desiré Charles Emanuel van,
1680**
Monckhoven formula, 1453
Monet, Claude, 1757
Monobaths, 1681. *See also:* Developers and
developing
Monochrome line screens, 1587–1588
Monoculars, taking picture through, 2382–
2383
Monopod, 344, 345
Monorail view camera, 2530
Montage, 428, 536, **1681–1684.** *See also:*
Collage; Combination printing; Spe-
cial effects
basic methods of, 1682–1684
from different negatives, 1684
uses of, 1681–1682
Monthly Abstract Bulletin, 1638
Moon, Photography of, 144, 1685–1687.
See also: Astrophotography; Eclipse
photography
Moonlight Photography, 1684–1685. *See
also:* Available-light photography;
Existing-light photography; Moon,
photography of
Morgan, Barbara, 1682
Morse, R.S., 1265
Morse, Samuel Finley Breese, 1687
Mortensen, William, 1351
Mosaic Systems, 865, **1687–1688.** *See also:*
Additive color synthesis; Color the-
ory; Dufaycolor; Line-screen sys-
tems; Lumière color processes
Motion-picture and TV camera movements, 333
diagram of, 333
Motion-picture cameras, 2587–2588
Motion-picture films, 1056, 1057–1058
models and miniatures, 1668–1669
Motion-picture formats, 1158–1159
Motion-picture photography, 2539
Motion-Picture Production, 1688–1705.
See also: A and B roll editing; Audiovisual planning; Lenses; Magnetic
sound for motion pictures; Model
release; Synchronization; Telephotography; Wide-angle photography; Zoom lens
budgeting, 1689
camera angles, 1697–1699
continuity, 1701–1702
double-system sound, 1705
editing, 1702–1703
equipment for, 1690–1695
film editing, 1702–1703
film script, 1689–1690
film treatment, 1688–1689
frame rate for, 1694
high-speed
camera running times for 16 mm films

2660

pp. 1–192 Vol. 1   pp. 193–376 Vol. 2   pp. 377–560 Vol. 3   pp. 561–744 Vol. 4
pp. 1481–1664 Vol. 9   pp. 1665–1848 Vol. 10   pp. 1849–2056 Vol. 11

negatives; Filing and storing negatives, prints, and transparencies; Graininess and granularity; Internegative; Paper negative; Push processing; Sabattier effect; Screened negatives and prints; Wet negatives, printing
black-and-white
  contrast, 574–592
  density, 317–318, 597, 705
  errors in processing, 983–987
  fungicides for, 2488
calotype, 319–320
character of, 1775
color, 445–446, 1774–1775
  black-and-white prints from, 269–271
color separation (chart), 511
contact printing, 555
copy, exposing and processing, 608–610
density range of, 1279
duplicate black-and-white, 866–868
duplicate color, 868–869
filing and storage of, 1051–1053, 1054
fixing, in archival processing, 114
halftone, 1257
intensification of, 1453–1456
paper, 1849–1852
preservation of, in the tropics, 2486
Sabattier effect, 1775
special-purpose, 1775
standard sizes (table), 1157
unblemished, 1775
underdevelopment, 2505–2506
underexposure and overexposure, 1775, 2506–2507
washing, 2560–2561
wet, printing, 2581–2582
Negative splice, 2297
Negative splicer, 1
Nepera Chemical Company, 217
Nepera solution, 217
Nettles, Bea, 1351
Neutral density, 712
  neutral density factors (table), 505
Neutral Density Filters, 1024, 1063, 1068, 1074–1075, 1094, 1502, **1776–1777,** 1952–1953, 2539. *See also:* Filters; Polarizers and neutral density filters; Wedge spectrogram
combining, 1777
density values of, 1776
dodging with, 1025
exposure with, 1024, 1025
home-made, 1777
neutral density versus transmission (table), 1776
special-purpose, 1777
tables, 921, 1075
uses, 1776
Neutralization (chemistry), 379
  acid, 8
Neutral oxalate of potash. *See* Potassium oxalate
Neutral test card, *Kodak,* 710–711, 1017, 1020, 1094, 1265, 1524, 1525, 1930, 2456
  outdoor exposure metering with (table) 1266
Newhall, Nancy, 15
New Jersey Press Photographers Association, 1902
Newport Research Corporation, 1368
News agencies, 43–44
Newspaper Techniques, 1777–1781. *See also:* Color separation photography; Graphic arts photography; Halftone; Photomechanical reproduction methods; Phototypesetting

color reproduction, 1781
halftone copy, 1778–1779
line negatives for, 1779–1780
lithographic platemaking, 1780–1781
paste-up, 1779
phototypesetting, 1777–1778
screened paper prints, 1779
in theatrical photography, 2426
News Photography, 1348–1350, **1782–1791.** *See also:* Available-light photography; Flash photography; Newspaper techniques; Photojournalism
assignments, 1783–1789
documentary vs., 830
editing the pictures, 1791
equipment, 1782–1783
lighting, 1785–1786
at the office, 1783–1784
photojournalism, 1782
picture captions, 1791
press conference, 1786
processing the film, 1789–1791
on the road, 1784–1785
subjects of, 1786
Newton, Henry J., 1908
Newton, Isaac, 845, 1389, 1651, 2288, 2593
Newtonian telescope, 2385
Newton's Rings, 899, **1792,** 2270–2271
New York Daily Graphic, 1908
New York Press Photographers Association, 1902
New Zone System Manual, The (White, Zakia, and Lorenz), 2610, 2618
Nickel-Cadmium Battery, 1792
Nicol, William, 1471, 1489
Niépce, Joseph Nicéphore, 380, 647, 648, 1312, 1340, 1341, **1792–1793,** 1803. *See also:* Daguerre, Louis Jacques Mandé; History of photography
Night Photography, 1794–1803. *See also:* Available-light photography; Existing-light photography; Filters; Landscape photography
exposure meters for, 1794–1796
extreme contrast in, 1796–1797
floodlit landmarks, 1798–1799
light and light patterns in, 1799–1800
miscellaneous equipment for, 1796
pseudo-night pictures, 1800–1801, 1803
"scapes" in, 1797–1798
seascapes, 1797–1798
sports, 2308–2309, 2315
traffic accidents, 2471–2472
tripods for, 1796
Nikonos camera, 2507–2508
Nikor roll film reels, 2374
Nikor tank, 2374, 2375
Nilsson, 1630
Nitrate-base films, storage and care, 1719–1722
Nitric Acid, 1803
6-Nitrobenzimidazole Nitrate, 753, 768, **1803.** *See also:* Antifoggant
6-Nitrobenzimidazole nitrate (*Kodak* Antifog No. 2), 95. *See also:* Antifoggant
Nitrogen, 1200
Nodal points, 1207
Non-Silver Processes, 1803–1804. *See also:* Blueprint process; Bromoil process; Carbon and carbro printing; Cyanotype; Electrophotography; Gumbichromate printing; Kallitype; Photofabrication; Photoresist; Platinum print process; Xerography
Nonsynchronous sound, 1606
Nord camera, 2603

Notch Codes, 1804. *See also:* Films and plates
Nude photography, 1678
Nujol, 1888
Numerical Aperture, 1805, 1943. *See also:* *f*-Number; *f*-Stop; Photomicrography
relationship to *f*-number (table), 1805

O

Objective filming, 1696
Objective lens, 1941, 1942–1943, 1947
  achromat, 1943
  apochromat, 1943
  fluorite, 1943
  numerical aperture, 1943
  resolving power, 1943
Object-overlap perspective, 1872, 1874
Oblique perspective, 1881
Obscene pictures, 1533
Off-camera flash, 1104, 1115
Offset lithography, 1251
Offset printing, 1251
Ohio News Photographers Association, 1902
Oil of vitriol. *See* Sulfuric acid
Oil paintings, copying, 611–612
O'Keefe, Georgia, 1357, 1360
Oklahoma News Photographers Association, 1902
Omnidirectional microphones, 1608–1610
On-camera flash, 1101, 1104
100th Street (Davidson), 838
Opacity (O), 699, 1560, 1595
Opal flashed glass, *Kodak,* 872, 876
Opal-glass diffusion, 968
Opaque, *Kodak,* 2211
Opaque projectors, 2085
Open flash, 1110–1111
Ophymograph, 1622
Optical-emission spectroscopy, 2287
Optical filters, 1058, 1059
Optical glass and plastic lenses, 1820–1821
Optical Industry and Systems Directory, The, 1907
Optical inhomogeneity. *See* Schlieren photography
Optical mixture, 2553
Optical printing, 2034–2035
Optical scanning, 1265
Optical Society of America, 1473, 1490
Optical viewfinders, 337, 339
Opticap discs, 211
Optics, 1807–1826. *See also:* Aberration; Achromatic; Anastigmat; Aperture; Apochromatic; Astrophotography; Back focus; Barrel distortion; Brightness; Close-up photography; Depth of field; Depth of focus; Diffraction; Field lens; *f*-Number; Fresnel lenses; *f*-Stop; Hyperfocal distance; Lenses; Light; Light: units of measurement; Microphotography; Pinhole camera; Prisms; Rangefinder; Sharpness; Telephotography; T-Stop
geometrical, 1807–1809
illumination of images, 1824–1825
image formation with a pinhole, 1807–1809
lens, 1809–1824
nature of a photographic subject, 1807
optical glass and plastic, 1820–1821
thin lenses, characteristics of, 1812–1820
of vision, 2542–2544
Oriel Corporation of America, 1368
Orthoboric acid. *See* Boric acid

2662

pp. 1–192 Vol. 1   pp. 193–376 Vol. 2   pp. 377–560 Vol. 3   pp. 561–744 Vol. 4
pp. 1481–1664 Vol. 9   pp. 1665–1848 Vol. 10   pp. 1849–2056 Vol. 11

pp. 745–936 Vol. 5   pp. 937–1112 Vol. 6   pp. 1113–1396 Vol. 7   pp. 1297–1480 Vol. 8
pp. 2057–2264 Vol. 12   pp. 2265–2472 Vol. 13   pp. 2473–2629 Vol. 14

2663

pp. 745–936 Vol. 5   pp. 937–1112 Vol. 6   pp. 1113–1396 Vol. 7   pp. 1297–1480 Vol. 8
pp. 2057–2264 Vol. 12   pp. 2265–2472 Vol. 13   pp. 2473–2629 Vol. 14

2665

pp. 745–936 Vol. 5   pp. 937–1112 Vol. 6   pp. 1113–1396 Vol. 7   pp. 1297–1480 Vol. 8
pp. 2057–2264 Vol. 12   pp. 2265–2472 Vol. 13   pp. 2473–2629 Vol. 14

2669

2670

pp. 1–192 Vol. 1   pp. 193–376 Vol. 2   pp. 377–560 Vol. 3   pp. 561–744 Vol. 4
pp. 1481–1664 Vol. 9   pp. 1665–1848 Vol. 10   pp. 1849–2056 Vol. 11

pp. 745– 936 Vol. 5   pp. 937–1112 Vol. 6   pp. 1113–1396 Vol. 7   pp. 1297–1480 Vol. 8
pp. 2057–2264 Vol. 12   pp. 2265–2472 Vol. 13   pp. 2473–2629 Vol. 14

2671

pp. 745–936 Vol. 5   pp. 937–1112 Vol. 6   pp. 1113–1396 Vol. 7   pp. 1297–1480 Vol. 8
pp. 2057–2264 Vol. 12   pp. 2265–2472 Vol. 13   pp. 2473–2629 Vol. 14

2673

2674

pp. 1–192 Vol. 1   pp. 193–376 Vol. 2   pp. 377–560 Vol. 3   pp. 561–744 Vol. 4
pp. 1481–1664 Vol. 9   pp. 1665–1848 Vol. 10   pp. 1849–2056 Vol. 11

pp. 745–936 Vol. 5   pp. 937–1112 Vol. 6   pp. 1113–1396 Vol. 7   pp. 1297–1480 Vol. 8
pp. 2057–2264 Vol. 12   pp. 2265–2472 Vol. 13   pp. 2473–2629 Vol. 14

2675

2676

pp. 1–192 Vol. 1   pp. 193–376 Vol. 2   pp. 377–560 Vol. 3   pp. 561–744 Vol. 4
pp. 1481–1664 Vol. 9   pp. 1665–1848 Vol. 10   pp. 1849–2056 Vol. 11

pp. 745–936 Vol. 5   pp. 937–1112 Vol. 6   pp. 1113–1396 Vol. 7   pp. 1297–1480 Vol. 8
pp. 2057–2264 Vol. 12   pp. 2265–2472 Vol. 13   pp. 2473–2629 Vol. 14

2677